ISLAM: THE ENEMY

THE ISLAMOPHOBIA SERIES

VOLUME I

Richard C. Crandall

Isn't it about time someone finally said it is not a war against Islamic extremism, Islamic fundamentalism, Islamic terrorism, Islamic fascism, Islamofascism, Muslim extremism, Muslim fundamentalism, Muslim terrorism, radical Islam, or stateless terrorists? Rather, it is a war against Islam, a bloody, intolerant, and violent ideology currently masquerading as a religion!

Islam: The Enemy
The Islamophobia Series Volume I
by Richard C. Crandall

Printed in the United States of America

ISBN 978-1-60647-307-8

www.xulonpress.com

DEDICATION

To the men and women of our armed forces who have recognized the enemy that confronts us, and who have successfully confronted it so our children and grandchildren will not have to and can live in freedom and peace.

TABLE OF CONTENTS

CHAPTER 1: WAKE UP, AMERICA!

Muhammad, the prophet of Islam, was an assassin, bandit, murderer, pedophile, rapist, robber, slave owner, thief, thug, and warlord. He called for and engaged in the mass slaughter of those who refused to convert or submit to Islam. And, for readers who are vegetarians or who belong to the Humane Society, Muhammad also engaged in animal sacrifice.

Islam is not a religion of peace. It is a religion of hatred, intolerance, and violence, as is easily demonstrated by its prophet's behavior and teachings, by its religious doctrines, as well as by its fourteen hundred-year history. Shortly before his death in 632, Muhammad told his followers, "I have been ordered by Allah to fight against the people till they testify that none has the right to be worshiped but Allah, and that Muhammad is the Messenger of Allah" (B25, B6924, B6925, 1:193, 9:5, 9:29).[1] Muslims have echoed these words many times over the last fourteen hundred years as they engaged in *jihad* to force others to accept Islam. In November 2001, Osama bin Laden (OBL) paraphrased them once again when he stated, "I was ordered to fight the people until they say there is no god but Allah and his prophet Muhammad."

It is not a coincidence that contemporary Muslims quote Muhammad when they are cutting off heads in Afghanistan, Iraq, Pakistan, and Saudi Arabia; murdering and raping school children in Russia; blowing up buses in England, trains in Spain, and resorts in Indonesia; or flying planes into buildings in the United States.

Nor is it coincidence that as the World Trade Center (WTC) towers were collapsing, Muslims throughout the world were dancing in the streets and shouting "death to America" and "*Allahu Akbar*" ("god is greater," "god is greatest" or "god is most great"). This is because *all* Muslims are ordered to follow the behavior or path of their prophet, and the beliefs and dictates of Islam as illustrated by Islamic religious documents such as the *Koran (Coran, Kor'an, Kuran, Kur'an Quran, Qur'an, Qurân)*, the *hadith* reports, and *sharia* (*shari'a, shariah*) or Islamic law.

Islam means submission or surrender to the will of the Islamic god and has become the name of the religion or ideology. The word Islam does *not* mean peace. A Muslim is someone who has submitted or surrendered to the will of the Islamic god. Muhammad often noted he was a slave of the Islamic god, as are all Muslims. As will be seen, the submission penetrates extensively into both the private and public aspects of life since there is no separation of church and state in Islam. Muhammad, for example, was not just a religious leader but was also the military and political leader of Islam, something similar to someone who had the power of a king, a military leader, and a pope.

A question that is seldom asked is, "If Muslims need to submit or surrender to the will of the Islamic god, what is this god's will?" To some extent the question can be answered by examining the way Islam separates the world. Essentially, it is separated into three areas. The first area is called *dar al-Islam*, which means "the House of Islam," "the Land of Islam," or "the Land of Submission." In the House of Islam, individuals live in submission and are under the control of and governed by *sharia*. *Sharia* is considered to be divine law which most Muslims believe is eternal, unchanging, and universal. Thus, Muslims seek to replace laws made by mere humans with laws made by the Islamic god. Under *sharia*, adulterers are stoned to death, thieves have their hands cut off and hung around their necks, and those who leave Islam are killed for apostasy. For women living under *sharia*, there are a number of consequences such as child marriages, forced marriages, genital mutilations, honor murders, and wife beatings.

The second area is *dar al-harb*, which means "the House of War" or "the House of non-Muslims." The House of War is an area which is not under the control of the House of Islam. That is, it is not in a state of submission or surrender to Islam, and it is not governed by *sharia.* It is the duty and obligation of Muslims to bring the House of War into the House of Islam. The only exception is if the enemy is temporarily too powerful to confront, or if Islam is temporarily too weak to wage war.

The earlier quotes by Muhammad and OBL command Muslims to fight until all stated there is no god but Allah and that Muhammad is his messenger. Until this is accomplished there will be perpetual war between the House of Islam and the House of War. Islamofascists, Islamic extremists, Islamic fundamentalists, Muslim terrorists, or Islamic terrorists are attempting to bring about "peace" by bringing the House of War into the House of Islam. *Jihad* is one of the techniques used to bring the two houses together through the conversion, death, or subjugation of non-Muslims who live in the House of War.

The third area is called the House of *dar al-sulh* (*sohl*). This is an area which has generally been conquered by Muslims who have imposed a treaty which can be revoked at anytime. The non-Muslims living in *dar al-sulh*, called *dhimmis,* do not have to convert to Islam as long as they are willing to live in de-humanizing, humiliating, and oppressive conditions as a conquered people in their own country with low status, few rights, and high taxes. This state of *dhimmitude* is a form of "modified" slavery.[2]

Earlier the question was asked, "If Muslims need to submit to the will of the Islamic god, what is this god's will?" The answer is that the will of the Islamic god is to have everyone living in the House of Islam or living in the house of *dar al-sulh* in *dhimmitude.*

This is it! Within Islam there are no other options such as Islam living side-by-side in harmony and peace with non-Muslims or non-Islamic countries. Thus, Islam is in a perpetual state of war until it places the world under its domination, or until it is destroyed.

Those who claim that Islam has been hijacked by extremists are either being deceitful or they are ignorant, liars, or stupid. In fact, these same individuals would have to claim that Muhammad, the prophet of Islam, was an extremist who hijacked his own religion. Those who hope that "moderates" will take over the religion or who hope for some type of reformation are naive. When the basis of the religion and the behavior and teachings of its prophet are to convert, kill, or subjugate non-Muslims, there is no moderate path to follow. The intolerant and violent basis of the religion can also be seen in Islam's bloody, intolerant, and violent fourteen hundred-year history.

Rather than saying extremists have hijacked Islam, it would be more correct to state that Islam has hijacked and corrupted the behavior, morals, and souls of its followers. Thus, Muslims who engage in acts of terrorism are not extremists. They are following the beliefs, commands, dictates, ideologies, principles, and teachings of their religion and following the behavior of its prophet as they are commanded and obligated to do. Moderate Muslims are the ones outside the boundaries of Islam and are considered hypocrites who will be eternally tormented in hell. In fact, if you take the hatred, intolerance, and violence out of Islam, there is not much left for moderates to follow.

Where Are We At?

We are at war with an unrelenting and unforgiving enemy which goes by names such as Islamic terrorism, Islamofascism, extremist Islam, or radical Islam. However, out of fear of offending Muslims, some prefer to associate the enemy with specific groups such as al-Qaeda or the Taliban. Others, out of political correctness, use generic names such as global terrorists or stateless terrorists, making it uncertain if the "global war on terrorism" is against those motivated to kill all non-Muslims or those trying to liberate Northern Ireland.

The name of the enemy is Islam, and it is time to identify the enemy and to call it by its name. The first step in any war is to identify the enemy. The time is over for ignoring the war, pretending it isn't really a war, providing false reasons for the war, saying we are losing the war, claiming the war is taking place in the wrong country, stating the war is a mistake, advocating withdrawal from the war, proclaiming the war a failure, or failing to recognize the real enemy in the war. These are no longer options if we want to keep our way of life and our lives. The war has been going on for fourteen hundred years, and the enemy is a seventh century ideology called Islam, which is currently masquerading as a religion.

Previously, many recognized the existence of the war and that the enemy was Islam. Thus, they mobilized to fight the war. Currently, many refuse to recognize the existence of the war and that the enemy is Islam. Nor do they recognize the magnitude of the danger that confronts us. As with any war, failure to act in an appropriate and timely manner can be disastrous. Every delay in recognizing and responding simply prolongs the war. It also places the outcome of the war in jeopardy.

This book is separated into two sections. The first section of the book illustrates that the attacks on 9/11 were simply the continuation of the Islamic *jihad* that has been taking place for fourteen hundred years, and that it will continue until either the world has been placed under Islamic domination or until Islam ceases to exist in its current form. This will be shown by examining Islam's holiest religious documents such as the *Koran*, the *hadith* reports, and *sharia* or Islamic law. The behavior of its prophet Muhammad, which Muslims are obligated to follow, will also be examined. The biography of Muhammad will also illustrate Islam's early bloody, intolerant, and violent history. At the conclusion of this section, readers will realize that Islam and Muslims have only one path to follow, which is that all must worship the Islamic god and believe Muhammad was his prophet.

The second section of the book examines why the American public has returned to a pre-9/11 mentality. The purpose of this section is to illustrate the factors that have prevented Americans from recognizing the reality of the war. It also examines the Islamic infestation of education and the community.

Islamophobic? Islamophobe?

Some will claim this book is bigoted or hateful. In fact, this book is simply citing Islam's holiest documents to demonstrate how Islam demands Muslims behave if they expect to go to paradise and be exempt from the fires of hell. It also provides a biography of the incredibly disgusting, vile, and violent behavior of Islam's prophet Muhammad, which Muslims are compelled to follow.

Others will claim the author is Islamophobic. If Islamophobia refers to the fear of losing one's life or liberty if placed under Islamic rule, then this claim is correct! However, generally the charge of Islamophobia is simply a technique of religious bullying by Muslims to discredit those who are disseminating the truth about Islam or stripping the *burka* or covering off Islam. The charge of Islamophobia is an attempt to prevent any criticism or examination of Islam. And it is an attempt to delay any response to *jihad*. It is time Americans stand up and stop being afraid of criticizing a barbaric seventh century ideology or of offending those who believe in it!

The Mandatory Elusive Moderate Muslim Section

In all religions, believers have different levels of commitment. This applies to Islam. There are millions of individuals who call themselves Muslims who would never engage in a *jihad* against non-Muslims. These Muslims want to be able to raise their children in peace in an environment where they are free, happy, and safe. They are more concerned with the character of their friends and neighbors than with their religion. They have adopted a reformed version of Islam by interpreting certain Islamic religious passages to fit their needs and by ignoring other passages. The issue of moderate Muslims is further addressed in Chapter 4.

CHAPTER 2: WHERE TO START I: THE *HADITH* REPORTS

The attacks on 9/11 by nineteen Muslims were not isolated, random, or unique. Rather, the nineteen Muslims were simply part of the fourteen hundred-year Islamic *jihad* against Western civilization and all else that is not Islamic, with the ultimate goal of placing the world under Islamic subjugation. The nineteen Muslims were obeying the documents that form the basis of Islam, and they were following the behavior of Islam's prophet Muhammad as they are commanded and obligated to do.

This is a difficult concept for most Americans to accept since the chant of liberals and the mainstream media, literally starting as the World Trade Center (WTC) towers were collapsing, is that Islam is a religion of peace and a few extremists have hijacked the religion. To support this position, they remind us that millions of Muslims live law-abiding lives and do not engage in terrorism. However, recent studies on the attitudes of Muslims living in Western countries such as Australia, Germany, Great Britain, and the United States are not encouraging since many law-abiding Muslims support suicide bombings and would like to see *sharia*, or Islamic law, replace Judeo-Christian laws.

Accepting Islam as the cause of the attacks on 9/11 is difficult for another reason. For those holding Judeo-Christian beliefs, it is difficult to believe that a religion such as Islam could be so depraved and vile as to mandate the conversion, death, or subjugation of all non-Muslims. Therefore, it is logical for those with

Judeo-Christian beliefs to accept that Muslim terrorists must be in violation of Islam's core beliefs and that "moderate" Muslims, who do not openly engage in *jihad,* must be living according to Islam's core beliefs. The religiously-challenged also have a difficult time accepting Islam as the cause of 9/11. They simply cannot believe a religion could be such a powerful force in an individual's life.

However, Islam as the cause of 9/11 makes sense after one understands Islam. It will be seen that Muslim assassins, bandits, butchers, murderers, rapists, terrorists, and thugs rely on the *Koran* and other Islamic religious documents to justify their behavior. And they are following the behavior of Muhammad, Islam's prophet, which they are obligated to do.

When confronted with Islamic passages which mandate the conversion, death, or subjugation of non-Muslims, Islamic apologists claim the passages are taken out of context. They also cite less violent passages, failing to mention they were abrogated or superseded by later passages demanding violence toward non-Muslims. When critics of Islam bring up Muhammad's violent behavior, Islamic apologists claim he was simply a "man of his times." In response, critics note that a prophet should *not* be someone of the times but someone of a different time, someone leading people away from a barbaric, intolerant, misogynistic, uncivilized, vile, and violent way of life. Also, Saddam Hussein was a man of Muhammad's time. Because of this he was executed!

As will be seen after examining Islamic religious documents and its prophet's behavior, it is "moderate Muslims" who are living outside the core beliefs of Islam. This chapter, and the three which follow, examine the religious documents that form the basis of Islam. These documents are important because they provide Muslims with the guidelines and the ideology for living their lives. We need to ask, for example, do these documents require that Muslims engage in war until all "testify that none has the right to be worshiped but Allah, and that Muhammad is the Messenger of Allah"? After the documents that form the basis of Islam have been examined, the following four chapters provide a biography of Muhammad. As already noted, Muhammad's behavior is important since all Muslims are obligated to follow his behavior or path. In fact, he stated in his last speech in

Mecca that if Muslims followed his behavior and words, they would never go wrong. The last chapters will examine why those under attack by the Islamic *jihad* have returned to a pre-9/11 mentality.

The *Hadith* Reports

Most readers have probably never heard of the *hadith* reports.[3] This section starts with the *hadith* reports because they provide the basis for understanding the other two documents which form the basis of Islam, and they are the source for his biographies. The *hadith* reports describe Muhammad's life such as his actions, behaviors, deeds, sayings, teachings, and what he allowed and forbade. They also include what he liked and did not like. The *hadith* reports are organized by topics such as divorce, funerals, inheritance, *jihad*, marriage, prayer, and war.

Those who obey and follow the *hadith* reports are said to be following the *sunnah* (*sunna*) or the path of Muhammad. One *hadith* report may contain several *sunnah*. The *hadith* reports also include information on the actions, behavior, deeds, sayings, and teachings of Muhammad's companions and wives. Most *hadith* reports are short, usually a sentence or a paragraph.

The *hadith* reports and *sunnah* are closely related but are not the same. The *sunnah* is the correct path or the correct model of behavior as illustrated by Muhammad. It is the behavior expected of all Muslims. The *hadith* is the report of the behavior.

The Shites and Sunni each have their own collections of *hadith* reports. The Sunni, who take their name from the *sunnah*, or "path," have six major collections. The Shites have what is known as the four books, meaning their best known collections of *hadith* reports. As would be expected, the two major branches of Islam have some disagreements over certain *hadith* reports.

The *hadith* reports have thousands of passages on many aspects of Muhammad's life which are to be followed as closely in the present as they were in the past. In more than forty verses the *Koran* demands Muslims follow the behavior, or *sunnah*, of Muhammad. For example, if Muslims want to go to paradise, Muhammad is a "good example to follow" (33:21). In another passage in the *Koran*,

Muhammad states, "If you (really) love Allah, then follow me (i.e., accept Islamic Monotheism, follow the *Koran* and the *Sunnah*), Allah will love you and forgive you your sins" (3:31). In fact, the *Koran* states that those who follow Muhammad are also obeying or following the Islamic god (4:80). The *hadith* reports have similar passages. For example, "Whoever obeys Muhammad obeys Allah; and whoever disobeys Muhammad disobeys Allah" (B2957, B7137). And, "whoever obeys me [Muhammad] he obeys Allah, and whoever disobeys me [Muhammad] disobeys Allah..." (B7137, B7281).

The *hadith* reports are considered the second holy "book" in Islam, the *Koran* being the first. The *hadith* reports are presented first since much of the *Koran* cannot be understood without them, and they are the basis for *sharia* and for the biographies of Muhammad.

The collection of *hadith* reports started more than one hundred years after Muhammad's death, with the major collections not appearing until more than two hundred years after his death. Since this was largely an illiterate society, many ask, "How were they collected?" Well, the *hadith* report collectors used what is known as the "chain of transmission method." The chain of transmission method relied on material being passed down orally from one generation to the next. For example, the *hadith* report collectors would have individuals relate the stories they had heard about Muhammad. They would then ascertain if the storytellers were "trustworthy." If the storytellers were deemed trustworthy, the *hadith* report collectors would find out from whom they had heard the stories. They would then ascertain if these individuals were trustworthy. This process would be repeated until the stories had been traced back to the original sources. This obviously meant there was always more than one transmitter. The *hadith* report collectors would only consider stories accurate if all the transmitters were deemed trustworthy.

The chains of transmitters were the footnotes of the era, and the *hadith* report collectors developed a list of "trustworthy transmitters." In the *hadith* report collections, almost every report starts with the list of transmitters, which for Western readers often makes the reports cumbersome to read. After the list of transmitters, the *hadith* report begins. Sometimes the same *hadith* report is repeated more than once with the same list of transmitters. Other times the same *hadith* report is repeated but with a different series of transmitters. This was designed to give specific *hadith* reports greater credibility since there was more than one series of trustworthy transmitters.

The use of the chain of transmission method to collect the *hadith* reports has been criticized. A major criticism deals with ascertaining the "trustworthiness" of the transmitters. Obviously, ascertaining the trustworthiness of those who were alive was possible, but ascertaining the same for those who had been dead, some for more than a century, must have been difficult if not impossible. Also, the *hadith* report collectors must have been influenced or pressured by the current political and religious climate, as well as by the political and religious beliefs of those who were assisting them financially in their work. Additionally, the political and religious beliefs of the *hadith* report collectors certainly influenced the collection. Because of these influences and pressures, the *hadith* report collectors were probably very selective in determining those who were considered "trustworthy transmitters" and what *hadith* reports were considered true. As will be seen, the *hadith* report collectors discarded the vast majority of what they collected. Some *hadith* report collectors may have fabricated *hadith* reports for political or religious reasons.

The chain of transmission method is suspect for other reasons. Over time, the memories of the transmitters must have failed. And, just as the *hadith* report collectors were influenced and pressured by the political and religious climate, so too were the transmitters.

Critics of the chain of the transmission method have asked readers to imagine if there were no documents from the American Civil War, and then this year someone decided to write the war's definitive history using the chain of transmission method. With no survivors from the era, the researcher would probably start by asking older Americans what they remember their parents and grandparents telling them about the Civil War. Certainly a variety of factors, such as the outcome of the war, would result in distorted, selective, and perhaps even created memories being transmitted. Defenders of the chain of transmission method claim that in an oral society, one with a low literacy rate such as that found in early Islam, memories were accurately and commonly used to transmit information.

While some collectors of *hadith* reports were considered reliable, others were deemed less reliable. For example, Waqidi an early *hadith* collector and historian who died in 822, was alleged to have fabricated twenty thousand *hadith* reports. One of the more widely respected and quoted collections is by Bukhari (Bokhari), who died in 870 well over two hundred years after Muhammad. His nine-volume Sunni collection was completed around 850 and is titled *Sahih al-Bukhari: The True Traditions.*[4] Al-Bukhari is reported to have collected six hundred thousand *hadith* reports during a sixteen-year period, or more than one hundred per day. The collection by Bukhari only has 7,563 *hadith* reports, which means he rejected the vast majority as being unreliable. Of the *hadith* reports in the collection, many are repeated several times.

Another *hadith* report collector was a Muslim who died in 875.[5] He collected three hundred thousand *hadith* reports, of which he only kept 3,033. Dawud was another *hadith* report collector who died in 888.[6] He is reported to have collected five hundred thousand *hadith* reports, of which he only kept about four thousand. The Bukhari, Dawud, and Muslim collections are Sunni collections and are considered by many Muslims to be the "correct" *hadith* reports. As can be seen, given what was collected and rejected, about ninety-nine percent of what Muslims believed about Muhammad and early Islam was "false" at the time the *hadith* reports were being collected.

There are *hadith* reports dealing with almost every aspect of Muhammad's life. For example, there is a section on the foods he liked and another on the foods he did not like. There are *hadith* reports dealing with Muhammad having his moustache trimmed. Other *hadith* reports deal with his clothing, bedding, shoes, socks, swords, coats of mail, shields, and his milk-yielding camels and goats. There is also a section that deals with how he cleaned his teeth. Different types of *hadith* reports will be examined.

Examples of *Hadith* Reports

1. Trivial. If individuals are expecting great philosophical thoughts or examples of an inspirational lifestyle while reading the

hadith reports, they are likely to be disappointed. For example, one *hadith* report deals with Muhammad spitting a mouthful of water in a young boy's face (B77). We also learn Muhammad snored (B117).

A man who was fixing a roof related that he saw Muhammad defecating while facing Palestine with his back to Mecca (B148, B3102, M266). While Muhammad did not have any difficulty "answering the call of nature" when and where he wanted, it was more difficult for Muslim women, especially Muhammad's wives. They had to go into the fields at night to attend to their needs. One of Muhammad's wives was rebuked for being out at night to attend to her needs, presumably because she was alone. Fortunately, Muhammad received a revelation from the Islamic god granting his wives permission to go out at night and attend to their needs (M2170).

We learn that men are forbidden from having sexual intercourse with their wives during menses since it would be "harmful" (B Book 6; 2:222). In fact, husbands are to keep away from women while they are menstruating. However, after Muhammad's child-bride started menstruating, he allowed her to comb his hair (B295), he fondled her (B300), and he had sexual intercourse with her during her menses (M293, M294).

The *hadith* reports instruct Muslims that when attending to bathroom needs, they need to clean their private parts using an odd number of stones (B161, B162, M237, M262). Readers also learn that Muhammad ate using the thumb, index finger, and middle finger of his right hand. When Muhammad was finished eating, he first licked his middle finger, then his index finger, and finally his thumb. Or someone else licked his fingers (D3838, M2031). One inspirational *hadith* report (B5969) is "I saw the Prophet lying down in the mosque and placing one leg on the other."

Muslims should avoid yawning since it is from the devil (M2994). Muslims are also commanded not to drink water when standing (M2024) and to drink water while standing (M2027). There are many cases where *hadith* reports contradict each other.

From the *hadith* reports, Muslims are commanded not to urinate where individuals take baths (B4842). We also learn that Muhammad cursed women who practiced tattooing or who had tattoos (B4886,

B5931, B5944, M2125). In this same *hadith* report he expressed his outrage at women who had eyebrow hair removed because they were changing Allah's creation. However, they were allowed to change Allah's creation by removing beard and moustache hair and through female genital mutilation, where Muhammad suggested they not be cut too severely (D5251).

Muslims are instructed to not laugh when someone "breaks wind" since you should not laugh at what you do (B4942). If someone "breaks wind" while praying, the prayer is nullified and the individual needs to start the prayer from the beginning (M1000). Muslims should not "pass wind" while in a mosque (B445) or go near a mosque if they have been eating garlic or onions (B854).

The *hadith* reports regulate most forms of behavior. For example, when spitting, Muslims must spit to the left, not to the front or to the right (B412). There are instructions on what to do if a Muslim purchases and milks an animal and then wants to return it. Basically, the buyer needs to pay for the milk with dates (B2151). There are also instructions on how to handle a transaction involving a camel with a skin disease (B2099).

Readers probably learn more than we want about shoes. For example, never wear just one shoe (B5855) and put the right shoe on first and take it off last (B5856). Also, Muhammad's sandals each had two straps (B5857).

According to the *hadith* reports, Muhammad had lice (B2788, B2789). And for some reason Muhammad became angry when a young boy passed in front of him while he was praying and he cursed the boy, who then became "crippled" (D707).

The smallest details are included in the *hadith* reports. For example, in the Dawud collection, Chapters 26-30 deal with "how to use the tooth-stick," "using others' tooth-sticks," "washing the tooth-stick," and "using the tooth-stick after getting up in the night."

If you are ever taking sacrificial camels to Mecca, there are *hadith* reports to guide you. Dawud has a chapter on what to do if the camels become fatigued and cannot continue to Mecca where the sacrifice should occur (D586). The following chapter deals with how to immobilize the sacrificial camels before they are killed. Also included in this *hadith* report is whether the sacrificial camels should be sitting, standing, or lying down during sacrifice. Dawud also has chapters on the animals that are recommended for sacrifice (D1032), the appropriate age of sacrificial animals (D1033), and how to kill sacrificial animals (D1043).

2. Islamic tolerance. There are many *hadith* reports dealing with Muhammad's followers asking him questions. For example, after a prayer session, Muhammad said, "Ask me any question." One man asked about paradise. Muhammad told him he was going to hell. Muhammad kept angrily asking for more questions and then responding bitterly to those asking them. Finally, one of his followers realized this was a trick and they were not supposed to be asking questions. The follower said, "We accept Allah as (our) Lord, Islam as (our) religion, and Muhammad as (our) Messenger" (B7294). The following *hadith* report has Muhammad stating, "O you who believe ask not about things." This theme is repeated where it is stated that Muhammad disliked those who asked too many questions (B7291), and at times he forbade his followers from asking too many questions (B7292). Muhammad explained his reasoning in another *hadith* report where he told his followers not to ask about things he had not mentioned or which he had explained (B7288). This was because previous religions had been ruined by those who had asked too many questions. Muhammad believed that too many questions created differences of opinions, especially about prophets. He told his followers to simply obey him (see M1337R1).

Muhammad ordered dogs kept as pets be killed (B3323, M1570, M1572). Some claim he meant rabid dogs, however, in other *hadith* reports he specifically mentioned killing rabid dogs (B1826, B1827, B1828, B1829). If the dogs kept as pets were not killed, their owners should as a minimum be fined (B3324, B3325). Muhammad did not believe angels would enter a house with dogs (B3325, B3228). The exception was working dogs, such as those used in herding and hunting (M1571, M1573). In fact, there is a section in the *hadith* reports on hunting with trained dogs (M1929).

While most dogs are "out," cats are "in." There is even a *hadith* report chapter titled "Forbiddance of Tormenting the Cat." In this *hadith* report we learn that women who torment cats will go to hell (M2242R2).

Readers of the *hadith* reports will learn that Muhammad did not like pictures (B4002, B5181, B5949, B5950, B5951, B5954, B5955, B6109, B7558, D227, D3746). In fact, he refused to enter his house after his child-bride purchased a cushion with the picture of an animal on it. He stated, "The people who will receive the severest punishment from Allah will be the picture-makers." Muhammad stated that in hell the picture-makers would have to make alive what they had drawn (B7558). He did not like poetry. He said, "It is better for a man to fill the inside of his body with pus than to fill it with poetry" (B6154, B6155, D4991, 26:224-226). Chess was also forbidden (M2260), perhaps because the queen, the only female piece on the board, was the most powerful figure in the game.

3. More serious stuff. Although passing wind, the order of shoe removal, and the direction of defecation seem trivial, there are a number of *hadith* reports that are more serious. For example, some deal with stoning to death those guilty of adultery (B4556, B5270, B5271, B5272, B6815, B7260, B7332, B7543, M1690). Other *hadith* reports have those who are guilty of "illegal sexual intercourse" stoned to death (B6815, B6816, B6819, B6820). Dawud has *hadith* reports on the stoning to death of "fornicators" (D4399-D4404). In one *hadith* report, a woman who became pregnant as a result of adultery was not stoned until she had given birth (D4426), and in another case a pregnant adulterous woman was not stoned to death until the infant was weaned (D4428, M1965R1). Once a man came to Muhammad and announced he was guilty of "illegal sexual intercourse." When Muhammad turned his head, the man repeated his statement. Muhammad once again turned his head. After announcing his guilt four times, Muhammad had him taken out and stoned to death (B6815, B6820). To be guilty of adultery there need to be four witnesses, and in this case the adulterer's four confessions sufficed as four witnesses. Stoning should not take place on the insane until they become sane, on children until they become adults, or on the sleeping until they awake (B Chapter 22).

Those reading about stoning will note that prior to being stoned, a woman's clothes are to be tied on her. This means that a woman's clothing is secured so that if she struggles while being stoned to death, no private parts, such as an arm or leg, will become exposed.

If a husband catches his wife in the act of adultery, it is acceptable to kill the adulterous man. In fact, Muhammad said this indicated the husband had *ghaira*, which is a fury and anger emanating from having one's honor challenged or injured. This is the basis for the "honor murders" of young Muslim women who defy Islamic traditions.

Others *hadith* reports deal with Muhammad ordering prisoners to have their hands and feet cut off, their eyes gouged out, and to then be left in the desert pleading for water until they died (B3018, B5686, B5727, B6802-6805, B6899, D4370-4398). Those who commit theft have their right hand cut off (B3733, B6787-6801, 5:38). If they steal again, the left foot is cut off (D4396). A third offense results in the amputation of the left hand and a fourth offense results in the amputation of the right foot. After a hand is amputated, it is hung around the thief's neck (D4398). The *hadith* reports are silent on where an amputated foot is hung. Muhammad even noted he would cut off the hand of his favorite daughter if she stole (B6787, B6788, and M1688). Muhammad did some of the amputations (B6789-B6800, M1684, M2686).

What needs to be stolen for amputation to occur varies in the *hadith* reports. Sometimes it is specified in *dinars*, a coinage system in use at the time, and is between twenty to thirty dollars. However, in one *hadith* report, amputation is to occur if the thief steals an egg or a rope (M1687).

We learn that Muhammad had sexual intercourse with a "wife" when she was nine years old (B3896, B5133, B5134, B5158).

There is a prohibition on consuming intoxicating beverages. The first through fourth violations bring the individual a flogging. The penalty for the fifth violation is death (D4468).

Those who commit suicide are prohibited from entering paradise (B1364, B1365, 4:29). The question naturally asked is, "Do Muslim suicide bombers enter paradise?" Muslim suicide bombers answer the question in the affirmative because they do not see the act of blowing themselves up as an act of suicide. Since the intent of the act is not to kill themselves but to kill non-Muslims, blowing themselves up is simply a means of killing as many non-Muslims as possible. Thus, suicide bombers are more correctly labeled homicide bombers. The *hadith* reports make it clear that those whose motivation in *jihad* is to advance Islam and who die in its cause will immediately enter paradise (see B3123). Additionally, deception in war is justified, and the homicide bomber is using deception to advance the cause of Islam.

The ever modest Muhammad told his followers, "None of you will have faith till he loves me more than his father, his children, and all mankind" (B15).

Muhammad cursed effeminate men and masculine women (B5885-86). Banditry is sanctioned in the *hadith* reports (B Book 57, Chapter 8). One chapter is subtitled "Booty Has Been Made Legal for You Muslims." And it is acceptable to break an oath if a Muslims finds another oath that is better (M1650R2, M1651, M1651R).

4. Women. Dawud has a chapter on "beating women" (D709). Basically, it is acceptable to beat "emboldened" women. If the emboldened women complain about being beaten, this means they are not the best among women. One of the footnotes in this section states this *hadith* report requires that women obey men. If preaching or educating emboldened women does not change their behavior, then beating them is acceptable. The beating is a last resort and is not to occur without reason, such as disobeying or being "emboldened toward her husband." A husband who beats his wife is not asked why the beating took place (M2142).

We know Muhammad hit his child-wife, Aisha (M974R1). Also, after her marriage to Muhammad, Aisha's father hit her (B6845). She described the episode as one in which he "struck me violently with his fist," and she said the blow was "very painful."

Evidently the beating of women by their Muslim husbands did little to save them from hell since Muhammad noted that when he was shown "hell-fire," the majority of dwellers were women (B304, B1052, B1462, B3241, B5197, B5916, B5918, M907). Most were there because they were "ungrateful to their husbands and are ungrateful for the favors and the good (charitable deeds) done for them" (B29, M2737). Muhammad stated, "They are ungrateful to their husbands and ungrateful to *Al-Ihsan* (good favors done to them)." In addition to being in hell for being ungrateful to their husbands, women were also the majority in hell because they "curse frequently" (B304). "Even if you do good to one of them all your life, when she sees something (not of her liking) from you, she will say, 'I have never seen any good from you'"(B5197).

Muhammad did not think much of women rulers. After learning Persia had made a woman its ruler, he stated, "Never will succeed such a nation as makes a woman their ruler." Perhaps this is because, according to the *hadith* reports, women are "deficient in intelligence" (B304, B1462).

Muhammad also believed women were evil omens. Muhammad stated, "There is an evil omen in a woman, a house and a horse" (B5093, B 5094, B5095). In fact, women were so evil they nullified prayers if they passed in front of a praying man. Dogs and donkeys also annulled prayers. However, after his child-wife reached puberty, she was exempt from this policy even during her menses (B379, B508, B511, B512, B513).

5. Offending Islam or Muhammad. What do the *hadith* reports say about those who insult Islam or Muhammad? There are numerous *hadith* reports in which Muhammad requested his followers kill those who offended him or Islam. Kab bin Al-Ashraf was a poet who offended Muhammad. Muhammad asked his followers, "Who will kill Kab bin Al-Ashraf who has hurt Allah and His Messenger?" (B4037). Kab was dead later that evening (see B3031, B3032, M1801). After a victorious battle, Muhammad had the captured poet, Uqba Abu Muayt, who had offended Muhammad, brought before him. Fearing for his life, Muayt asked, "Who will look after my children?" Muhammad replied, "Hell," and then had him decapitated (B2934, M1794, M1794R1-3). In another account, a man killed his wife because she slandered Muhammad (D4348). Muhammad stated there would be "no retaliation" for the murder. The footnote to this *hadith* report states it is "unanimously agreed that if a Muslim abuses or insults the Prophet he should be killed." It continues by noting there is a difference of opinion about killing non-Muslims who insult Muhammad. In another *hadith* report, a Jewish woman was murdered because she "disparaged" Muhammad. Muhammad said, "no recompense was payable" for her murder (D4349).

The *Koran* supports the *hadith* reports in this area. In fact, "who can be more unjust than he who invents a lie against Allah...?" It continues by saying, "This day you shall be recompensed with the torment of degradation because of what you used to utter against Allah other than the truth" (6:93). Verse 33:57 reads, "Verily, those who annoy Allah and His Messenger, Allah has cursed them in this world and the Hereafter, and has prepared for them a humiliating torment." The footnote for the word *annoy* includes "abusing or telling lies against Allah and his Messenger, by making pictures—imitating Allah's creations, and by disobeying Allah and His Messenger." The verse continues stating that those who spread false news "shall be seized wherever found and killed with a terrible slaughter" (33:58-61). Another verse reads that those who "annoy" Allah or Muhammad will have a "painful torment" (9:61).

Although Islam and Muhammad appeared to be immune from criticism, Muhammad satirized those who "spoke against the Apostle of Allah" (D4997). As will be seen in the chapters providing a biography of Muhammad, there are other examples of individuals being killed for criticizing Islam or Muhammad.

6. *Jihad.* What do the *hadith* reports say about *jihad*? Because of its importance, *jihad* will also be examined in the chapters which deal with the *Koran* and *sharia.* We learn that the second best deed a Muslim can do is to participate in *jihad*, or "holy fighting in Allah's cause" (B26). Several other *hadith* reports note that *jihad* is one of the best deeds or actions of Muslims (B26, B527, B1519, B2782, B5970, B7534). The importance of *jihad* can be seen in the amount of space the *hadith* report collectors devote to it. Also, the editors of the *hadith* report collections often have additional material on *jihad.*

Bukhari has an entire chapter on *jihad* (Chapter 56) which is titled "Fighting in Allah's Cause." The editors of the *hadith* reports define *jihad* as "(Holy fighting) in Allah's Cause (with full force of numbers and weaponry), is given the utmost importance in Islam, and is one of its pillars (on which it stands). By *jihad* Islam is established, Allah's Word is made superior." The passage continues by saying, "Which means none has the right to be worshiped except Allah." If *jihad* is abandoned, Muslims will lose their land, honor, and authority and will fall into an "inferior position." "*Jihad* is an obligatory duty in Islam, on every Muslim..." The definition concludes by stating that those who try to escape from *jihad* die a hypocrite, which means their torment in hell will be especially severe.

Note that the fighting is with numbers and weapons, not ideas. The belief that *jihad* is a military struggle and not a personal struggle is further illustrated by the *hadith* reports, which exempt those who are blind, lame, or otherwise disabled (B2832). If *jihad* is a personal struggle, then why are the blind, lame, and otherwise disabled exempt?

Muhammad said, "Allah assigns for a person who participates in (holy battles) in Allah's Cause and nothing causes him to do so except belief in Allah and in His Messengers, that he will be recompensed by Allah either with a reward, or booty (if he survives) or will be admitted to Paradise (if he is killed in battle as a martyr)" (B36). "In paradise, none will want to come back, even if he were given the entire world and whatever is in it, except martyrs who on seeing the superiority of martyrdom, would like to come back to the world and get killed again (in Allah's cause)" (B2795, B2817).

The *jihad* is to continue until all "testify that (none has the right to be worshiped but Allah and that Muhammad is the Messenger of Allah..." (B25).

The importance of *jihad* can be seen in the *hadith* collection of Bukhari, where the editors have included an appendix titled "The Call to *Jihad* in the *Koran* (Holy Fighting for Allah's Cause)."

Dawud's *hadith* collection also has a large section on *jihad* (Chapters 848-1028). Again, the editors have provided a definition of *jihad* which reads, "In the Islamic context, it stands for fighting against the infidels to promote the cause of Islam." This section continues and states that the fighting may be in several areas, such as the battlefield, the classroom, or in making public speeches. However, in reading this section, there is no information on taking the *jihad* into the classroom or incorporating it into public speeches. There are chapters with titles suggesting that *jihad* is by the sword: "Excellence of Killing an Infidel" (858), "On the Troops of Warriors Who Return Without Obtaining Booty" (860), "On Shooting" (871), "On a Man Who Embraces Islam and Is Killed on the Same Spot in the Path of Allah, the Exalted" (885), "On a Person Who Is Killed with His Own Weapon" (886), "Wearing Coats of Mail" (921), "Burning Enemy Territory" (937), "To Attack the Enemy at Night" (948), "Flying from Enemy in a Battle" (952), "On Lying in Ambush" (962), "To Draw Swords When Fighting" (964), "Prohibition of Mutilation" (966), "On Killing Women" (967), and "On Killing a Captive When Islam Is Not Presented to Him" (973). These chapter titles, and many others, suggest that *jihad* is a military struggle, not a personal struggle.

The *hadith* collection by Muslim also has a large section on *jihad*. The *hadith* reports are in Chapter 32, which is titled the "Book of the Holy Struggle" (1730-1816). Again, the subtitles in the chapter suggest that *jihad* is a military struggle, not a personal struggle: "Permission to Make a Raid," "Prohibition of Killing Women and Children in War," "Permissibility of Killing Women and Children in the Night Raids, Provided It Is Not Deliberate," "The Spoils of War," "Binding the Prisoners," "Battle of Hunain," "Battle of Taif," "Battle of Badr," "Battle of the Ditch," "Battle of Uhud," and the "Battle of Khaibar."

For Muslim *jihadists* to receive paradise, their motivation for *jihad* must be to make Islam superior over other religions. It cannot be for booty, for fame, or for showing off (B2810). If the motivations of *jihadists* are only to promote Islam, then when they are killed their sins are blotted out and they go directly to paradise (M1885).

In the three *hadith* collections cited above, *jihad* is presented as a military struggle, not a personal struggle. This is important since recently Muslim apologists have attempted to portray two types of *jihad*: the lesser *jihad*, which is by the sword, and the greater *jihad*, which is a personal struggle. Islamic apologists stress that the personal struggle is more important than the military struggle, even though there is more material on the military struggle and literally none on the personal struggle. If the personal struggle is so important, we need to ask, "Why there is so little material on it?" If we make the assumption there is a "greater *jihad*" which involves a personal struggle, perhaps we need to ask, "What is involved in this struggle?" We first need to remember that Muhammad is seen as the perfect model of behavior and that Muslims are obligated to follow in his path if they want to go to paradise. Given some of the *hadith* reports examined so far, is it possible some Muslims have a personal struggle with stoning to death those accused of adultery? Do some Muslims struggle with cutting off the hands of thieves? Is there a personal struggle with assassinating poets or of chopping off the heads of prisoners? And then there is the sex with a nine-year-old, which hopefully all are going to struggle with.

Comment on *Hadith* Reports

Islamic apologists will complain that the above is a selective sampling of *hadith* reports. This is correct, and there are some *hadith* reports which are commendable even by contemporary standards. For example, don't steal or engage in illegal sexual intercourse. Muslims have a unique understand of when taking another's property by force is stealing and when rape constitutes illegal sexual intercourse. Additionally, Muslims are advised to visit the sick and generally not to lie. They are also instructed not to bury their infant daughters alive (B5975, B7292), a common practice in pre-Islamic Arabia. [Note to self: Remember to look for the asterisk allowing the murder of infant daughters before burying them and of allowing "honor murders" of daughters when they are older.]

Again, we need to remember that Muslims are required to follow Muhammad's behavior. This is made clear in the statement "and whoever obeys Muhammad obeys Allah; and who disobeys Muhammad disobeys Allah" (B7281). Thus, it is acceptable to have sex with a nine-year-old, to cut off the hands of thieves, and to stone adulterers to death. It is also acceptable to force non-Muslims, through *jihad*, to convert or submit to Islam, and if they refuse they can be killed.

One of the reasons Muslims are to follow Muhammad's behavior is because it was influenced by the Islamic god. Verse 7:203 reads, "I but follow what is revealed to me from my Lord." Thus, all aspects of Muhammad's life are seen by Muslims as divinely inspired and are the path, or *sunnah*, to follow.

One last point needs to be made about the *hadith* reports. Remember that there are thousands of *hadith* reports, and in a true Islamic society, one governed by *sharia* law, all would need to be followed. Most of our artwork would need to be destroyed, as would books other than those approved by Islam. Women would be relegated to the house, except when accompanied by a male relative. The list of rules would cover almost all aspects of daily life.

What's Next?

The following two chapters will examine the *Koran,* which is followed by an examination of *sharia*, or Islamic law.

CHAPTER 3: WHERE TO START II: THE *KORAN* (PART I)

The best way to understand Islam and the behavior of Muslims is by examining Islam's religious documents, the behavior and sayings of its prophet Muhammad, and its bloody and violent fourteen hundred-year history. The last chapter examined the *hadith* reports, which detailed the actions, behaviors, deeds, sayings, and teachings of Muhammad. The *hadith* reports also assist in providing an explanation and an understanding of Islam's holiest document, the *Koran*, which will be examined in this and the following chapter.

The *Koran*

For Muslims, the *Koran* is the eternal, exact, final, perfect, timeless, and unchanged words of the Islamic god.[7] These words constitute "an absolute truth with certainty" (70:51), about which there can be no doubt (2:2). In fact, the *Koran* is without any crookedness or flaws (39:28). In addition, the Islamic god protects the *Koran* from corruption (41:41) and will not allow falsehoods to enter into it (41:42). The words of the Islamic god are "exalted" and "full of wisdom" (43:4). Muslims believe these words of the Islamic god have always existed on "eternal" stone tablets in heaven (85:22). The angel Gabriel (Jibreel, Jibril) came and revealed the words of the Islamic god to Muhammad in installments over twenty-three years. The revelations started in 610 while Muhammad was living in Mecca. They continued after Muhammad left Mecca in 622 and went to live in Medina. They ceased with his death in 632, and since Muhammad was the last prophet (33:40) and he had perfected the religion (5:3), there will be no more revelations. Muhammad noted he was different from earlier prophets who had been sent to specific nations in that he had been sent for all mankind (see footnote for 2:252, B335, w4.2).

It is estimated that of the one hundred and fourteen *suras*, or chapters, in the *Koran*, eighty-six to ninety were revealed in Mecca. Since at this point in time Arab society was primarily an "oral" society, and since it is generally acknowledged Muhammad could not read or write (7:157-158), many of the revelations were initially memorized by Muhammad and his followers. In fact, Muhammad is known as the "illiterate prophet," which has been used as the basis for the claim the *Koran* must have been divinely inspired since someone who was illiterate could not have produced such a document. [Note to self: The claim of "divine inspiration" would have greater credibility if the illiterate prophet Muhammad had been "divinely inspired" to read and write, or if Muhammad was a mute who had been "divinely inspired" to speak.] Some have suggested that Muhammad could read and write, and the allegations of his illiteracy were simply a technique used to increase his prestige in producing the *Koran*. It is possible that over the course of his prophecy he learned to read and write. Examples of his "literacy" will be noted in a later chapter.

The argument over whether Muhammad was illiterate or literate is not important. What is important is that the *Koran* is not Muhammad's message or even his words. As will be seen, Muhammad was simply the "messenger of God." Muhammad received the words of the Islamic god through the angel Gabriel. Basically, Muhammad went into a trance and the angel Gabriel came and revealed to him a chapter or verses of the *Koran*. Muhammad would then recite the revelation to his followers. Thus, it is questionable if Muhammad meets the definition of a "prophet" since his behavior, ideas, and speech were not divinely inspired. Rather, he was nothing more than a loud speaker for the Islamic god or an actor reciting a script. Although he is often referred to as a prophet, even the Islamic god said, "Muhammad is no more than a messenger..."

(3:144). It should also be noted that the Islamic god did not give Muhammad the ability to produce any miracles (6:109, 29:49-50).

The root of the word *koran* means "to read" or "to recite," and the word *koran*, according to many, means "the book," "the recitation," or "the recitation from god." In reciting the *Koran*, Muslims believe they are reciting the exact words of the Islamic god, and each *sura*, or chapter, is intended to be a single recitation. For Muslims, the *Koran* is not only the word of the Islamic god untouched by human intervention, but it is also the final word since, as mentioned above, Muhammad was the last prophet (33:40). Thus, all knowledge is in the *Koran*. Muslims believe that previous holy books, such as the *Torah* and the *Bible*, were corrupted and distorted by the followers of earlier prophets (2:75; 3:78; 4:46). For example, Muslims believe Jewish rabbis took out material from the *Old Testament* (5:13) and Christians took out material from the *New Testament* (5:14) which prophesied the coming of Muhammad. In fact, according to the *Koran*, Islam came before Judaism and Christianity, and their prophets, such as Abraham and Jesus, were Muslims. Thus, Muhammad was not "the" prophet of Islam but "a" prophet. Because of the corruption and the failure to worship Allah properly, the revelations were revealed once again to Muhammad. Thus, the Islamic god was sending down "what came before" (3:3). The Islamic god told Muhammad, "Nothing is said to you (Muhammad) except what was said to the messengers before you" (41:43).

There are several stories of how the *Koran* came into existence as a book, rather than as a series of revelations Muhammad and his followers memorized and recited. One story is that Abu Bakr (Bekr), the man who followed Muhammad as the leader of Islam (c. 632-634), directed that the revelations be compiled because in the battle at Yamana, five months to a year after Muhammad's death, more than four hundred of the best reciters of the *Koran* were killed (B4679, B4986, B7191). The young man entrusted with the task was Zayd (Zaid), who had been one of Muhammad's secretaries. He initially questioned the propriety and even the legality of collecting the revelations since Muhammad had not requested that it be done. Abu Bakr finally convinced him it should be done, and Zayd enthusiastically went about the task. He later said it would have been easier to move a mountain than to collect the revelations. This probably meant there was no one person alive who had memorized all the revelations from whom they could have been transcribed, and that there may have been disagreements concerning the content of certain verses. The revelations were in different locations and were written on flat stones, animal bones, palm leafs, pieces of papyrus, pieces of wood, and scraps of leather. They were also found in the "minds of men." After being collected, they were given to one of Muhammad's widows, Hafsa, for safekeeping. Many have wondered why after being collected the *Koran* was treated as a private document rather than as a public religious document.

Although the initial treatment of the revelations was at best casual, current practices are very different. Because Muslims believe the *Koran* is the literal word of the Islamic god, it is treated with tremendous respect and reverence. Before touching the *Koran*, Muslims must wash, they cannot hold it below the waist, and it cannot be placed under other books. It is forbidden to take the *Koran* into the land of the enemy since a copy might fall into their hands (M1869, M1869R1). Additional material on handling or reading from the *Koran* will be covered in the chapter on *sharia*.

Other concerns dealing with the collection of the revelations have been raised. Some have speculated that Muhammad did not want the revelations collected because of the inconsistencies or because many were embarrassingly self-serving. Other writers have pointed out the rather casual treatment of the Islamic god's revelations for much of the twenty-three-year period they were being received. One example of the casual treatment of the revelations deals with the adultery stoning verse, which is not included in most versions of the *Koran*. It is missing because it was written on a palm leaf that was eaten by a goat which wandered into the apartment of one of Muhammad's wives.

Another group believes it was the second leader of Islam after Muhammad, Omar (Umar), who initiated the collection of the *Koran* (c. 634-644), and the collection was completed under the reign of Othman (c. 644-656), the third leader of Islam after Muhammad. After the revelations were collected, Othman realized there were at least four versions of the *Koran*, which was causing conflict and tension among Muslims. Thus, he had three of the four versions destroyed.

There is another group who believes the collection of the revelations took place under Ali (c. 656-661), the fourth leader of Islam after Muhammad. Some believe Ali started the collection under the rule of Abu Bakr. Ali was Muhammad's cousin and son-in-law and was uniquely qualified to compile the *Koran* since he had been one of the first converts to Islam and he had memorized all of the revelations, although, as noted earlier, Zayd did not find one person who could recite the entire *Koran*.

There are other stories of how the *Koran* came into existence. One is that the *Koran* was created two hundred to three hundred years after Muhammad's death to justify a growing "religion." It may have been used to support Arab nationalism or to unite and provide a common religious identity for diverse cultural and religious groups that had been brought under Islamic control. It may also have been used to justify the murdering, pillaging, raping, and robbing being engaged in by Muslims.

Support for this last story of how the *Koran* came into existence comes from a number of areas. For example, there are no early versions of the *Koran* although there are thousands of surviving documents dealing with the *Bible*. There is also the curious paucity of early non-Muslim writings about the spread of Islam. It would seem as though a growing religious movement would have generated more attention, concern, notice, and writing than what has been found.[8] Some of these same critics even challenge if Muhammad was a real person or simply a prophet who was created to justify a growing religious movement.[9]

Obviously, this is an important area for discussion since the political and religious views of those collecting the revelations or destroying different versions of the *Koran* had the ability to shape the image of certain individuals and events. However, this discussion is beyond the scope of this book. And, to some extent, it does not matter when or who compiled the *Koran* or how the versions that were destroyed differed from the version that remains. What matters is what Muslims believe, and Muslims believe the *Koran* is the actual word of the Islamic god, and they act accordingly.

The *Koran* is a book of guidance for Muslims. Verse 2:2 states, "This is the Book (the *Koran*), whereof there is no doubt, a guidance to those who are *Al-Muttaqun* [the pious believers of Islamic monotheism who fear Allah much (abstain from all kinds of sins and evil deeds which He has forbidden) and love Allah much (perform all kinds of good deeds which he has ordained)]." Later, in the same *sura*, Muslims are provided specific instructions of what the Islamic god expects of them. Verse 2:190 states, "And fight in the way of Allah those who fight you..." *Sura* 2 continues by saying, "And kill them wherever you find them, and turn them out from where they have turned you out" (2:191). This section concludes with, "And fight them until there is no more *Fitnah* (disbelief and worshiping of others along with Allah) and (all and every kind of) worship is for Allah (Alone)" (2:193). If this guidance is not specific enough, verse 9:29, one of the last revealed, states, "Fight against those who (1) believe not in Allah, (2) nor in the Last Day, (3) nor forbid that which has been forbidden by Allah and His Messenger (Muhammad), (4) and those who acknowledge not the religion of truth (i.e., Islam) among the people of the Scripture (Jews and Christians), until they pay the *Jizyah* [a heavy tax] with willing submission, and feel themselves subdued."

Muslims are critical and often violent toward those who criticize the *Koran*. This is in part because of verse 21:23, which states, "He cannot be questioned as to what He does, while they will be questioned." However, there are some questions or problems with the *Koran* which need to be addressed.

Problems with the *Koran*

1. Failure to document revelations. As noted earlier, the *Koran* was revealed to Muhammad in a series of revelations over twenty-three years. When receiving a revelation, Muhammad went into a trance-like state, which some have claimed was really an epileptic seizure. After the revelation was received, he would recite it to his followers.

Early in his prophecy, the revelations were not written down. Muhammad simply told his followers the revelation, which they memorized and recited. The five daily prayers were in part so that revelations would be frequently repeated and not forgotten. This is supported by a *hadith* report (B5032) where Muhammad said, "So you must keep on reciting the *Koran* because it escapes from the hearts of men faster than camels do when they are released from their tying ropes."

One example of a verse being forgotten deals with the "stoning verse" which, as mentioned earlier, is not in all versions of the *Koran*. One *hadith* report (M1691) noted the stoning verse was "sent down" and "recited." The report continues by saying, "I am afraid that with the lapse of time, the people (may forget it) and may say: We do not find the punishment of stoning in the book of Allah, and thus go astray by abandoning this duty prescribed by Allah." Another *hadith* report (B6829) is similar and reads, "Umar said, 'I am afraid that after a long time has passed, people may say, "We do not find the Verses of the *Rajm* (stoning to death) in Allah's book (the *Koran*)," and consequently they may go astray by leaving an obligation that Allah has revealed.'" This is repeated in the next *hadith* report (B6830).

Even Muhammad would forget and have to be reminded of certain revelations by his followers. Muhammad's explanation was that for some reason the Islamic god had caused him to forget the revelation. For example, the *Koran* (87:6-7) states, "We shall make you to recite (the *Koran*), so you (Muhammad) shall not forget (it), except what Allah may will. He knows what is apparent and what is hidden." There is a similar passage in a *hadith* report (B5038) where one of Muhammad's wives was reminded of a verse she was "caused to forget." In another *hadith* report (B5039), Muhammad said, "Why does anyone of the people say, 'I have forgotten such and such Verses (of the *Koran*)?' He, in fact, is caused (by Allah) to forget."

Another similar incident is revealed in the *hadith* reports (B4992, B5041, B6936) when a Muslim was reciting a *sura* in a way that was different from the way Muhammad had recited it. Another follower took the man to Muhammad and announced that the man had been telling a lie by reciting the *sura* incorrectly. Muhammad asked the man to recite the *sura*. After listening to the recitation, Muhammad said, "It has been revealed like this" or "It was revealed to be recited in this way." He then asked the second man to recite the *sura* as he had heard it. After reciting the *sura* in a different way, Muhammad repeated, "It has been revealed like this" or "It was revealed to be recited in this way." Muhammad then added, "This *Koran* has been revealed to be recited in seven different ways, so recite it whichever way is easier for you." In another *hadith* report (B5062), a Muslim heard someone reciting the *Koran* in a way that differed from the way he recited it. The two men went to Muhammad and explained their disagreement. Muhammad said, "Both of you are reciting in a correct way, so carry on reciting" or "The *Koran* has been revealed to be recited in seven different ways, so recite of it that which is easier for you." In fact, Muhammad had the angel Gabriel revel each *sura* in seven ways (B3219, B4991).

In another *hadith* report (B4943), two Muslims recited a verse the way they had heard it recited by Muhammad. But then one said, "Many do not consider this recitation as the correct one." If Muhammad did not know the correct recitation, then who did? There is also an instance where a scribe could not find a revelation he had recorded the previous evening. Muhammad said it had been recalled to heaven.

After Muhammad died, one of his followers, Abu Bakr, recited an important section of the *Koran* which another follower, Omar, said he had never heard before. And one of Muhammad's wives noted that *Sura* 39 (The Groups) had two hundred verses when it was recited orally, but in written form there were only seventy-five verses. This, of course, raises the questions, "If there were omissions, were there also additions? And, if memories failed, is the *Koran* the exact word of the Islamic god?"

One of Muhammad's scribes, Abdullah Sa'd, left Islam after Muhammad allowed him to add words, phrases, or sentences to revelations. Muhammad allowed Sa'd to add the last sentence to verse 23:14 which states, "So blessed is Allah, the Best of Creators." Other times he made suggestions in the wording of revelations to which Muhammad agreed. There were also times he did not record exactly what Muhammad recited. One example was when Muhammad told him to write "Most High, All-Wise," and he wrote

"All-Wise," to which Muhammad said, "Yes it is all the same." The scribe then sarcastically announced that both of them must have been inspired by Allah, and if Muhammad was a liar, then the scribe was an equally good liar. After being allowed to make other changes, the scribe left Islam asking how a mere scribe could change the words of the Islamic god. The *Koran* (6:93) has a section on this scribe which starts, "And who can be more unjust than he who invents a lie against Allah, or says: 'A revelation has come to me' whereas no revelation has come to him in anything; and who says, 'I will reveal the like of what Allah has revealed.'" Muhammad's hatred of this scribe was so great that when he conquered Mecca in 632, he ordered that ten people be killed, including this scribe.

There is also the question, "What is a revelation?" Or, more specifically, which revelations from the angel Gabriel went into the *Koran* and which did not? The chapters with the biography of Muhammad have several instances where the angel Gabriel came to Muhammad with revelations which are not in the *Koran*. Thus, there are reports of revelations and the basic content of the revelations, but there are no corresponding verses in the *Koran*.

Six "revelations" that do not appear in the *Koran* will be mentioned. First, the angel Gabriel came to Muhammad and asked, "What is faith?" Muhammad replied, "Faith is to believe in Allah, His angels, (the) meeting with Him, His Messengers, and to believe in Resurrection." The angel Gabriel then asked, "What is Islam?" Muhammad said, "To worship Allah alone and none else, to perform the *salat* (prayers), to pay the *zakat* and to observe *saum* [fast (according to Islamic teachings)] during the month of Ramadan" (B56).

In the second example, Muhammad was on a mountain when the angel Gabriel came to him and said, "Whoever amongst your followers dies, worshiping none along with Allah, will enter paradise." This was even if the follower stole or committed illegal intercourse (B2388, B3222, B6443, B6444).

The third instance occurred in Medina after the Battle of the Trench when Muhammad was taking a bath. The angel Gabriel came to him and said, "You have put down your arms! By Allah, I have not put down my arms yet." Based on this revelation, Muhammad attacked a Jewish tribe (B2813).

The fourth example deals with an instance where the angel Gabriel had not honored his promise to visit Muhammad. When he finally came, he announced, "We angels do not enter a house in where there is a picture or a dog" (B3227).

The fifth example deals with an episode where the angel Gabriel offered Muhammad two cups, one with milk and the other with wine. Muhammad drank the cup with milk. The Angel Gabriel stated, "Praise be to Allah who guided you to *al-Fitrah* (Islam and the right path); if you had taken (the cup of) wine your nation would have gone astray" (B5576).

The sixth and last example deals with a *hadith* report described in the last chapter. Here it was mentioned that Muslim women attended to their bathroom needs by going out into the fields at night. One night one of Muhammad's wives, described as a tall and bulky lady, went out to attend to her needs and was chastised because she was so easily identified. The woman ran back to see Muhammad, who was having dinner with his child-wife Aisha. She related what had happened, and Aisha noted that a revelation came to him and he said, "Permission has been granted to you that you may go out for your needs" (M2170, M2170R3).

The above examples illustrate the possibility that revelations were omitted from the *Koran.*

Although many believe the collection of the revelations started soon after Muhammad's death, it was probably at least twenty years before this collection of palm leafs, flat stones, pieces of dried leather, animal bones, and the memories of followers were collected into the *Koran.* The word *probably* is used since, as noted earlier, there are varying accounts of who was responsible for the collection of the revelations and when, or if, it took place. The prevalent view is that there were at least four early versions of the *Koran*, and certainly some of the final verses were not original but were inserted by scribes. Eventually, three of the versions were destroyed and there was only one *Koran.* From the *Koran* we learn Muhammad was to make Islam "superior over all other religions" (9:33) and Muslims were obligated to believe in and obey Allah and Muhammad (B7137, 3:32,

3:53, 3:132, 4:13, 4:14, 4:42, 4:59, 4:69, 4:80, 4:115, 4:170, 5:92, 8:1, 8:13, 8:20, 8:46, 9:63, 9:71, 24:51, 24:52, 24:54, 24:56, 33:21, 33:31, 33:33, 47:33, 48:13, 49:14, 58:13, 58:20, 61:11, 64:12, 68:4, 72:23). We also know that "And verily, you (Muhammad) are on an exalted (standard of) character" (68:29). And, if Muslims wanted to reach paradise, they should follow Muhammad's behavior since "in the Messenger of Allah (Muhammad) you have a good example to follow for him who hopes for (the meeting with) Allah and the Last Day, and remembers Allah much" (33:21).

Although Muhammad was not divine, his behavior and character were perfect because everything he did and said was divinely inspired. Verse 53:3 states, "He (Muhammad) does not speak of his own desire." And in verse 7:203 Muhammad states, "I but follow what is revealed to me from my Lord."

2. Confusion. About twenty percent of the *Koran* is so poorly written that the passages, phrases, and sentences cannot be understood in any language even though the *Koran* has passages stating it is clear (16:103, 24:46, 39:28, 43:2, 44:2, 75:19). The following passage in the *Koran* (3:7) states that there are clear and unclear passages:

> It is He Who has sent down to you (Muhammad) the Book (*Koran*). In it are Verses that are entirely clear, they are the foundation of the Book [and those are the Verses of *Al-Ahkam* (commandments), *Al-Fara'id* (obligatory duties), *Al-Hudud* (laws for the punishment of thieves, adulterers, etc.)] and others not entirely clear. So, as for those in whose hearts there is a deviation (from the truth) they follow that which is not entirely clear thereof, seeking *Al-Fitnah* (polytheism and trials) and seeking for it hidden meanings; but none knows its hidden meanings except Allah. And those who are firmly grounded in knowledge say: "We believe in it; the whole of it (clear and unclear verses) are from our Lord." And none receive admonition except men of understanding.

This passage is repeated in a *hadith* report (B4547).

In 29 *suras*, the first verse starts with a combination of letters "no one" understands (*Suras* 2, 3, 7, 10-15, 19, 20, 26 - 32, 36, 38, 40-46, 50, 68). Some of the "words" are *Alif-Lam-Mim*, *Ta-Ha*, *Ta-Sin-Mim*, *Nun*, *Qaf*, *Ya-Sin*, and *Sad*. In a document that is "clear," this lack of clarity is explained by the footnote that says, "These letters are one of the miracles of the *Koran*, and none but Allah (Alone) knows their meanings." We also learn that "God knows best what He means by these [letters]" (2:1).

Part of the confusion is because there are many non-Arabic words, meaningless Arabic words, words that do not seem to exist in any language, or words where the meaning is not clear or has been lost. In other parts of the *Koran*, the person or event being referred to is not clear. This may be because the reference is to persons or events that were known in an oral society but which have been forgotten.

There are also areas where a document supposedly dictated by the Islamic god does not have god as the speaker. For example, 1:1 is a prayer to the Islamic god, probably spoken by Muhammad. In more than three hundred other verses, editors have inserted the word *say* generally at the beginning of the revelation. Thus, the Islamic god is asking Muhammad to recite or "say" the verse. For example, verse 9:51 reads, "Say: 'Nothing shall ever happen to us except what Allah has ordained for us.'" As can be seen, without the "say," Muhammad or someone else is the speaker. By inserting the "say," the Islamic god is telling Muhammad to recite the verse. A basic question is who decided which verses needed to have "say" inserted?

There are other examples where the Islamic god is not the speaker, a few of which will be mentioned. Verse 6:104 is spoken by Muhammad and says, "And I (Muhammad) am not a watcher over you." The speaker in verse 17:1 is probably Muhammad and starts, "Glorified (and Exalted) be He (Allah)..." Verse 27:91 is also spoken by Muhammad and reads, "I (Muhammad) have been commanded only to worship the Lord of this city (Makkah)..." In another passage, angels are the speakers, and it starts by saying, "And we (angels) descend not except by the Command of your Lord (Muhammad)..." (19:64). Islamic apologists claim that these are examples of the Islamic god instructing Muhammad on how to say certain verses.

In other verses, there are grammatical errors. And, given the interruption in the flow or rhyme of certain verses, it appears that words were inserted by later writers.

As noted with the insertion of the word *say*, there are also other missing words which editors have inserted to make the thought or sentence complete. Readers have probably already noticed the cited verses often have a word or words in brackets or parentheses. For example, verse 17.1 was cited above where Muhammad was the speaker. Muhammad was inserted by the editors as the speaker. How did they know Muhammad was the speaker? Verse 3:60 reads, "(This is) the truth from your Lord, so be not of those who doubt." How did the "editors" know "this is" were the missing words from the Islamic god? Numerous critics have asked, "How could an all-knowing, all-wise god produce such an incoherent manuscript?"

The liberty of inserting words can also be seen in the *Noble Koran* in verse 8:60, which reads in part, "And make ready against them all you can of power, including steeds of war (tanks, planes, missiles, artillery) to threaten the enemy of Allah..." The inclusion of tanks, planes, missiles, and artillery in a seventh century document either indicates an incredibly perceptive Islamic god of future developments not found in other sections of the *Koran* or of editors inserting words.

Adding to the confusion is the fact that many of the *suras* have a random assortment of verses. Readers often find there are several verses that are logically connected, but then there is no transition to the next set of verses, which again are logically connected but not to the prior set of verses or those which follow.

Another source of confusion is that rather than being a story that is presented with context in chronological order, the *Koran* is a series of random verses which cannot be understood without consulting either the biographies of Muhammad or the *hadith* reports. For example, verses 111:1-3 read, "Perish the two hands of Abu Lahab (an uncle of the Prophet) and perish he. His wealth and his children will not benefit him! He will be burnt in a Fire of blazing flames!" Unless it is an annotated *Koran,* such as the one being used here which notes Abu Lahab is Muhammad's uncle, or if readers have read biographies of Muhammad, they will not know who Abu Lahab was and why he was going to be cast into blazing flames. Even though readers do not know why Abu Lahab, which some passages claim means "father of the flames," was going to burn in blazing flames, other passages claim that nothing has been left out of the *Koran.* For example, "We have neglected nothing in the book..." (6:38), the Islamic god has sent down a "book (the *Koran*) explained in detail" (6:114), the *Koran* is "a detailed explanation of everything" (12:111), and the *Koran* is "an exposition of everything" (16:89). This brings us back to the question, "If the *Koran* is perfect and complete, why do readers need to consult other sources to understand it?"

To illustrate the lack of context, some have suggested taking several novels, perhaps one in a foreign language, ripping out all the pages, randomly throwing ninety percent of the pages away, and then randomly putting the remaining pages together. Then start to read the "book." Few, if any, readers would be able to understand what was taking place as they read this "book." This is the equivalent of reading the *Koran.*

Some of the above criticisms are challenged by Islamic apologists who claim that to be understood, the *Koran* needs to be read in its original classical Arabic. In fact, they claim that the *Koran* is only the *Koran* as it was originally written. However, since there are no early editions of the *Koran,* and since later "editors" added diacritical points to the text, the "original" *Koran* no longer exists except on eternal tablets in heaven. Also, many of those making the above criticisms are fluent in classical Arabic and still find the *Koran* either does not make sense or is incomprehensible. Additionally, most Muslims do not read or understand classical Arabic and, thus, need a translated copy of the *Koran.* It would also be difficult to attract converts if the first demand was they learn classical Arabic, the equivalent of learning Chaucer's Middle English. This also raises the question of whether those who are illiterate can be Muslims.

Other defenders of the *Koran* address issues such as grammatical errors by stating humans have created a flawed grammatical system which does not understand the words of the Islamic god.

Because the *Koran* is so confusing, Muslim writers have developed the *tafsir*, or explanation. One is the multi-volume set titled *Tafsir Ibn Kathir*, which means "the explanation by Ibn Kathir" (c. 1301-1373). In a *tafsir*, an author takes each verse in the *Koran* and explains it using the *hadith* reports, the reports by Muhammad's companions, the reports of those who knew the companions, and through scholarly reasoning.

One specific example of the confusion and the need for an explanation can be seen in verse 2:256, which states in part, "There is no compulsion in religion." Apologists for Islam cite this verse endlessly to demonstrate that Islam is a religion of tolerance. Critics claim it has been abrogated by later verses such as verse 9:33, which strives to make Islam superior to all other religions, and by verse 9:73, which instructs Muhammad to "Strive hard against the disbelievers and the hypocrites, and be harsh against them, their abode is Hell..." According to the *Tafsir Ibn Kathir*[10] this verse was revealed in Medina when a Muslim woman whose children had all died shortly after birth swore she would convert any future children to Judaism with the hope this would prevent them from dying. With this revelation, Muhammad informed the woman she was not compelled to do this. Thus, this verse is only applicable in this instance.

There are several other interpretations of verse 2:256. One is that it was revealed shortly after Muhammad came to Medina so as to not upset the Jewish tribes, and it was later abrogated. Others believe this verse is one of the mandatory verses appearing in religious documents since few religious leaders desire a congregation of forced converts. For others, this verse only relates to Muslims. Thus, non-Muslims can be forced to convert. But others believe the verse is only for non-Muslims who may attempt to force Muslims to become apostates. Perhaps Muslims must fight to make Islam superior (92:193), but they cannot force anyone to accept Islam. Finally, it comes down to what the word *compulsion* means. Is there a compulsion to convert if the consequence for not converting to Islam is death or subjugation?

Another source of confusion occurs when verses are only partially cited. Perhaps the most frequently partially cited verse by Islamic apologists is verse 5:32, which is used to illustrate that the

Koran has its own version of "thou shall not kill." It is generally cited as, "If any one slew a person it would be as if he killed all mankind." The entire verse is as follows:

> Because of that, We ordained for the Children of Israel that if anyone killed a person not in retaliation of murder, or (and) to spread mischief in the land—it would be as if he killed all mankind, and if anyone saved a life, it would be as if he saved the life of all mankind. And indeed, there came to them Our Messenger with clear proofs, evidences, and signs, even then after that many of them continued to exceed the limits (e.g., by doing oppression unjustly and exceeding beyond the limits set by Allah by committing the major sins) in the land.

First, note that this verse does not apply to Muslims but is related to a rule handed down to Jews and is chastising them for violating the rule. The next verse (5:33) continues by saying, "The recompense of those who wage war against Allah and His Messenger and do mischief in the land is only that they shall be killed or crucified or their hands and their feet be cut off from opposite sides, or be exiled from the land. That is their disgrace in this world, and a great torment is theirs in the Hereafter." Here we see that non-Muslims can be "killed or crucified" for "exceeding beyond the limits set by Allah." This does not sound like a "thou shalt not kill" verse but a "kill the non-Muslims verse."

There are examples where the initial revelations were so confusing that the Islamic god had to issue a clarification. One example deals with verse 4:95, which starts, "Not equal are those of the believers who sit (at home) except those who are disabled (by injury or are blind or lame)..." Two *hadith* reports (B2831, B4490) note that the initial verse was, "Not equal are those of the believers who sit (at home)..." Then a blind follower asked Muhammad the question, "O Allah's Messenger! What is your order for me?" Another verse was quickly revealed which gave an "exception clause" for those disabled by blindness, injury, or lameness.

There is a similar *hadith* report (B4511) concerning verse 2:187 which reads in part, "Eat and drink until the white thread (light) of dawn appears to you distinct from the black thread (darkness of night)..." The *hadith* report states that originally the revelation just dealt with the white thread and the black thread. However, some followers did not understand the white thread was dawn and the black thread was night. Therefore, another revelation partially clarified the matter by adding "of dawn." As can be seen, apparently some Muslims still did not understand the revelation, so editors added "darkness of night."

Edward Gibbons, the author of the *Decline and Fall of the Roman Empire*, said the *Koran* is an "incoherent rhapsody of fable and precept, and declamation, which seldom excites a sentiment or an idea, which sometimes crawls in the dust, and is sometimes lost in the clouds."[11] Others have noted it is a collection of disorganized statements that only the most dedicated can spend any time reading. Many believe, with good reason, that many passages in the *Koran* were plagiarized from early Christian, Jewish, or Zoroastrian sources. Critics ask, "Why did the Islamic god need to plagiarize?" Apologists respond that the Islamic god was simply restating what had been presented earlier to Jews and Christians who had distorted the revelations.

3. Failure to organize chronologically. As noted earlier, the *Koran* is not arranged chronologically. The first *sura*, or chapter, is titled the "*fatihah*," or opening, and is considered by some to be the equivalent of the Christian "Lord's Prayer." It is one of the shortest *suras* in the *Koran*, with only seven verses. This *sura* is recited during each of the five daily prayer sessions. In fact, if it is not recited, the prayers are invalid (B756). After the first *sura*, the *Koran's* additional one hundred and thirteen *suras*, or chapters, are "generally" arranged by length, with the longest *suras* coming first and the shorter coming last. The word *generally* was used because it uncertain what is meant by length. After the first *sura*, the *Koran* is not ordered by the number of verses in each *sura*. For example, the second *sura* has two hundred and eighty six verses, the third has two hundred verses, the fourth has one hundred and seventy-six verses, and the fifth has one hundred and twenty verses. But the

sixth *sura* increases to one hundred and sixty-five verses, and the seventh increases to two hundred and eighty-six verses. There are several other examples, such as the thirteenth *sura* has forty-three verses, but the thirty-seventh has one hundred and eighty-two verses. Perhaps those who claim that the *suras* in the *Koran* are ordered by length are not referring to the number of verses in each *sura* but the number of words. Measuring word count is difficult because editors have inserted additional words to clarify the *Koran.*

The previous paragraph mentioned the *Koran* is not arranged chronologically. For example, the first revelation Muhammad received is the ninety-sixth *sura* in the *Koran*, and the ninety-first revelation is the second *sura.* And the last or second to last revelation became the ninth *sura*, which contains the *Koran's* most intolerant and violent passages. Several scholars have attempted to order the *suras* chronologically. In these attempts at placing the *suras* in chronological order, it is often difficult to provide a specific date for a *sura*, but many can be placed into general categories. For example, the revelations received in Mecca can be separated into early and late. After leaving Mecca and going to Medina, the revelations generally fall into early, Battle of Badr, Battle of Uhud, and the pre-conquest of Mecca.

Three comments are needed on the attempts to place the *suras* in chronological order. First, there is disagreement among scholars on when certain *suras* were revealed. Second, although scholars do not agree on the chronological ordering of the *suras*, there is general agreement that over time the nature of the *suras* changed, with the earlier *suras* being more peaceful and tolerant, while the later *suras* were more intolerant and violent. Third, some of the *suras* have verses from different periods.

4. Repetition. Much of the *Koran* is repetitious, with stories being presented several times. For example, the Exodus story is repeated twenty-seven times.

5. Contradictions. There are at least four verses in the *Koran* stating it is perfect and cannot be changed. Verse 6:34 says in part, "None can alter the words (Decisions) of Allah." Verse 6:115 is similar, saying, "None can change His words." Verse 10:64 says, "No change can there be in the Words of Allah." And verse 18:27 states

in full, "And recite what has been revealed to you (Muhammad) of the Book (*Koran*) of your Lord (i.e., recite it, understand and follow its teachings and act on its orders and preach it to men). None can change His Words, and none will you find as a refuge other than Him."

As noted earlier, the *Koran* is without "crookedness" (39:28). In fact, it is being guarded from corruption (15:9) and it has not been "corrupted" (41:41). Not only is it perfect and cannot be changed, but it is also without contradictions. Verse 4:82 says, "Had it been from other than Allah, they would surely, have found therein many a contradiction." Well, "they" have found numerous contradictory passages in the *Koran*, which brings up the controversial area of "abrogation." Basically, sometimes the Islamic god issued contradictory revelations. The reasoning was that the Islamic god was bringing a better revelation. Verse 2.106 says, "Whatever a verse [revelation] do We [God] abrogate or cause to be forgotten, We bring a better one or similar to it." And verse 16:101 states, "And when We change a verse (of the *Koran*) in place of another—and Allah knows best what He sends down—they (the disbelievers) say: 'You (Muhammad) are but a *Muftari* (forger, liar).' Nay, but most of them know not." An additional verse (22:52) reads, "Never did We send a Messenger or a Prophet before you but when he did recite the Revelation or narrated or spoke, *Shaitan* (Satan) threw (some falsehood) in it. Then Allah established His Revelations. And Allah is All-Knower, All-Wise." This verse relates to the Satanic Verses, discussed in a later chapter, where the verses inserted by Satan were abrogated and removed from the *Koran* (see B4481 and B4762).

Thus, according to apologists for Islam there are no contradictions in the *Koran* because the earlier verses which contradicted the later verses were eliminated or abrogated by the later verses. One of the problems is that most of the abrogated verses were *not* removed from the *Koran*. The process of having later passages abrogate or cancel out earlier passages is a unique feature among sacred manuscripts. Islamic apologists claim that an abrogation is not a contradiction but an improvement. Many critics claim that Muhammad created new revelations to meet current circumstances.

Abrogation is a complex and controversial area within Islam. The number of abrogated verses ranges from five to five hundred. An additional problem deals with contradictions between the *Koran* and the *hadith* reports. Does the *Koran* abrogate contradictory passages in the *hadith* reports or do the *hadith* reports abrogate contradictory verses in the *Koran*? We also need to ask which prevails if there are contradictions among the *sunnah* (Muhammad's actions and behavior), the *hadith* reports, and the *Koran*. It would have been simpler if the Islamic god would have had Muslims "forget" the abrogated verses prior to their inclusion in the *Koran*.

Another explanation for abrogation is in verse 13:39, which states, "Allah blots out what He wills and confirms (what He wills): And with Him is the Mother of the Book." There are additional verses allowing for the abrogation of verses. For example, verse 17:86 states, "And if We willed, We could surely, take away that which We have revealed to you (i.e., this *Koran*). Then you would find no protector for you against Us in that respect." As noted earlier, because the *Koran* is not organized chronologically, it is sometimes difficult to ascertain which passages came first and are to be cancelled and replaced by later passages. Scholars have noted that in the chronologically earlier passages where Muhammad had the least power, he tended to preach tolerance and non-violence. In the chronologically later passages after Muhammad had gained more military and political power, he preached intolerance and violence. Muslim apologists often cite the early chronological verses which have been abrogated to demonstrate that Islam is a religion of peace and tolerance, rather than the later chronological verses which stress intolerance and violence. For example, there are more than one hundred and twenty verses calling for tolerance and patience, however, these have been abrogated by verses such as 9:5, which states, "kill the *Mushrikūn* [disbelievers] wherever you find them, and capture them and besiege them, and lie in wait for them in every ambush," and by verse 5:33, which says, "The recompense of those who wage war against Allah and His Messenger and do mischief in the land is only that they shall be killed or crucified or their hands and their feet be cut off from opposite sides, or be exiled from the land."

Critics of the *Koran* ask, "Why does a divine revelation need to be abrogated?" or "Why does an all-wise god need to develop something better? Couldn't the Islamic god have developed the better verses first?" Islamic apologists claim the need for progressive revelations, to which critics respond, "Then why isn't this found in other areas?" For example, the polytheistic Arabs were *not* told to progressively reduce the number of gods they believed in to one.

Islamic apologists claim that abrogation refers to the *Bible* being abrogated by the *Koran*.

As noted earlier, the verse "there is no compulsion in religion" (2:256) was abrogated by several later verses. In addition to 9.5, cited earlier, there is also verse 9:29, which says, "Fight against those who (1) believe not in Allah, (2) nor in the Last Day, (3) nor forbid that which has been forbidden by Allah and His Messenger [Muhammad], (4) and those who acknowledge not the religion of truth [Islam]." Those who believe verse 2:256 was abrogated also cite verse 8:39, which states, "And fight them until there is no more *Fitnah* (disbelief and polytheism or those who worship others besides Allah), and the religion will all be for Allah Alone." And for those who still do not believe verse 2:256 was abrogated, critics cite 9:3, which says, "Then know that you cannot escape (from the punishment of) Allah."

The title of the ninth *sura* is "The Repentance." It is also called the "Verses of the Sword." Other than the first *sura*, this is the only one that does not have the preface "In the Name of Allah, the Most Gracious, the Most Merciful." Islamic apologists claim the missing preface is because *Suras* 8 and 9 were actually one *sura* and became separated when editing the *Koran*. If this is true, it means the *Koran* is not the perfect and unchanged word of the Islamic god. Critics of Islam believe that by the time this revelation was received, Muhammad's power was such that the Islamic god did not have to be gracious or merciful.

Another contradiction is, "Who is the *Koran* for?" Some verses claim it is for Arabs (14:4, 42:7, 43:3, 46:12). This is supported by verse 12.2, which claims it is an Arabic *Koran* "in order that you may understand" (see also 13:37). Also, 16:103 concludes, "This (the *Koran*) is a clear Arabic tongue" (see 20:113, 26:195, 39:28,

41:3, 41:44, 42:7, 43:3). Yet other verses claim the *Koran* is for all mankind (3:138, 34:28, B335, B438).

There is a contradiction on who was the first Muslim. In verses 6:14 and 6:163, it is Muhammad; in verse 7:143, it is Moses; and in verses 2:131 and 3:67, it is Abraham.

Verses on the consumption of alcoholic beverages provide more contradictions. Early in its development, Islam allowed the consumption of alcoholic beverages although the sin of drinking was greater than the benefit it provided (2:219). A progression then came in verse 4:43, which prohibited Muslims from going to prayer drunk, among other things. Then before the Battle of Uhud, which the Muslims lost, some Muslims consumed wine prior to the battle. Verse 5:90 was then revealed, which states, "O you who believe! Intoxicants (all kinds of alcoholic drinks)...are an abomination of *Shaitan's* (Satan's) handiwork. So avoid (strictly all) that (abomination) in order that you may be successful." This verse abrogated the earlier ones and ended the legal consumption of alcoholic beverages by Muslims. Although wine is prohibited in the secular world, in paradise there are "rivers of wine delicious to those who drink" (47:15), and a place where "they will be given to drink of pure sealed wine" (83:25, see B4616-4620). Critics ask, "If alcohol is an abomination of Satan, then how did it get into paradise?"

There is even a contradiction in the number of daily prayers. Currently, most pious Muslims pray five times per day. However, the *Koran* does not specify five prayer sessions per day. Verse 11:114 mentions at "the two ends of the day and in some hours of the night..." Verse 17:78 has "mid-day" and "early dawn." Verse 20:130 requires prayers at sunrise, sunset, night, and "the ends of the day." And while verse 30:17 calls for prayers at sunset, night, and morning, verse 30:18 calls for them in the afternoon and at sunset.

There are also contradictions in the number of days it took the Islamic god to create heaven and earth. In some verses, it is six days (7:54, 10:3, 11:7). In verse 41:9, it took two days to create the earth, but in the next verse (41:10) it is four days. It apparently took two days to create the heavens (41:12).

Although the *Koran* is supposed to be the complete and final word of the Islamic god, which has "neglected nothing" (6:38), there is a contradictory verse. Verse 31:27 states, "And if all the trees on the earth were pens and the seas (were ink wherewith to write), with seven seas behind it to add to its (supply), yet the Words of Allah would not be exhausted" (see B Book 97, Chapter 30).

One last area on abrogation deals with verse 2:23, which commands Christians and Jews who doubt Muhammad to compose a *sura* "the like" of which is in the *Koran.* An issue that will be examined in a later chapter deals with the Satanic Verses, where Satan sent revelations to Muhammad. Although the Satanic Verses were not sent by Christians or Jews, Satan sent revelations which must have been "the like" of what is in the *Koran* because both Muhammad and his followers initially believed them to be from the Islamic god.

Not only can verses be abrogated but, as noted earlier, apparently some can be cancelled or recalled. One of the *hadith* reports (B4090) states, "We used to read a verse of the *Koran* revealed in their connection, but later the verse was cancelled." A *hadith* report (B2801) states that at one time Muslims recited, "Inform our people that we have met our Lord, He is pleased with us and He has made us pleased." The report continues by saying, "Later on this Koranic verse was abrogated (cancelled)."

6. No early versions. It has already been mentioned that there are no early versions of the *Koran.* There are fragments dated to about one hundred years after Muhammad's death. The earliest complete copy of the *Koran* is from the ninth century. Unlike the current versions of the *Koran,* the early fragments do not have vowels or diacritical dots, markings, or points which, depending on their absence or placement, can change the meaning of a word. These were added in the eighth and ninth centuries. There are numerous discussions on this issue, and one example will suffice. Many *jihadists* assume that after death they will go to paradise where there will be an abundance of promiscuous virgins. By changing the diacritical dots, one writer has noted they are actually getting white raisins. Given the image of paradise as a large garden, this seems logical. This again brings up the question of who decided where to place the markings. Different markings can change the word and its meaning. This brings up another question. Namely, the *Koran* states

the Islamic god previously sent down both prophets and the revelations. However, the revelations were corrupted, and thus, there was a need to send down a final prophet and once again the revelations. Why would the Islamic god allow humans to corrupt the revelations a third time by adding diacritical and punctuation marks? Apologists claim there is no need for punctuation marks since the word of the Islamic god has "syntactic precision."

As noted earlier, some scholars speculate that the lack of early versions is because the *Koran* was a later Islamic invention, something created for a growing religion. Just as the *Koran* could be created, the accounts of its development could also have been created and, as will be seen, tied as closely as possible to the time of Muhammad.

7. Different translations and Arabic versions. As with any translated work, different translations can present problems. For example, one translation might say, "Strike off their heads..." while another will soften the words by saying, "Smite their necks..." Another example deals with the consumption of alcohol, which is prohibited in Islam, at least in the secular world. Verse 16.67 says, "And from the fruits of date palms and grapes, you derive strong drink and a goodly provision. Verily, therein is indeed a sign for people who have wisdom." In other translations, the word for *wine* can mean "intoxicating drink," "inebriating drink," "strong drink," or "wholesome drink." Apologists who agree that there are rivers of wine in paradise claim that the wine is not intoxicating and does not produce a hangover.

8. Self-serving verses. As will be seen in the chapters presenting a biography of Muhammad, some of the verses in the *Koran* appeared in a timely manner to defend Muhammad's behavior, which offended or violated the traditional cultural and religious beliefs of the time. For example, Muhammad's Islamic god was not above quickly issuing "revelations" to quiet nagging wives (66:1-12), allowing him an exception to the rule prohibiting more than four wives (33:50), allowing him to marry his son's wife (33:37-38), or dismissing allegations of adultery against his child-wife (24:11).

This brings up another interesting question. Namely, if the *Koran* has always existed on eternal tablets, then how did the Islamic god anticipate that Muhammad would have so many personal problems that would need to be dealt with?

9. Inaccuracies in science, history, and theology. There are many inaccuracies in the *Koran* in areas such as history, science, and theology. Two examples will suffice. In verse 27:61, the earth is seen as fixed, and verse 4:157 states that Christ was not crucified.

10. Nothing new. Most of the *Koran* is unoriginal. It is a mixture of tribal customs and a variety of religions, such as Christianity and Judaism, of which Muhammad had a poor understanding. Verse 16:103 reads in part, "It is only a human who teaches him." This relates to what non-Muslims were saying about Muhammad, who did not consider his "revelations" to be inspired by god. Verses 25:4-5 have the non-Muslims claiming Muhammad invented the *Koran* or that it was nothing more than the "tales of the ancients" which he had written down.

Where Are We At?

The following chapter will continue the examination of Islam's holiest document, the *Koran*, by providing commentary on how it deals with certain issues. This will then be followed by a chapter dealing with *sharia*, or Islamic law, which will conclude the examination of the ideological foundations of Islam.

CHAPTER 4: WHERE TO START III: THE *KORAN* (PART II)

The last chapter started by examining the origins of the *Koran* and ended after reviewing some problems with the *Koran*. This chapter will provide commentary on the *Koran*.

Commentary on the *Koran*

According to Muslims, the *Koran* is the eternal, exact, final, perfect, and unchanged words of the Islamic god. It is the holiest book in Islam. To understand Islam and the danger it presents, we need to understand the *Koran*.

The *Koran* is very blunt about Muhammad's purpose in life. Muhammad was to explain "clearly" to non-Muslims (16:44) that the Islamic god was the only god who had the right to be worshiped (3:18). Furthermore, Muhammad was to guide all non-Muslims to Islam and to make Islam superior over all other religions (9:33, see 48:28, 61:9). Thus, Islam is at war until all embrace Islam, are killed, or are placed in a slave-like status called *dhimmitude* (47:4).

Not only is the *Koran* very clear on Muhammad's purpose in life, but it is also very clear on why humans were created. Verse 3:31 reads, "And I (Allah) created not...mankind except that they should worship Me (Alone)." Those who surrendered to Islam and worshiped the Islamic god would have their sins forgiven and be admitted to paradise.

From the *Koran*, we know humans were created to worship the Islamic god. We also know Muhammad was to guide non-Muslims to Islam and to make Islam superior over other religions. In this chapter, the *Koran's* position on paradise, free will and predestination, apostasy, *jihad*, women, moderate Muslims, Islam and democracy, and accommodation (or "can't we all just get along?") will be examined.

1. Paradise. There have been many questions about the Islamic paradise, especially if each male entering paradise really has seventy-two promiscuous virgins waiting for him. A corresponding question is what do women get—unlimited shopping for one-size, one-color, one-style *burkas*?

Paradise is a major theme in the *Koran*, and there are more than one hundred and twenty verses describing its characteristics. While Muhammad's Arabia must have been a barren, desolate, hostile, and poor land, the Islamic paradise is the opposite. While most of Arabia is dry, paradise has rivers and springs of water (3:15, 3:198, 4:57, 7:43, 9:72, 16:31, 18:31, 20:76, 22:23, 39:20, 44:52, 47:15, 55:50, 55:66, 56:31, 57:12, 76:6, 88:12, 98:8). There are also rivers of honey, milk, and wine (47:15). There is every kind of fruit (43:73, 44:55, 55:52, 55:68, 56:20, 56:29, 56:32, 77:42), which only grows low on trees or bushes so it can be easily picked (69:23, 76:14). Fruit trees or bushes that have thorns in Arabia do not have thorns in paradise (56:28). There is the flesh of any fowl desired (56:21). There is also ample shade and the temperature is never too hot or too cold (56:30, 76:13, 76:14). And while in Arabia there are times of drought and famine, in paradise there is a never-ending supply of drink and food (9:21, 50:35, 52:22). In paradise there is no bitterness (15:47); taxes (7:42); or talk that is dirty, evil, false, or vain (19:62, 56:25, 88:11).

Muhammad placed a limit on the number who could enter paradise, which is either seventy thousand or seven hundred thousand (B3247). At the time the revelations were being received, and with few followers, this must have seemed like a huge number. However, after fourteen hundred years and millions of followers, there are going to be some surprised Muslims when they encounter the "no vacancy" sign in front of paradise. Also, Muhammad received a revelation which could be titled "If You Are One of the First 100 Callers" in that most of those entering paradise would be from the first generation to embrace Islam (56:13). Only a few would be admitted from later generations (56:14). [Note to self: It must come as a surprise to *jihadists* who have recently died in the name of the Islamic god to find that paradise is full.]

To be admitted to paradise, the individual has to believe in and become a slave of the Islamic god. Islamic slaves or Muslims also have to follow Muhammad's behavior, which includes doing "good deeds" such as engaging in *jihad.* However, to be admitted into paradise there are a couple of conditions in small print which should be mentioned. First, simply doing good deeds is not enough to gain admittance to paradise. It is the intent of the deeds which matters (B6953). The intent of the deeds has to be *only* for the sake of the Islamic god. For example, the intent of the deeds cannot be to gain booty, to show off, or to gain praise. Second, in doing deeds, a Muslim has to follow Muhammad's behavior or *sunnah.* Those who violate either condition are "losers," their deeds are in vain, and they go to hell (18:103-107). The *hadith* reports also support this position. One *hadith* report notes there can be no innovation in how to do a deed. In fact, all innovation is rejected (B2697). Also, if someone does a good deed which has not been ordered or in a way that does not follow Muhammad's behavior, then the deed is not accepted (see B Book 96, Chapter 20). Another *hadith* report has Muhammad stating, "You must then follow my *sunnah...* Hold to it and stick fast to it. Avoid novelties, for every novelty is an innovation, and every innovation is an error" (D4590, see D4589, D4595, D4596). Innovative forms of behavior mean that Muhammad's followers are denying the proofs and signs they have been given by Muhammad, and they are engaging in behavior that is not in accordance with what the Islamic god has prescribed. Thus, they are hypocrites for not accepting what has been prescribed, and they go to hell.

There is an additional condition in small print which must be met for Muslims to enter paradise. Verse 48:14 states in part, "He forgives whom He wills, and punishes whom He wills." Verse 77:31 is similar and says, "He will admit to His Mercy whom He wills..." And another verse says, "Allah will accept the repentance of whom

He wills" (9:27). These verses indicate the Islamic god can make subjective decisions on who goes to hell and who goes to paradise, regardless of the deed or its intent.

A "fast-track" to paradise can be obtained by killing an infidel in *jihad* (D2489, D2493). Verse 9:111 states, "Those who fight in Allah's Cause, so they kill (others) and are killed, go to paradise" (see B3123).

Paradise is better than an earthly existence. It is noted, for example, that the life in paradise is much better than the "life of this world" (9:38). This is supported in a *hadith* report where Muhammad says, "Nobody who dies and finds good from Allah (in the Hereafter) would wish to come back to this world, even if he were given the whole world and whatever is in it..." (B2795, see B2817).

Although drinking wine is forbidden in the mortal world, there is ample wine in paradise, which is consumed from vessels of silver and cups of crystal. In paradise, drinking wine is "lawful" (52:23), and it will not produce either a hangover or intoxication (37:47, 56:19, 78:34, 83:25). Even with all the eating and drinking, there are no bodily secretions such as sweat or urine (2:25, 3:15, 4:47).

Those in paradise are clothed in silks and wear gold bracelets. It should be mentioned that under *sharia,* Islamic law, it is unlawful for men to wear silk in the mortal world (p53.1). Those in paradise recline on thrones covered in silk and woven with gold and precious stones. They recline in circles or rows and immortal boys serve them from golden trays (18:31, 43:71, 44:53, 44:54, 52:20, 52:24, 55:54, 55:76, 56:15, 56:16, 56:17, 56:34, 76:12, 76:13, 76:19, 76:21, 83:23).

Paradise seems to have been designed with men in mind. Men are married to wives, or *hurs*, who are beautiful, chase, full-breasted, and young. *Hurs* have wide, lovely eyes and desire none but their husbands (52:20, 55:56, 55:58, 55:70, 55:72, 55:74, 56:22, 56:23, 56:24, 56:35, 56:36, 56:37, 78:33). Is there sex in paradise? According to *Tafsir Ibn Kathir*, in paradise each man will have sex with one hundred virgins a day (V9, p429). Fortunately, there is no fatigue in paradise (15:48). [Note to self: Sex more than four times an hour! Perhaps the term that best describes the sexual ability of *jihadists* who enter paradise is "minute man."]

Other than being whores for Allah, there is little mention of what Muslim women obtain in paradise. Some of the Muslim women who have become homicide bombers have stated the reason for blowing themselves up and killing non-Muslims is to get into paradise to become a *hur*. Some of these women have dishonored their families through sexual activity and are attempting to regain their virginity to regain family honor. [Note to self: What a depraved, misogynist, and vile ideology where women have to kill themselves and others and become a whore to obtain honor.]

2. Free will and predetermination. This is another confusing and controversial area within Islam. Are human beings predestined, predetermined, or preordained? Or do they have free will? On the one hand, there are many passages where the Islamic god seems to have predetermined all aspects of life. Thus, there is no free will. On the other hand, there are numerous passages invoking humans to obey the Islamic god and Muhammad, or else there will be hell to pay—literally. Thus, there seems to be free will since individuals have the choice to either obey the Islamic god and Muhammad or to consciously follow a different path. First, the concept of predetermination will be examined, and then we will examine free will.

Verse 44:3-4 informs readers that after the *Koran* was "sent down," every matter of ordainment was decreed. This means that areas such as births, calamities, and deaths have been decreed by the Islamic god. This is supported by verse 3:145, which states, "And no person can ever die except by Allah's Leave and at an appointed term." Verse 9:51 has Muhammad saying in part, "Nothing shall ever happen to us except what Allah has ordained for us." Even Muhammad's behavior was predetermined according to verse 7:203, which states, "I but follow what is revealed to me from my Lord."

In the previous section, the conditions for entry into paradise were mentioned. Here it was stated that to enter paradise there are some conditions in small print, one of which gave the Islamic god a great deal of discretion in deciding who entered or did not enter paradise. There are several verses suggesting the Islamic god also has discretion in predetermining human lives. Some of these verses suggest that humans are little more than objects which the Islamic god can manipulate in any manner desired. For example, according to verse 7:178, "Whomsoever Allah guides, he is the guided one, and whomsoever He sends astray, then those! They are the losers." This line of thinking is continued in verse 14:4, which states, "Then Allah misleads whom He wills and guides whom He wills." Verse 3:284 is similar and states, "Then He forgives whom He wills and punishes whom He wills." In verse 18:17, we learn that, "He whom Allah guides, he is the rightly-guided; but he whom He sends astray, for him you will find no *wali* (guiding friend) to lead him (to the right path)." Verse 74:31 states the Islamic god "leads astray who He wills and guides whom He wills." What is remarkable is that the Islamic god has the ability to guide everyone to the right path but consciously selects for some the path to eternal hell (16:9). Those who go astray because of the Islamic god's will, become little more than "firewood for hell" (72:15).

In other cases, the Islamic god actively prevents individuals from receiving guidance. Verse 2:7 states, "Allah has set a seal on their hearts and on their hearing (i.e., they are closed from accepting Allah's Guidance) and over their eyes there is a covering."

There are additional passages suggesting predetermination over free will. Verse 9:51 reads, "Say: 'Nothing shall ever happen to us except what Allah has ordained for us.'" In verse 57:22, we read, "No calamity befalls on the earth or in yourselves but it is inscribed in the Book of Decrees before We bring it into existence." The case for predetermination continues with, "Allah gives you life and then causes you to die" (45:26). Verse 54:49 is even more specific and states, "Verily, We have created all things with *Qadar* (Divine Preordainments of all things before their creation as written in the Book of Decrees...)." Verse 64:11 is similar and states, "No calamity befalls, but by the Leave [i.e., Decision and *Qadar* (Divine Preordainments)] of Allah, and whosoever believes in Allah, He guides his heart [to the true Faith with certainty, i.e., what has befallen him was already written for him by Allah from the *Qadar* (Divine Preordainments)]." And when asked about the torment that is going to fall on disbelievers, the response is "There is none that can avert it" (52:8). There is more in verse 76:30, which reads, "But you cannot will, unless Allah wills," and verse 81:29 reads, "And you cannot will unless it be what Allah wills..."

There are also examples in the *hadith* reports which support predetermination. One of the most famous examples deals with the rape of female captives. After the conquest of a Jewish tribe, Muhammad's bandit-rapists asked if they should practice coitus interrupts when raping female captives. The Muslim rapists did not want their victims to become pregnant since it would lower their value on the slave market or when they held them for ransom. Muhammad told the Muslim-rapists not to practice coitus interrupts since the Islamic god had already determined who was going to exist (B2229, B2542, B4318, B5075, B5210, B6603, B7409, D2167). Note that the prophet and religious leader of Islam, Muhammad, was not giving advice on the morality of rape but on the sexual technique that should be used during the rape.

Additional material on preordainment can be found in Bukhari in a chapter titled "Book of Divine Preordainment" (B6594-6620).

So far, the *Koran* appears to be suggesting that the world and everyone in it is predestined, predetermined, or preordained. The Islamic god has determined who will be born, how they will live their lives, and when they will die. Although there seems to be little room for free will, it is an area that needs to be discussed.

It does not take much thought to realize that Islam and free will do not seem compatible. After all, why would there be free will in a religion whose name means "submission" or "surrender"? Why would those who want to be the slaves of the Islamic god even want to have free will? Yet we find numerous passages suggesting that humans have free will. This is found early in the *Koran* in verse 1:6, which states, "Guide us to the Straight Way," and verse 1:7, which mentions those who have earned the Islamic god's anger by going astray. In verse 1:6 we need to ask, "Why would humans need to be guided if their behavior was predetermined?" And in verse 1:7 the question becomes, "If humans are predetermined to go astray, why would the Islamic god be angry with them?"

The concept of guidance was mentioned earlier in this chapter with verse 9:33, which states Muhammad is to guide all non-Muslims to Islam and to make it superior to all other religions. Why do individuals need to be guided if their lives are predetermined?

Free will is also suggested by the numerous verses which threaten humans if they do not submit to the will of the Islamic god. For example, verses 3:131-132 read, "And fear the Fire, which is prepared for the disbelievers. And obey Allah and the Messenger (Muhammad) that you may obtain mercy." This same theme is in verse 4:115, which informs readers that "whoever contradicts and opposes the Messenger (Muhammad)" will "burn in Hell." Verse 5:7 instructs humans to "hear and obey" the Islamic god. Followers are also warned to not disobey Allah or Muhammad (4:14, 59:4). Verse 8:19 claims that "if you cease (to do wrong), it will be better for you..."

Other verses demand that believers follow and obey the Islamic god and Muhammad (3:53, 4:59, 4:69, 4:80, 4:170, 5:92, 8:13, 8:24, 24:51, 25:54, 47:33, 48:13, 64:12). Verse 33:36 states, "It is not for a believer, man or woman, when Allah and His Messenger have decreed a matter that they should have any option in their decision." Verse 4:64 states that Muhammad was sent to be obeyed.

Those who "strive hard in Us (Our Cause), We will surely guide them to Our paths (i.e., Allah's religion - Islamic Monotheism)." This is in verse 29:69 and indicates individuals have free will and can be guided. In verse 3:138, it says the *Koran* was sent down to guide and instruct mankind. Why would those who are predetermined need guidance and instruction unless they had free will? And verse 47:4 demands that followers fight non-Muslims until they become Muslims. Why fight non-Muslims if they are predetermined to be either Muslim or non-Muslim? It continues by informing followers that the Islamic god could have done the fighting, but "(He lets you fight) in order to test some of you with others." Why would the Islamic god have to test individuals if their lives were predetermined?

So far we have seen there are verses suggesting humans are predetermined. There are other verses suggesting humans have free will. Sometimes we can find both free will and predetermination in connecting verses. For example, in verses 77:29-30, we read, "Whosoever wills, let him take a Path to his Lord. But, you cannot will, unless Allah wills."

3. Leaving Islam—apostasy.[12] Apostasy relates to the prior section on free will and predetermination. Do humans have free will to select or not to select a religion, or is it predetermined for them? Although this is an important question, in this section we are more interested in the question, "Is death mandated for those who leave Islam?"

Basically, there are two types of verses which deal with the consequences for apostasy. First, there are verses in the *Koran* stating that punishment for leaving Islam will occur after death and that the punishment is harsh (3:90-91). Second, there are verses requiring that individuals be killed immediately after leaving Islam. For example, verse 4:89 states, "But if they turn back (from Islam), take (hold of) them and kill them wherever you find them..." Verse 9:29 is more generic in that it mandates fighting against all non-Muslims, which would include apostates. This is reinforced in a *hadith* report which states, "The Prophet said, 'If someone changes his (Islamic) religion, then kill him'" (see B Book 96, Chapter 28).

In the *hadith* reports, we find that apostates were burned to death (D4337).

Apostasy means more than just leaving Islam. Other examples of apostasy are desecrating the *Koran* and insulting Allah or Muhammad.

4. *Jihad. Jihad* has been examined in the chapter on *hadith* reports. Here we will examine *jihad* in the *Koran*. Later *jihad* in *sharia*, or Islamic law, will be discussed.

Is Islam really a religion of peace as many Islamic apologists claim? Is *jihad* an inner struggle against temptation or a military struggle against non-Muslims? Before these questions can be answered, we need to distinguish between the early and later verses in the *Koran* dealing with *jihad*. It is worth repeating that early in his prophecy, while in Mecca (c. 610-622), Muhammad had little power and few followers. To a large degree the early verses told Muslims to be patient. Verse 73:10 states, "And be patient (Muhammad) with what they say, and keep away from them in a good way." In verse 52:48, Muhammad is told, "So wait patiently (Muhammad) for the Decision of your Lord..." This same theme is repeated in verse 38:17, which states in part, "Be patient (Muhammad) of what they say..."

Verse 20:130 is similar and reads, "So bear patiently (Muhammad) what they say and glorify the praises of your Lord..." In verse 19:84, Muhammad is told, "So make no haste against them..."

In addition to being told to wait patiently, Muhammad was portrayed as a prophet whose task was to warn non-Muslims of what would happen to them if they did not convert to Islam. For example, verse 22:49 states, "Say (Muhammad): 'O mankind! I am (sent) to you only as a plain warner.'" This same theme is repeated in verse 67:26, which says, "Say (Muhammad): 'The knowledge (of it exact time) is with Allah only, and I am only a plain warner.'" See also 15:89, which states, "And say (Muhammad): 'I am indeed a plain warner.'"

Initially Muhammad was told to turn away from non-Muslims (43:89) although this verse was abrogated by a later verse which made it a duty of Muslims to fight and kill non-Muslims (9:5). Muhammad was also initially told not to argue with non-Muslims (29:46) but to leave them in ignorance at least for a time (23:54).

Either shortly before leaving Mecca or after arriving in Medina in 622, Muhammad received the "defensive" or "revenge" *jihad* verses. For example, in 22:39 permission was given to fight against non-Muslims who had "wronged" the believers by forcing them to leave their homes in Mecca. At this time, *jihad* was not mandatory.

The *jihad* revelations then expanded from fighting non-Muslims who had wronged Muslims to simply fighting non-Muslims. This can be seen in verse 2:191, which reads, "And kill them wherever you find them, and turn them out from where they have turned you out. And *Al-Fitnah* [not believing in Allah] is worse than killing." The footnote in the *Koran* on "fighting in the way of Allah" for verse 2:190 has interesting insights into the meaning of *jihad*. It states that *jihad* is holy fighting in "Allah's Cause (with full force of numbers and weaponry)." *Jihad* is given the "upmost importance in Islam and is one of its pillars." Islam and Allah's word are established by *jihad*. "By abandoning *jihad* (may Allah protect us from that) Islam is destroyed and Muslims fall into an inferior position; their honor is lost, their lands are stolen, their rule and authority vanish." *Jihad* is an obligation in Islam, and those who try and escape from *jihad* are hypocrites and will die with those qualities. There is nothing here about *jihad* being an inner struggle, and *jihad* is no longer optional but is mandatory.

There are several verses demonstrating that *jihad* is to continue until all non-Muslim land has been placed under Islamic control. This is because all land belongs to the Islamic god as seen in verse 48:14, which starts by saying, "And to Allah belongs the sovereignty of the heavens and the earth." The gradual acquisition of the land can be seen in verse 13:41, which states, "See they not that We gradually reduce the land (of the disbelievers, by giving it to the believers, in war victories) from its outlying boarders." Verse 21:44 is almost identical.

In addition to placing all land under Islamic domination, the *jihad* is also to convert, kill, or place all humans under Islamic subjugation. Verse 2:193 states, "And fight them until there is no more *Fitnah* (disbelief and worshiping of others along with Allah) and (all and every kind of) worship is for Allah (Alone)." Verse 8:39 is similar and reads, "And fight them until there is no more *Fitnah* (disbelief and polytheism, i.e., worshiping others besides Allah), and the religion (worship) will all be for Allah Alone [in the whole of the world]." The *jihad* is to ensure that Islam is made superior over all other religions (9:33, 9:73, 9:123, 48:28, 61:9).

Another later verse also states *jihad* is no longer optional but mandatory and reads, "*Jihad* (holy fighting in Allah's Cause) is ordained for you (Muslims) though you dislike it, and it may be that you dislike a thing which is good for you and that you like a thing which is bad for you. Allah knows but you do not know" (2:216). Verse 2:217 concerns fighting in the holy months. Basically, it is allowed since it is "a greater (transgression) with Allah...to prevent mankind from following the way of Allah..."

One reason writers believe *jihad* refers to physical aggression is because of verses 4:95 and 48:17. These verses exempt the blind, lame, and sick from *jihad.* If *jihad* is an inner struggle, then why would these individuals be exempt (see 9:91, B2832)?

In verse 8:12, the Islamic god informs followers he will cast terror into the hearts of non-Muslims, and they are to be struck on their fingers, necks, and toes. In battle, individuals often wore body armor and a helmet. Here the Islamic god is telling his followers to strike at areas not protected by armor, such as the feet, hands, and neck. In verse 2:190, Muslims are ordered to "fight in the way of Allah those who fight you, but transgress not the limits." In some ways this sounds like the Islamic god was mandating a humane war with the "transgress not the limits" phrase. This actually means the dead non-Muslims are not to be mutilated, the Muslim bandits are not to steal stolen booty from other Muslim bandits, and animals should not be killed unless there is some benefit.

Muslims are to fight until there had been great slaughter. It is only after the slaughter they are allowed to take prisoners (8:67).

To encourage believers to aggressively, fearlessly, and recklessly engage in *jihad*, the revelations made it clear it was a no-lose position. If successful, the Muslim bandits get loot and women. And as seen in the section on paradise, if killed they go to paradise and get loot and women in greater quantities. In fact, those who die in *jihad* get an express ticket to paradise (4:95). In the *hadith* reports, Muhammad stated, "Allah guarantees him who strives in His Cause and whose motivation for going out is nothing but *Jihad* in His Cause and belief in His Words (Islamic Monotheism), that He will admit him into Paradise (if martyred) or bring him back to his dwelling place whence he has come out with what he gains of reward or booty" (B3123). There are even examples in the *hadith* reports of Muslims willing to be martyred to enter paradise. In one *hadith* report, Muhammad was asked by a follower moments before a battle, "Can you tell me where I will be if I should get martyred?" Muhammad replied, "In Paradise." The man threw away some dates he was eating, ran toward the opposing force and was quickly martyred (B4046).

Still, however, Muhammad found many Muslims who were unwilling to engage in *jihad*. And there were Muslims who engaged in *jihad* but who, out of a natural fear of death or an agnostic approach to paradise, were not as aggressive as Muhammad had hoped. Thus, further verses were revealed. Verse 9:38 asks believers, "What is the matter with you, that when you are asked to march forth in the Cause of Allah (i.e., *Jihad*) you cling heavily to the earth? Are you pleased with the life of this world rather than the Hereafter? But little is the enjoyment of the life of this world as compared to the

Hereafter." Verse 9:111 continues with, "Verily, Allah has purchased of the believers their lives and their properties for (the price) that theirs shall be the Paradise. They fight in Allah's Cause, so they kill (others) and are killed... Then rejoice in the bargain which you have concluded. That is the supreme success." To assist the tepid, verse 3:169 was revealed, which states, "Think not of those as dead who are killed in the way of Allah. Nay they are alive, with the Lord, and they have provision."

The *hadith* reports reinforce these verses. For example, Muhammad stated, "Nobody who dies and finds good from Allah (in the Hereafter) would wish to come back to this world, even if he were given the whole world and whatever is in it except the martyr who, on seeing the superiority of martyrdom would like to come back to the world and get killed again (in Allah's Cause)" (B2795).

Muslims who make up excuses to avoid participating in *jihad* will go to hell, where they will suffer an intense heat (9:81). In fact, for those who do not "march forth" in *jihad*, "He will punish you with a painful torment and will replace you by another people; and you cannot harm Him at all, and Allah is Able to do all things" (9:39). The *hadith* reports also comment on those who avoided *jihad*. Muhammad said, "He who dies without having fought or having felt fighting (against the infidels) to be his duty will die guilty of a kind of hypocrisy" (D2496).

As noted previously, *Sura* 9 was one of the last *suras* to be revealed. Thus, it abrogated or cancelled the earlier more "peaceful" verses. There are about thirty "violent" verses in *Sura* 9. It opens by giving Muslims permission to cancel all oaths and treaties with non-Muslims (9:1). One of the most widely quoted verses is 9:5, which states in part, "Kill the *Mushrikun* [nonbelievers] wherever you find them, and capture them and besiege them, and lie in wait for them in every ambush." And verse 9:29 states, "Fight against those who (1) believe not in Allah, (2) nor in the Last Day, (3) nor forbid that which has been forbidden by Allah and his Messenger (Muhammad), (4) and those who acknowledge not the religion of truth (Islam) among the people of the Scripture (Jews and Christians), until they pay the *Jizyah* [a tax imposed on non-Muslims living under the domination of Muslims] with willing submission, and feel themselves subdued."

The penalty for those who "wage war against Allah and his Messenger" is severe. They are to be crucified or killed or "their hands and feet be cut off from opposite sides, or be exiled from the land" (5:33).

One of the most powerful verses is 9:111, which reinforces that Muslims are nothing more than slaves of the Islamic god. It reads in part, "Verily, Allah has purchased of the believers their lives and their properties for (the price) that theirs shall be the Paradise. They fight in Allah's Cause, so they kill (others) and are killed."

There is to be no cessation of the *jihad* through peace treaties, especially if Islam has the "upper hand" (47:35).

While killing non-Muslims is not a problem, killing other Muslims is severely punished. Muhammad knew there were many clan, family, and tribal feuds his followers would try and violently resolve. He wanted the violence directed outside of Islam, not inside. Thus, verse 4:93 was revealed, which says, "And whoever kills a believer intentionally, his recompense is Hell to abide therein, and the Wrath and the Curse of Allah are upon him, and a great punishment is prepared for him." This is also in the *hadith* reports, one of which reads, "A Muslim is one who avoids harming Muslims with his tongue and hands" (B10, see B11).

At the beginning of the discussion on *jihad*, two questions were posed. The first was, "Is Islam a religion of peace?" Based on the later verses that were revealed, the answer is a resounding no! The second question asked if *jihad* was an inner struggle or a physical one. There are some verses which "suggest" *jihad* is an inner struggle. In one verse, Muhammad was told not to invite non-Muslims to Islam through arguing and preaching (16:125). In another verse (25:52), he was told to strive against non-Muslims by preaching "with the upmost endeavor with it (the *Koran*)." Some also interpret verse 22:78 as an example of an inner struggle. This verse reads, "And strive hard in Allah's Cause as you ought to strive (with sincerity and with all your efforts that His Name should be superior)." Some claim the struggle is to follow the *Koran* by struggling against committing illegal sexual intercourse, being too lazy to engage in *jihad* or the five daily prayers, or by being too cheap to pay the mandatory taxes.

There are, however, three reasons why the answer to the second question, on whether *jihad* is an inner struggle or a military struggle, is that it is a military struggle. First, there are more than one hundred verses which deal with the military aspects of *jihad* and few—if any—that deal with it as an inner struggle. The second reason deals with the specificity of the verses. While the military *jihad* verses are very specific in what needs to be done, such as "kill the non-Muslims," the inner struggle verses can be interpreted in a variety of ways. For example, does "strive hard" mean to strive hard militarily or spiritually? The third and last reason *jihad* is a military struggle is that these verses were revealed late in Muhammad's prophecy and cancelled out the earlier more "peaceful" verses.

There is one other area that needs to be mentioned when apologists for Islam state *jihad* is an inner struggle. Namely, to win the war it is acceptable to use deceit or to lie (B3028, B3029, 3030, B3031, B3032).

5. Women in Islam. There are few who were not repulsed by the brutal treatment of women under the Taliban in Afghanistan. In other predominantly Muslim countries we read about females being beaten, forced into marriages (often as children), sexually mutilated, and murdered to protect the family "honor." The recent biographies by Ayaan Hirsi Ali, *Infidel* (2007), and Azar Nafisi, *Now They Call Me Infidel: Why I Renounced Jihad for America, Israel, and the War on Terror* (2006), portray the life of women in Muslim societies as something few Western women would willingly accept. Several writers have asked, "Why does the mainstream media loudly denounce racial apartheid, but remain silent on Islam's sexual apartheid?"

Several writers have noted the dearth of material on the "legal" abuse of Muslim women, both in Islamic and non-Islamic societies, in women's studies departments across university campuses. While liberal women in these departments can discuss endlessly the phony wage gap between men and women or the imaginary flooding of emergency rooms by abused women during Super Bowl weekend, the amount and extent of abuse of Muslim women make women's grievances in the United States seem trivial by comparison.

The question that needs to be asked is, "Is the treatment of women by the Taliban and the sexual apartheid found in Islamic countries an aberration, or is it in accordance with the *Koran*?" Some of the laws concerning women will also be examined in the chapter on *sharia.*

Part of the demeaning treatment of women in Muslim societies is because of verse 4:34, which reads,

> Men are the protectors and maintainers of women, because Allah has made one of them to excel the other, and because they spend (to support them) from their means. Therefore the righteous women are devoutly obedient (to Allah and to their husbands), and guard in the husband's absence what Allah orders them to guard (e.g., their chastity and their husband's property). As to those women on whose part you see ill-conduct, admonish them (first), (next) refuse to share their beds, (and last) beat them (lightly, if it is useful); but if they return to obedience, seek not against them means (of annoyance).

This states clearly that men are superior to women and that husbands can beat their wives.

There are also questions about the way Muslim women dress. Some are completely covered, with the slit for the eyes having a mesh covering, and with gloves covering the hands. [Note to self: Based on the Islamic god-sanctioned beating of wives, perhaps this style of dress is to cover the bruising.] Other Muslim women make little or no attempt to cover themselves in "traditional" ways. And some only wear a head scarf. The question is, "How does the *Koran* mandate that women dress?"

In verse 24:31, women are instructed "not show off their adornment except only that which is apparent (like both eyes for necessity to see the way, or outer palms of hands or one eye or dress like veil, gloves, head cover, apron), and to draw their veils all over *Juyubihinna* (i.e., their bodies, faces, necks and bosoms)..." The verse continues by listing exceptions to the rule, such as that husbands are allowed to see their wives' "adornments." Verse 33:59 seems more severe and was one of the later verses to be revealed. It reads, "Tell your wives and your daughters and the women of the believers to draw their cloaks (veils) all over their bodies (i.e., screen themselves completely except the eyes or one eye to see the way)."

In his *tafsir*, or explanation, Ibn Kathir states that because of their position of honor, in public Muslim women need to be covered with just the left eye showing. This will distinguish them from non-Muslim women, slaves, servants, and whores (Volume 7, p.67, Volume 8, page 45). Post-menopausal women who do not plan to marry can discard the veil (24:60).

As with many "primitive" societies, menstruating women are considered "unclean" (2:222). In fact, Bukhari has an entire book on menstruation (Book 6, B294 - 333).

Muslim wives have little control over their sex lives. Verse 2:223 informs Muslim husbands that their wives "are a tilth for you, so go to your tilth." In different versions of the *Koran*, this is expressed as wives are there for their husbands to seed or to cultivate as they desire. The exception is during menstruation, when wives are off-limits sexually until they purify themselves (2:222). There are some instructions on sexual techniques. All sex is to be penile-vaginal, and the male is not to have vaginal intercourse from behind his wife since the child will be born squint-eyed (M1435). The footnote for this *hadith* report also states that "the act of sexual intercourse should be directed at some fruitful end and should not be a vain delight." Muslim men are allowed up to four wives (4:3).

In terms of illegal sexual intercourse, initially women are to be confined to a house until death, presumably from starvation (4:15). This was abrogated by verse 24:2, which has unmarried individuals flogged with one hundred stripes, and married individuals stoned to death. The stoning verse is not in all versions of the *Koran*, but it is in the *Noble Quran*, which is being used for this book. Thus, there are prohibitions on adultery, with the exception of slaves, where sex or rape is not considered adultery and is acceptable (4:24, 23:6, 33:50, 70:30). While female slaves can be raped, it is not considered adultery since married women who are taken captive, and thus are slaves, have their marriages abrogated (M1456, M1456R3). The accepted and relaxed attitude toward the rape of captive women can be seen in the *hadith* reports. In one *hadith* report, a man was upset when he found Muhammad's son-in-law, Ali, having sex with a female captive. The captive had been given to Ali by Muhammad. Muhammad told the man Ali deserved even more from the conquered tribe (B4350). Ali was married to Muhammad's daughter Fatima.

Female slaves cannot be forced into prostitution (24:33). However, if female slaves are forced into prostitution, they are forgiven because they were forced to do an "evil act." There is no punishment specified for those who forced them into prostitution.

As can be seen, there is an Islamic image of women which emerges. They need to be covered from head to foot. They need to be mutilated sexually. They need to be seen as inferior to men. It is noted in the *hadith* reports that most of those in hell are women because they were ungrateful to their husbands (B29, B304, B1052, B1462, B3241, B5196, B6449, B6546, M2736). According to Muhammad, women are also "deficient in intelligence" (B304, B1462).

As noted earlier, in verse 4:34 men are given permission to "lightly" beat their wives for ill conduct if admonishment and refusing to sleep with them did not change their behavior. Ill conduct is described as disliking, disobeying, or ignoring a husband. Beating wives is also in the *hadith* reports. For example, after being told by a follower that many Muslim wives had become "emboldened toward their husbands" Muhammad gave the husbands permission to beat their wives. When the abused women complained to Muhammad about being beaten, he said of them, "They are not the best among you" (D2141). Additionally, if a husband beats his wife it is assumed that she deserved the beating since "a man will not be asked as to why he beat his wife" (D2142). Even Muhammad's child bride, Aisha, noted that Muhammad hit her (M974R1).

In business transactions, the testimony of one man is equal to that of two women (2:282). The same principle applies to inheritance: Males inherit twice as much as females (4:11, 4:176).

The allowance for child marriage is in verse 65:4, which deals with divorce from females who are too young or old to have "monthly courses." When a Muslim man divorces his wife, she cannot remarry for three months if she is still having menstrual cycles. But what about divorced women who are too old or too young to have menstrual cycles? For those who "have passed the age of monthly courses" or for those "who have no courses (i.e., they are still immature)," the waiting period is still three months.

Muhammad had some observations about women in leadership positions. In *Tafsir Ibn Kathir* (v2, pp. 442-447), Muhammad states, "People who appoint a woman to be their leader, will never achieve success." According to Kathir, this meant that women should never be appointed to positions of leadership, such as that of a judge.

6. The myth of the moderate Muslims. A question which needs to be asked is, "Can there be such a thing as a moderate Muslim?" The answer is no! This does not mean that all Muslims keep a sharpened scimitar while waiting for the call to *jihad.* Islam is like most, if not all, religions in that individuals have different degrees of commitment. Presumably, many Muslims adhere to a "reformed" version of Islam. Here they try and live everyday lives by making Islam compatible with contemporary Western society. This can be accomplished by interpreting certain passages in ways that fit their needs and by ignoring other passages. Islamic fundamentalists would obviously criticize the reformist approach by asking, "How can truth change from one time to another?"

Early in his prophecy, Muhammad recognized there were many tepid or convenient Muslims. That is, it was easier to openly pretend to be Muslim and do the minimum to "pass" rather than to openly oppose Islam and be killed. For men, this simply meant turning the baseball cap around so the brim did not hit the ground when praying, letting one's beard grow, and taking on a couple of extra wives—including one who was pre-pubescent—to follow Muhammad's behavior. To Muhammad, these "Muslims" were hypocrites. They were not to be forgiven for their hypocrisy (4:137), and he foresaw a hell for them that was worse than for non-Muslims such as Christians and Jews (9:101). Verse 48:11 states many say with their "tongues what is not in their hearts." However, the Islamic god knows the truth and will test them before they are allowed into paradise (3:141). For these individuals, there is a blazing fire (4:97, 48:13). For Muhammad, hypocrites were the vilest of the vile, the worst of the worst. The Islamic god curses hypocrites (63:1-4), and hypocrites are promised the fire of hell as a lasting torment (4:140, 9:68, 9:81, 9:90, 59:15).

It also needs to be asked why would Muslims, moderate or not, want to get along with non-Muslims? After all, non-Muslims are the "worst of moving (living) creatures..." (8:55).

"Moderate" Muslims have three options. First, they can continue to practice a toned-down or cafeteria-style of Islam which makes them hypocrites. And hypocrites will go to hell where they will suffer a torment far worse than that of non-Muslims. Second, they can become apostates and leave Islam, which means they will be killed for being an apostate, and as apostates they will go to hell, where they will receive extra torment. The third option is to become a pious Muslim.

An additional problem with those who claim to be "moderate Muslims" is there are verses which allow the Islamic god, Muhammad, and Muslims to dissolve obligations and vows (9:3, 66:2). In verse 4:142, we read that just as the hypocrites want to deceive the Islamic god, the Islamic god will retaliate by deceiving them. And in the *hadith* reports we read, "And whenever you take an oath to do something and later you find that something else is better than the first, then do the better one and make expiation for your oath" (B6622, see B6623, B6680, B6721). And, of course, we have the classic statement by Muhammad that "war is deceit" (B3027-3030). There is a well-known episode in Muhammad's life where he wanted one of his followers to kill someone who had been critical of Islam. Muhammad approved of the assassins telling a lie to lure the victim out of his house (B3032).

Some cling to the hope that moderate Muslims will reform Islam. This is not likely to happen for three reasons. First, why would a Muslim want to change or reform a religion that is eternal, exact, final, perfect, and timeless? Why would a Muslim want to reform what is "an absolute truth with certainty" and is without any "crookedness or flaws"? Why would Muslims want to deviate from Muhammad's behavior since it was inspired by the Islamic god? Second, Muhammad anticipated that there might be followers who would want to change Islam. Thus, shortly before his death he announced that the religion had been perfected and that there would be no further revelations. In the event that followers attempted to change Islam he said that any changes were "heresies" and those proposing changes were "Far removed (from mercy), far removed (from mercy), those who changed, did new thing in (the religion) after me" (B7051). Emphasizing twice that they were "far removed from mercy" meant they were going to hell. Muhammad did not want his followers changing the religion probably because he did not have much respect for them. Muhammad told the Islamic god that "my followers are weak in their bodies, hearts, hearing, and constitution..." (B7517). The third reason there is little hope for a reformation of Islam is because Muslims are not supposed to be critical of Islam. After all, it is hardly the role of the slave of the Islamic god to be asking questions or changing the religion. This area was addressed in Chapter 2 under "Islamic Tolerance." Muhammad forbid asking too many questions about disputed religious matters (B7292). To prevent any questioning of Islam Muhammad stated, "The worst crime among the Muslims is the one who asked about something which had not been prohibited, but was prohibited because of his asking" (B7289). Essentially, Muhammad told his followers that they were not to ask any questions about things he had not mentioned. And, they were not to ask questions about things he had mentioned because these things had already been explained to them. Muhammad feared that one question would lead to another. He noted, for example, that his followers would eventually be asking "If the Islamic god is the 'Creator of everything, then who created' the Islamic god?" Muhammad's solution was to tell his followers that if they had questions about certain passages in the *Koran* they were simply to stop reciting the passages (B7364, B7365). Thus, there is not much hope that Islam going to undergo a reformation.

A recent Muslim leader in the Middle East stated that, "There is no radical or moderate Islam. This is an insult to Muslims. There is only Islam."

Bottom line, "moderate" Muslims have approval from their god to deceive and lie, even about being "moderate" Muslims!

7. Is Islam compatible with the U.S. Constitution? The answer to the question is, "Don't be ridiculous; of course not!" This ques-

tion takes on added significance because two Muslims are currently serving in the U.S. Congress.

There are numerous areas of incompatibility between Islam and democracy, a few of which will be mentioned.

The Declaration of Independence states, "All men are created equal." It will be assumed that in contemporary usage the word *men* refers to males and females. In an earlier section, it was pointed out that Islam considers females to be beneath, not equal, to males. Additionally, Islam does not consider all "men" to be equal. Under Islam, Muslim males are superior to non-Muslim males. In Islamic countries, all non-Muslims live under *dhimmitude*, which as noted earlier is an inferior, slave-like status. The *Koran* makes it clear that non-Muslims must pay a high tax called the *Jizyah*, and they must "feel themselves subdued" (9:29). Those under *dhimmitude*, the *dhimmis*, must feel themselves "subdued" in a variety of ways which differ in place and time. They often had to live in specific areas of a city, generally the most undesirable areas. Their homes had to be inferior to those of Muslims, and their entrance doors had to be low so non-Muslims had to bend before entering. A *dhimmi* male who married or had sex with a Muslim woman would be executed. They could not carry weapons. They could not ride on horses or camels, only donkeys. They could only ride these donkeys outside of a city and sometimes had to ride backward. And when approaching a Muslim, they had to dismount the donkey and bow until the Muslim had passed. Non-Muslims could only pass Muslims from the left, their unclean side. There were often clothing regulations distinguishing Muslims from non-Muslims. The restrictions placed on the *dhimmis* were severe, causing them to live under humiliating, inferior, and oppressive conditions with few legal rights.

In addition to the Declaration of Independence, there are also problems of compatibility between Islam and the Bill of Rights, a few of which will be mentioned.

The First Amendment deals with religion in two ways. The first is the "establishment" clause, and the second is the "free exercise" clause. The establishment clause, which is often incorrectly interpreted to mean a separation of church and state, simply states there will not be a state-mandated religion. In Islam, there is a state-mandated religion which is Islam. The free-exercise clause is also null and void in Islam. In fact, those who leave Islam are apostates who deserve to be killed (o8.1). In fact, there is no indemnity or expiation for killing an apostate since "it is killing someone who deserves to die" (o8.4). Although the early verses in the *Koran* were tolerant of other religions, these were abrogated by later verses which instructed Muslims to fight and kill non-Muslims. Non-Muslims living under *dhimmitude* have severe restrictions placed on their religious freedoms.

The First Amendment also deals with the freedom of speech. Within Islam there can be severe penalties for those who exercise freedom of speech. This is because apostasy, and hence being killed, includes more than leaving Islam. An apostate is also someone who speaks in a way that implies disbelief in Islam (o8.7.3), reviles the Islamic god (o8.7.4), denies the existence of the Islamic god (o8.7.5), is sarcastic about the Islamic god (o8.7.6), denies any part of the *Koran* (o8.7.7), reviles Islam (o8.7.16), is sarcastic about *sharia* (o8.7.19), or denies that all should follow Islam (o8.7.20).

The Second Amendment deals in part with the right to bear arms. This is not acceptable in Islam since it is illegal for non-Muslims to arm themselves.

There are also problems with the Eighth Amendment, which is against cruel and unusual punishment, unless liberals are going to consider amputations, flogging, and stoning to be "usual" forms of punishment, which they are under Islam.

And there is that pesky problem of slavery in the Thirteenth Amendment. Muhammad owned, traded, and had sex with slaves, and pious Muslim are obligated to follow in Muhammad's path. Sex with slaves is specifically allowed in the *Koran* (4:24, 16:77, 23:6, 30:28, 33:50, 70:30). Verse 24:32 approves of marrying and breeding "pious, fit, and capable" slaves.

Last, the Fourteenth Amendment guarantees citizens equal protection under the law. As noted earlier, non-Muslims are not considered "citizens," but *dhimmis* are not provided with equal protection under the law.

8. Accommodation. Accommodation simply refers to individuals living peacefully side by side while accepting the ethnic, racial,

and religious differences of others. This is obviously largely what is seen in Western societies.

The question is, "can Islam accommodate to other religions or to non-Muslims?" The answer is no, and several examples have already been provided in this chapter. For example, we saw in the area on apostasy that Islam does not allow for religious freedom. The discussion on *jihad* revealed Muslims are commanded to engage in a war against non-Muslims until they convert to Islam, are killed, or are placed in submission under Islamic control. The slave-like status of women in Islam was also discussed. We also saw Islam is not compatible with the U.S. Constitution.

There are additional verses in the *Koran* which will make "getting along" difficult. Verse 3:28 instructs Muslims not to take non-Muslims as friends. In verse 4:91, Muslims are told to kill non-Muslims, and in verse 5:30, non-Muslims are to be crucified. Non-Muslims are labeled as "confused" in verse 6:25 and later as behaving ignorantly (6:111). As such, they are to be annihilated (6:45). Non-Muslims are to be terrorized (8:12) and then seized and murdered (33:60). Non-Muslims are also *najasun*, or impure, both physically and spiritually (9:28).

Thus, there are religious doctrines which will prevent Muslims from accommodating to non-Muslims. Also, Muslims are compelled to follow the behavior of Muhammad which, as we will see in the chapters dealing with his biography, did not consist of accommodating to other religions or to non-Muslims. Rather, he literally destroyed other religions and their symbols. Non-Muslims had the option to convert, be killed, or live in *dhimmitude*.

What's Next?

To understand Islam, it is important to understand its ideological foundations. Thus, the *hadith* reports and the *Koran* have been examined. The next chapter examines *sharia*, or Islamic law. As will be seen, the law is based on the Islamic religious documents already examined, as well as on the behavior of Muhammad. A biography of Muhammad follows the chapter on *sharia*.

CHAPTER 5: WHERE TO START IV: *SHARIA*

The last three chapters have examined two of Islam's holiest documents, the *hadith* reports and the *Koran*. This chapter will deal with Islamic law, or *sharia*.

Sharia

Sharia is Islamic law and refers to following the correct path or way. It is an all-encompassing set of laws which controls and regulates both the private and the public aspects of life. It is the goal of Islam and of Muslims to have the world under *sharia*. *Sharia* is perceived by Muslims as law from the Islamic god, and it is to replace the laws created by mere humans. Because it is divinely inspired, humans may not understand the reasoning behind the laws but must unquestioningly accept them. Since *sharia* is divinely-inspired, most Muslims believe *sharia* is immutable and not evolving. That is, truth does not change from one time to another. Others, however, believe *sharia* can evolve to deal with a changing world. Among those who believe *sharia* can evolve there is disagreement as to the amount of evolution that is allowed as well as the areas in which evolution can take place.

Sharia is based on the *hadith* reports, the *Koran*, the behavior of Muhammad (*sunnah*), and centuries of debate among Muslim scholars. Muslim scholars used these sources to create laws which could be applied to everyday life. Prior to the development of *sharia*, each Muslim jurist dealing with an offense had to review the *hadith* reports, the *Koran*, and the *sunnah* before making a decision. Given the contradictions in these sources, there must have been different rulings for similar offenses. The development of *sharia* led to the development of specific guidelines which Muslim jurists could follow. For example, all three sources mention the amputation of the right hand for theft. The *Koran* has the following passage: "And (as for) the male thief and the female thief, cut off (from the wrist joint) their (right) hands as a recompense for that which they committed, a punishment by way of example from Allah" (5:38). The *hadith* reports also have material on the amputation of the right hand for theft. One report reads, "The hand should be cut off for stealing something that is worth a quarter of a *dinar* or more" (B6789, see B6790-B6799). And another report has the hand amputated for the theft of an egg or a rope (M1687). Islamic scholars took the general principle of amputation for theft specified in the *Koran* and, by using the *hadith* reports and the biographies of Muhammad, developed specific *sharia* guidelines. These guidelines dictate the amount that needs to be stolen for amputation to occur, and they say that the thief has to have reached puberty, be sane, and to have acted voluntarily.

Just as there are different collections of *hadith* reports, the same is true of the *sharia*. It is generally agreed, however, that the four major Sunni schools of Islamic law concur on about seventy-five percent of their legal opinions.

The source used for this book is *Reliance of the Traveller: A Classic Manual of Islamic Sacred Law*. The "travel" reference is to the path or the travel through life. Those who follow *sharia* can expect to spend eternity in paradise. Those who do not follow *sharia* will spend eternity in hell.

Sharia covers literally all aspects of life, including divorce, fasting, inheritance, justice, marriage, pilgrimages, prayer, and taxes. Some aspects of *sharia* will be examined.

In the discussion of the *hadith* reports, it was mentioned that Muhammad was obsessed with cleaning his teeth. Based on this information, *sharia* law has been developed for dental hygiene (e3.0). For example, the tooth-stick, similar to a toothbrush, should be used to remove unpleasant odors from the mouth. Toothpaste should not be used by those who are fasting since, if swallowed, it would nullify the fast. And Muslims must start by cleaning the teeth laterally on the right side, and they must pay special attention to the back teeth.

There is a section on the body which deals with matters such as trimming the beard, fingernails, mustache, and toenails (e4.0). It is forbidden to pluck out grey hair or to dye one's hair black. Hair dyes are to be either red or yellow.

Also, circumcision is mandatory for both males and females. The prepuce is to be removed from the penis and clitoris (e4.3). Several articles have claimed that this section has been "sanitized" for Western readers through an intentional mistranslation. Basically, the law says that in females the *bazr* must be removed, which the book translates as the prepuce, when in fact it should have been translated as the clitoris.

There is a large section on purification before prayer (e5.0). The parts of the body that are to be washed are specified, as is the number of times each needs to be washed and the order of washing. Washing starts with a prayer. The face is washed, a tooth-stick is used, and the mouth and nose are rinsed out. The hands and arms are washed up to the elbows. The head is then washed with wet hands, making certain to clean the ear canals with the little finger. The feet are then washed up to the ankle. This is repeated three times. There is then a prayer at the conclusion of the washing. Apparently Muslims drip dry after washing (e5.34.3). There is also information on washing for those who have had an arm or hand amputated. Washing is nullified for those who use nail polish since water cannot penetrate through the polish to the dirt. Also, if a man touches a woman after purification but before prayer, the purification is nullified and must be repeated (e7.3).

There are numerous laws about going into a bathroom (e9.0). When entering a bathroom, it is mandatory the Muslim wear shoes and cover the head with something such as a handkerchief. There is a prayer to be said when entering and exiting a bathroom. Enter a bathroom with the left foot and leave with the right foot. Once in the bathroom, do not linger or talk. If reading material is taken into the bathroom, it should not include any mention of the Islamic god or

Muhammad. If squatting, the weight should be on the left foot. The right hand is not used for wiping.

Although sexual intercourse is to be avoided during menstruation, if the husband does not believe his wife is menstruating, he is allowed to have sex with her (e13.5).

In Islam there are many filthy things, including pigs and dogs (e14.0).

Apostasy was discussed in the section dealing with the *Koran*. If an apostate returns to Islam, all missed prayers must be made up (f1.1). Children should start prayers by age seven. By age ten, they can be beaten for neglecting their prayers, although not severely and not more than three blows are to be applied (f1.2).

Men should remain armed during prayers (f16.9), and it is unlawful for men to wear silk (f17.2). It should be recalled that in paradise men are dressed in silk.

Just as the *hadith* reports had instructions for sacrificing animals, so does *sharia*. One section provides information on the types of animals that can be sacrificed (j14.2): camels, cattle, goats, and sheep. The age of the animals is also specified. Additionally, the animals should be free of defects. There are also instructions on how the animals should be killed (j17.6). Basically, push a knife into the hollow area in the neck between the collarbones, which will sever the windpipe. The sacrificial animals should be facing the *Kaaba* in Mecca when sacrificed. There is also a section on sacrificing animals after the birth of a child (j15.0). For male children, two sheep are sacrificed, and for female children, one sheep is sacrificed.

It is unlawful for a man to look at women other than his wives or other women he is not allowed to marry, such as his mother or sister (m2.3). A man can listen to women's voices unless temptation is likely. It is also unlawful for a man to be alone with a woman other than his wife or other women he is not allowed to marry. Women are obligated to have sex with their husbands on demand if they can physically endure it (m5.1). Also, husbands control when their wives are allowed to leave the home (m10.3). Women cannot leave their homes without permission unless there is a "pressing necessity." They cannot allow others to enter "his" home without "his" permission, even including family members they are not allowed to marry, such as a brother or a father (m10.12). Women are not allowed to travel outside the city unless it is with their husbands or with family members they are not allowed to marry. The conditions under which a husband can strike a "rebellious" wife are listed. Basically, a wife must obey her husband and allow him full sexual enjoyment of her. A wife who fails to meet these and other conditions is "rebellious" and should be guided to the right path by her husband first by admonition and advice, then by not sleeping with her, and finally by hitting her if her husband believes it will end the "rebelliousness" (m10.12, see also p42.0).

There are also rules for divorce for women who have reached puberty. A major concern dealt with the possibility of women being divorced while in the early stages of pregnancy. Since DNA testing was not available to determine paternity, divorced women must wait about three months before remarriage to make certain they are not pregnant by their former husbands. *Sharia* prescribes a waiting period after divorce even for prepubescent girls (n9.1, n9.9).

Justice is severe by civilized standards. Apostasy from Islam is punishable by death as long as the individual has reached puberty and is sane. Apostasy is seen as treason and deserving of death (o8.2). Apostasy is more than just leaving Islam. Apostasy, and hence the punishment of death, also includes reviling the Islamic god or Muhammad (o8.7.4), denying the existence of the Islamic god (o8.7.5), being sarcastic about the Islamic god (o8.7.6), denying any verse in the *Koran* (o8.7.7), reviling Islam (08.7.16), being sarcastic about *sharia* (o8.7.19), or denying that the entire world should follow Islam (o8.7.20).

There is a section on *jihad* (o9.0). It is defined as "to war against non-Muslims and is etymologically derived from the word *mujahada*, signifying warfare to establish religion and is the lesser *jihad*." The "greater *jihad*" is spiritual, which Muhammad experienced when returning from the lesser *jihad*. Even though there is a spiritual *jihad*, the basis for *jihad* is three verses in the *Koran*, all of which stress violence (2:216, 4:89, 9:36). Also, the specifics of *jihad* are found in the twenty-seven to twenty-nine *jihad* expeditions led personally by Muhammad. The "objectives of *jihad*" are to make war on other religions such as Christianity and Judaism. The fight will continue until all become Muslim.

The section on *jihad* covers several pages. Other than one mention of the spiritual or "greater *jihad*," all the material deals with the military or lesser *jihad.* This should provide an idea of which is the most important.

Married women who are captured have their marriages immediately annulled (o9.13).

There is a section dealing with non-Muslims living in an Islamic society (o11.0). Non-Muslims, *dhimmis*, are technically "protected" but do not have equal rights with Muslims. They have to pay a high tax (protection money), and they must comply with Islamic laws. Their clothing must identify them as non-Muslim and has varied by place and time. Non-Muslims are not allowed to build their homes as high as Muslim homes. They cannot display forbidden foods, such as alcohol and pork. They cannot build new religious structures, ring bells, openly recite religious material, or display religious symbols such as crosses. In some cases, non-Muslims are not allowed to repair existing religious structures.

The penalty for theft is the amputation of the right hand, as long as the thief has reached puberty, is sane, and has acted voluntarily (o14.1, see 5:38). *Sharia* provides guidelines in terms of the amount that needs to be taken for amputation to occur.

Intoxicants are prohibited, even in medicines (o16.6), and those who violate the law are to be scourged forty stripes. If the individual dies while being scourged, the scourger must pay an indemnity (o16.3).

There is a book on enormities (p). Muslims are reminded not to intentionally kill other Muslims or they will reside in hell (p2.1). Muslims can also go to hell for not praying (p.4.1). Muslims are instructed to treat their parents well (p6.1, 17:23-24, 29:8). Muslims who flee from combat will suffer in hell (p11.1, 8:16). For Muslims, drinking alcohol and gambling are sins (2:219, 5:90). Originally, those who violated the prohibition against drinking were scourged for the first three offenses and killed after a fourth offense. Later it appears the killing was reduced to another scourging. However, whoever buys, drinks, pours, produces, or sells alcohol will go to hell (p14.2).

Sharia is intolerant of homosexuality (see 7:81). Males are killed for engaging in sodomy. Females are killed for engaging in adultery (p17.2). The law is also critical of masculine women and effeminate men (p28.1). Muhammad stated that men are destroyed when they obey women, and he cursed effeminate men and masculine women.

Muslims who commit suicide will reside in hell (p25.1). Men are not allowed to wear gold or silk (p53.1). Women should not wear false hair, have tattoos, or remove facial hair (p59.1).

Earlier several *hadith* reports concerning Muhammad's dislike of pictures and artists were presented. This issue is also discussed in *sharia* (p44.0), where we learn that picture makers will go to hell. Muhammad also did not like music (r40.0), and he wanted to do away with most musical instruments. And it is noted that the Islamic god will pour molten lead into the ears of those who listen to a songstress.

Jokes and joking are largely out because they may hurt people (r19.0). "Excessive joking" is especially bad since it eliminates dignity and may cause "immoderate laughter, which kills the heart."

There is a list of thirty-seven rules for reading the *Koran* (w16.0). For example, it can only be touched or recited when in a state of purity, the reciter must be dressed as though meeting with a prince, and the reciter must stop reciting when yawning since yawning is from the devil.

And masturbation "with one's own hand" is unlawful (w37.1).

This is only a small sampling of what is in *sharia*. Islamic apologists will claim this is a selective presentation, and they are correct. In the voluminous *sharia*, there are certainly many "good" laws, such as don't disrespect your parents (p6.0), and don't bear false witness (p16.0). The problem is that as a whole, *sharia* is a barbaric, intolerant, and primitive set of laws. It does not allow for Muslims to follow those laws they like and not to follow those laws they do not like.

Based on *sharia*, Muslims are making increasing demands that Western laws give way to *sharia*. Many in the West try to accommodate, appease, and tolerate Muslims with regards to certain *sharia* laws. Thus, for example, Muslim cashiers do not have to scan alcohol or pork, and foot baths are installed for Muslims in schools and the workplace. What those in the West need to realize is that this is the beginning of a *sharia* society, not the end of demands by Muslims. Next, for example, Muslim cashiers will refuse to scan milk since "the milk of animals (other than human)" is considered filth (e14.2). This will be followed by their refusal to assist openly gay individuals or women who are dressed inappropriately or without a male escort. [Note to self: At some point they will demand that female genital mutilation be covered by their medical plan since, according to *sharia*, it is an "enormity not to be circumcised" (w52.1.368)]

There is a list of other enormities which include the following (w52.1): thinking badly about Muslims, tattooing or being tattooed, removing facial hair, men wearing gold or silk, shaving off or pulling out one's hair, ridicule or mockery of a Muslim, engaging in sodomy with one's wife, rebelliousness of a wife to her husband, swearing at a Muslim, suicide, engaging in lesbianism, engaging in sodomy, failing to be circumcised, gambling (including backgammon and chess), playing or listening to string or reed instruments, and reciting poetry which mocks Muslims. Engaging in any of these hundreds of enormities annuls any good deeds. All of this is leading to one conclusion, which is "that none has the right to be worshiped but Allah, and that Muhammad is the Messenger of Allah."

Part of one section (w4.1) deals with the "finality of Muhammad's message" and is to clarify any confusion "among Muslims as to Islam's place among world religions." Thus, readers are reminded that Muhammad was the last prophet and that anyone claiming to be a prophet after him with the intent of creating a new religion is a "fraud, misled and misleading." Even the *Koran* (33:40) states that "Muhammad is not the father of any of your men, but he is the Messenger of Allah and the last (end) of the Prophets." It is also states that certain religions were valid in their own times and eras but have been abrogated by the "universal message of Islam."

Muhammad also stated he was favored above all other prophets (w4.2). For example, he had a "succinctness of speech," he had war booty made lawful for him, he made the world purer to worship him, and he was made "triumphant through dread."

While many aspects of *sharia* are entrenched in the seventh century, there are some modifications dealing with contemporary issues. For example, one section deals with "performing the obligatory prayer in a vehicle" (w24.0). Basically, if traveling on a crowed vehicle, such as a bus, if Muslims cannot pray in the traditional manner, they are allowed to do the best they can. This even includes facing in the direction the vehicle is traveling.

So, Where Are We At?

To understand why Islam is an enemy which must be confronted, the book has examined the holiest documents in Islam, the *hadith* reports, and the *Koran*. These documents contributed to a third document, *sharia*, or Islamic law. Obviously, Muslims are compelled to follow all three.

The next area that needs to be examined is the *sunnah*, or the behavior of Muhammad. We need to remember that Muslims are commanded to follow in his path, or his *sunnah*. The next four chapters will provide a biography of Muhammad, the prophet of Islam.

CHAPTER 6: MUHAMMAD: MECCA (PART I OF II)

The examination of the ideological foundations of Islam in the prior four chapters allows for an understanding of the cause of the Islamic *jihad*. This chapter and the following three chapters will provide an additional reason Islam is in a perpetual war with all that is not Islamic, namely a biography of Muhammad. Again, it must be stressed that Muslims are obligated to followed Muhammad's behavior or path exactly and with no deviation, innovation, or variation. By doing this, they will go to paradise. Failure to do this assures them a place in hell. The basic question which few ask is, "What is the behavior of Muhammad which Muslims are obligated to follow?"

What Do We Know About Muhammad and How Do We Know It?

The thousands of articles and books on Muhammad's life all come from a few sources written more than one hundred years after his death. Because there is so little information on Muhammad's life, it would seem simple to write his biography, especially since some claim Muhammad was born "in the full light of history." However, in reality, writing about Muhammad is very difficult. The biographical material on his life contains many contradictions, omissions, and almost certainly later insertions. The dating of and sequencing of events is often uncertain. Even events and individuals can be viewed differently by the various branches within Islam. Readers need to understand there is more than one version of nearly every aspect of Muhammad's life. For example, writers differ on when he was born, the number and ordering of his wives and children, if he was literate, and even on whose breast his head rested when he died. In other words, almost anything written about Muhammad could be followed by as asterisk noting alternative views.

The early biographies of Muhammad are generally referred to as *Sirah Rasul Allah (Life of the Apostle of God*) or simply as the *sira* (*sirah*). Although the word *sira* may sound as though it has some type of spiritual meaning, it is simply an Arabic word meaning "biography" or "the life and times of." A second word that is often used in connection with *sira* is *sunnah. Sunnah*, which, as noted earlier, is the path Muslims are to follow, is based on Muhammad's behavior as portrayed in his biographies.

There appear to have been several early biographies of Muhammad which have all been lost. Ibn Ishaq (Ishak), who died in 768, wrote the first biography of Muhammad that has survived. This biography may have been published as a book or simply consisted of a collection of notes taken by his students around 750 or about one hundred and twenty years after Muhammad's death. Ishaq may have used material from some of the early biographies which were lost. Ishaq's biography is titled *Sirat Rasul Allah,* which as noted earlier loosely translates as *Life of the Apostle of God.* Although Ishaq's original work appears to have been "lost," perhaps because of the inclusion of the Satanic Verses, it is widely known through two authors who had copies of his "book" and used material from it to write their books.

The first was Ibn Hisham (d. 833), who edited Ishaq's "book" around 830 to 833, about two hundred years after Muhammad's death, and re-published it under the title *The Life of Muhammad.* Hisham admitted to omitting certain material, such as the Satanic Verses, because it was "disgraceful to discuss" and would "distress certain people." Given the material left in the book—such as assassination, genocide, murder, pedophilia, rape, and robbery—some have wondered what could have been left out that would be more disgraceful or distressing than what was included. Hisham's book is currently available as *The Life of Muhammad* by Alfred Guillaume.

Guillaume's book is an attempt to recreate Ishaq's work as closely as possible by including material removed by Hisam such as the Satanic Verses and by removing material inserted by Hisam.

Ishaq and Hisham's works were written prior to the *hadith* report collections of Bukhari, Dawud, and Muslim.

The second author to use Ishaq's book was Tabari (d. 923) who, from 870 to 922, more than two hundred and fifty years after Muhammad's death, wrote the *History of Prophets and Kings*. Tabari wrote about the early history of Islam and used Ishaq's "book" as one of his sources. He included the controversial Satanic Verses. By utilizing numerous sources, Tabari sometimes provided alternative views of events. Tabari's work has recently been republished in a series of thirty-eight volumes titled *The History of al-Tabari*. There is an additional volume in the series by the editors which contains a biography of Tabari and material related to the technical issues in completing the collection. This collection of books is considered the "most important universal history produced in the world of Islam." Volumes I, II, VI, VII, VIII, and IX have material on Muhammad.

In addition to the books mentioned above, there are some other early surviving works with biographical material on Muhammad. For example, Waqidi (d. 822) wrote about Muhammad's "expeditions"—his raids of banditry and of conquest after he left Mecca and went to Medina. His book is titled *Waqidi's Kitab al-Maghazi* (*Book of Wars*) and provides a chronology of the spread of Islam by *jihad*. Waqidi's book has been criticized since it contains far greater detail than the sources he cited. Either he had sources which he did not acknowledge or he embellished segments of his book. Again it needs to be noted that Waqidi's book was written almost two hundred years after Muhammad's death. Waqidi was a *hadith* report collector who some believe fabricated twenty thousand *hadith* reports.

Waqidi's secretary, Ibn Sa`d (Saad), who died in 845, wrote a two-volume biography of Muhammad which has survived. It is titled *Kitab al-Tabaqat al-Kabir* (*The Book of the Major Classes*). In addition to the biography, a book on the women of Medina and two volumes on the men of Medina have also survived. Once again, it needs to be pointed out that Sa`d's books were written more than two hundred years after Muhammad's death.

Ibn Kathir was a famous and well-respected Islamic scholar who was born in 1313 and died about 1373. He is perhaps most known for his fourteen-volume history of Islam. Although he did not publish an independent biography of Muhammad, Islamic scholars have recently taken sections of his history of Islam collection and incorporated the material dealing with Muhammad into a four-volume series titled *The Life of the Prophet Muhammad.* Kathir made extensive use of the *hadith* reports in writing about Muhammad.

Kathir's biography is not easy to read but is indispensable for more advanced and knowledgeable readers. The four-volume set rambles in terms of chronology. And the chain of transmitters which starts most sentences can be distracting, as seen by the following: "This wording is that of Ahmed. Abu Daud, al-Tirmidhi and al-Nasai related it through various lines from Sa'd Jamhar. Al-Tirmidhi stated." After the listing of the chain of transmitters, the *hadith* report would start. Because Kathir relied on several collections of *hadith* reports, the same story is often presented in several variations.

Kathir also made his opinion known about certain aspects of Muhammad's life. It is not uncommon to find phrases such as "My own comment [on the *hadith* reports] is that..." If he believed a *hadith* report was correct, he stated something like, "This chain of authorities is in accordance with the established criteria of..." Or if he saw a problem, he would write something like, "This tradition is devoid of a link from this line; indeed it is problematic." Another forthright comment includes: "There is dispute over the veracity of this. But god knows." He also cited when *hadith* reports were "weak," when there was a gap in the chain of transmission, or when only one *hadith* collector reported a certain *hadith* report.

In addition to the earlier biographies from Muslims who lived in Arabia during the development of early Islam, there are few fragmentary Western sources available which deal with the spread of Islam shortly after Muhammad's death.[13] One of the more recent Western sources on Islam and Muhammad is the four-volume set titled *The Life of Muhomet: From Original Sources* by Sir William Muir. The first volume appeared in 1856 and the last appeared in 1861. Although the four-volume set is difficult to obtain in print, a single abridged volume is readily available.[14]

Muir was born in Scotland in 1819 and spent a great deal of his life in India. Much of his research focused on studying the life of Muhammad. Muir was unhappy with the two types of biographies which had been written, the first by pious Muslims who exaggerated and fabricated material about Muhammad, the second by Christian missionaries whose scholarship was questionable and whose goal was to negatively distort the history of Muhammad. Muir's first chapter is almost one hundred pages and is devoted to presenting the early Muslim sources he used in writing the biography.

David Samuel Margoliouth was born in 1858. He became a professor of Arabic at the University of Oxford. He traveled extensively in the Middle East, and some believe he became more knowledgeable about Islam than many Islamic scholars. His first book on Muhammad came out in 1905 and was titled *Mohammed and the Rise of Islam*. It was followed by several others, including *Mohammedanism* (1912) and *The Early Development of Mohammedanism* (1914). Margoliouth's books also used the early Muslim sources. He often interjected his own views into his writing, and one frequently cited example is from his 1905 book. It reads as follows:

> The character attributed to Mohammed in the biography of Ibn Ishaq is exceedingly unfavorable. In order to gain his ends he recoils from no expedient, and he approves of similar unscrupulousness on the part of his adherents, when exercised in his interest. He profits to the utmost from the chivalry of the Meccans, but rarely requites it with the like. He organizes assassinations and wholesale massacres. His career as tyrant of Medina is that of a robber chief, whose political economy consists in securing and dividing plunder, the distribution of the latter being at times carried out on principles which fail to satisfy his follower's ideas of justice. He is himself an unbridled libertine and encourages the same passion in his followers. For whatever he does he is prepared to plead the express authorization of the deity. It is, however, impossible to find any doctrine which he is not prepared to abandon in order to secure a political end. At different points

> in his career he abandons the unity of God and his claim to the title of Prophet. That is a disagreeable picture for the founder of a religion, and it cannot be pleaded that it is a picture drawn by an enemy: and even though Ibn Ishaq's name was for some reason held in low esteem by the classical traditionalists of the third Islamic century, they have made no attempt to discredit those portions of the biography which bear hardest on the character of their prophet.

Another early book, seemingly one of the types Muir did not like, was written by the Reverend J. L. Menezes and is titled *The Life and Religion of Mohammed: The Prophet of Arabia.* First published in 1912, the author had a mission in writing the book in that as a Catholic priest in India, he wanted to show the "true colors" of Islam and Muhammad to his readers. He hoped to demonstrate to those who "blindly followed" Islam that they were being "deceived" and they needed to find a "better leader and a more certain way of salvation." It is a relatively short book, and although without citations, it portrays Muhammad as he was portrayed in the early Islamic literature which he must have used in writing the book.

William Montgomery Watt was born in 1909 and became an important historian on Islam and the West, although he was not without controversy. He wrote several influential books, including *Muhammad at Mecca* (1953); *Muhammad at Medina* (1956); and a synthesis of the two books, *Muhammad: Prophet and Statesman* (1961). His critics perceive Watt as "too apologetic" toward Islam, which affected his objectivity.

Bernard Lewis is another important figure who needs to be mentioned. Born in 1916, he has been a prolific writer. Rather than dealing specifically with Muhammad, his books have had a broader focus, such as his 1950 book, *The Arabs in History.* Two of his recent post-9/11 books have attracted a great deal of attention: *What Went Wrong? The Clash Between Islam and Modernity in the Middle East* (2002) and *The Crisis of Islam: Holy War and Unholy Terror* (2003). Lewis blames the backwardness of the Middle East on conditions imposed by their culture and religion rather than on conditions imposed by outsiders.

Martin Lings wrote a book titled *Muhammad: His Life Based on the Earliest Sources* (1983). Lings was born in 1909 and lived in Egypt for much of his life, where he converted to Islam. Being fluent in Arabic, he used the early Islamic sources to write this book. One interesting feature of this book is that in the biography on Muhammad, he notes when he believes the *suras*, or chapters, of the *Koran* were revealed to Muhammad, thus allowing readers to see the historical context in which they were revealed. As a devout Muslim, Lings has been criticized as being too accepting of questionable Islamic sources.

More recently, especially after 9/11, several writers such as Robert Spencer have been added to the list with books such as *The Truth about Muhammad: Founder of the World's Most Intolerant Religion*, *The Politically Incorrect Guide to Islam (And the Crusades)*, and *Religion of Peace? Why Christianity Is and Islam Isn't*. And the Center for the Study of Political Islam has an eleven-volume series on Islam: *Mohammed and the Unbelievers* (I), *The Political Traditions of Mohammed* (II), *A Simple Koran* (III), *An Abridged Koran* (IV), *Mohammed, Allah and the Jews* (V), *Mohammed, Allah, and the Christians* (VI), *Mohammed, Allah, and Hinduism* (VII), *Mohammed, Allah, and the Intellectuals* (VIII), *Mohammed, Allah, and the Mind of War* (IX), *Mohammed, Allah, and Politics* (X), and *The Submission of Women and Slaves* (XI).[15]

Muhammad: Early Life

Muhammad's purpose in life was described in the *Koran* (61:9), where it states, "He it is Who has sent His Messenger (Muhammad) with guidance and the religion of truth (Islamic Monotheism) to make it victorious over all (other) religions even though the *Mushrikun* (polytheists, pagans, idolaters, and disbelievers in the Oneness of Allah and in His Messenger Muhammad) hate (it)."

Muhammad was born on a Monday in either April or August 570 in Mecca (Bakka, Beccah, Makkah), the major commercial and religious center in Arabia. According to some sources, his linage could be traced back to Ishmael (Ismail), the son of the prophet Abraham.

The year of Muhammad's birth is important because of another event, namely the attempted conquest and destruction of Mecca by Abraha (Abrahah), the Abyssinian (Ethiopian) governor of Yemen. Abraha wanted to make Sanaa (Sa'a, San'a), the capital of Yemen, the major commercial and religious center in Arabia, and he used the desecration of a church by an Arab as the pretext to lead his army north to conquer and destroy Mecca. However, after his army had advanced to within two miles of Mecca, it was forced to withdraw after suffering a disaster. Some claim the disaster was an epidemic. Others believe the disaster was the result of the Islamic god directing birds to drop pebbles on the invading army. Each bird carried three pebbles, one in each claw and one in each of their beaks, which when dropped either killed or caused the flesh of the soldiers to rot. Whatever the cause of the disaster, the year was referred to as the "year of the elephant" since the Abyssinian army included a fighting elephant—or, in some accounts, thirteen fighting elephants—to terrorize the opposing Arab army (see 108:1-5). The year was also referred to as the "lucky one" since Muhammad was born and the invading army was destroyed.

As with so many "facts" about Muhammad and early Islam, there are controversies over Muhammad's birth. For example, some believe the "year of the elephant" or "the lucky one" occurred fifteen to twenty-five years prior to Muhammad's birth and was changed to link the "miracles" of Muhammad's birth with the defeat of the invading Abyssinian army.

It is recognized that the defeat of the invading Abyssinian army greatly elevated the power, prestige, and status of Muhammad's tribe, the *Quraysh* (*Kuraish*), among the other tribes in Mecca since their prayers were believed to be responsible for the destruction of the invading Abyssinian army. This was an era when tribal status was important in everyday life and belonging to a powerful tribe gave individuals greater power and respect than those belonging to less powerful tribes.

Muhammad's father, Abdullah, which means "the servant or the slave of god," died in Medina, then known as Yathrib, shortly before Muhammad was born, probably while returning with a trading caravan from Gaza or Syria. Some sources claim Muhammad's mother, Amina, heard a voice stating she was pregnant with "the lord of his people." Perhaps this is why she gave him a rare name among Arabs, Muhammad, which means "the praised."

Shortly after Muhammad's birth his mother sent him to live with a wet-nurse in a desert tribe. This was a common practice in Arabia for male children because it was believed they would become healthier and stronger living outside urban areas since the desert air was cleaner and healthier to breathe than urban air. Another reason was because urban areas were sources of epidemics from the unsanitary living conditions and because those traveling with passing caravans often carried contagious diseases. Parents also wanted their sons to learn a pure form of the Arabic language spoken by the desert tribes, rather than the pidgin Arabic that was spoken in urban areas which were the focal points of caravans from many areas. Some believe Muhammad was sent to live with a wet-nurse because the grief over his father's death had dried up his mother's milk.

It does not appear that wet-nurses were paid for their services. Rather, they would have another "son" who would have an obligation to take care of them in times of need. These "sons" would also be "brothers" to the children of the wet-nurses which created clan, family, and tribal bonds. Having additional bonds to more powerful or wealthy clans, families, and tribes was a way of enlarging the security network of wet-nurses in the event of disability, famine, old age, unemployment, or war. The bonds required that the "brother" or "son" protect his wet-nurse and her family in times of need. As will be seen, later in his life both the wet-nurse and her daughter sought Muhammad's assistance.

Muhammad was returned to his mother when he was two. She was so pleased by his healthy and robust appearance that she either told the wet-nurse to take him back or the wet-nurse suggested taking him back. After another two years, Muhammad had some sort of seizure, which some believe was an epileptic fit, and again he was brought back to his mother. Again, Muhammad's mother told the wet-nurse to take him back, which she did for another year. When he was between five and six years old he was finally returned to his mother. In 577, when returning with him from a trip to Medina, Muhammad's mother died. He then went to live with his paternal grandfather, and then after his grandfather died in 580 he went to live with his paternal uncle, Abu Talib (Taliba), a member of the powerful *Quraysh* tribe. Some claim he was a wealthy caravan merchant while others believe he was poor. Abu Talib had inherited his father's job as caretaker of the *Kaaba* (*Ka'ba, Ka'bah*), a religious shrine in Mecca. One of Muhammad's jobs for his uncle was that of a shepherd, where he cared for camels, goats, and sheep near Mt. Arafat. In 579 or 583, Muhammad traveled in a caravan with his uncle Abu Talib to Syria.

This is all that is known about Muhammad's early life. Other stories appear to have been created, some probably by Muhammad, which were designed to give him greater credibility as a prophet. Many of these stories are now accepted as fact. As noted earlier, allegedly Muhammad's mother heard a voice prior to his birth which announced she was pregnant with "the lord of his people." Muhammad's wet-nurse stated that after she received Muhammad, her breasts—which had been dry—suddenly overflowed with milk. It is seldom asked why Muhammad's mother would give her infant to a wet-nurse who could not nurse. The story continues that the wet-nurse's old female camel which had also been dry suddenly had unlimited milk. A story told by Muhammad was that when he was about three, two men dressed in white robes, or the angel Gabriel, came to him and opened his body, took out his heart, and removed a black clot of "hatred and impurity" which had been implanted by Satan. Other versions have the "devil's lot" removed.

Another story is that when he was traveling with his uncle Abu Talib, Muhammad met a Christian monk named Bahira near Bosra (Bostra, Busra) in southern Syria, which was at the juncture of several trade routes. Bahira recognized a mark on Muhammad's back between his shoulder blades which resembled a "cupping-glass" or "an apple" as that of a prophet. The mark was also described as "a collection of hair on his shoulders" and "a protruding lump of flesh." Bahira told Abu Talib, "Return with this boy and guard him against the hatred of the Jews, for a great career awaits your nephew." Another account has Bahira saying, "Take him back to your country, and be on your guard against the Jews, for, by god, they will seek to do him harm." Bahira also said, "Great things are in store for this brother's son of thine."

Although it is not documented, many assume that between 583 and 595 Muhammad traveled with caravans to areas such as Yemen, Syria, Persia, and perhaps even Egypt. He may also have traveled on sea voyages. On these travels he would have been exposed to and influenced by many cultures and religions. Others claim that because of Bahira's warning, Muhammad's did not leave Mecca for several years.

Muhammad participated in a tribal war in about 590, which was called the "Sacrilegious War" because it started during the sacred months. This appears to have been a blood feud, and it was reported that Muhammad was in a battle, and he was an excellent archer.

Marriage

When he was a young man, Muhammad asked Abu Talib for one of his daughters in marriage. Abu Talib refused the request, telling Muhammad he was not ready for marriage, meaning he was too poor.

In 594, Muhammad was hired by a forty-year-old woman named Khadijah (Khadeejah, Khadija) to take her camels loaded with trade goods such as dates, leather, olive oil, and spices in a caravan to Bosra to sell the goods, and then return with trade goods such as china and silk which would be sold in Mecca. Khadijah had been widowed and/or divorced two to four times and had children by these marriages. One early biographer wrote this was Muhammad's second trip to Bosra. Others have noted it does not seem logical that a business-savvy woman would entrust a fortune in trade goods to someone who had only been on one trading caravan to Bosra as a boy. She was trusting Muhammad to take her camels loaded with trade goods along a trade route where bandits lurked. Once Muhammad arrived in Bosra, he would have had to negotiate the best price for Khadijah's trade goods and then negotiate the best price for trade goods to bring back for sale in Mecca. Muhammad would then have to return safely to Mecca with the trade goods he had purchased. Thus, for Khadijah to trust her caravan to Muhammad meant he was seen as a man who was experienced, honest, intelligent, reliable, resourceful, and trustworthy. Khadijah's slave, Maysarah, who was described as a "lad," was the only person to accompany Muhammad on the trip.

Earlier it was noted that some believe Muhammad was illiterate. Others claim his role as a merchant would necessitate some math, reading, and writing skills. As will be seen, there are some indications he could read and write, although these skills may have been learned later in life.

While in Bosra, Muhammad sat under a tree and Nastur (Nestor), a monk who lived nearby, said, "No one has ever halted under this tree but a prophet," and "he [Muhammad] is the last of the prophets." Some believe this was the same place Muhammad had stopped several years earlier when he was with his uncle Abu Talib, and that the monk Bahira had died and been replaced by Nastur. Others believe the two stories are simply variations of the same story which became distorted, embellished, and enhanced over time. There are several variations of the two stories noted above. All have the same theme, which is an educated or religious individual stating that Muhammad had the characteristics of a prophet.

There are other stories indicating that Muhammad was a prophet. For example, Maysarah, the young slave who accompanied Muhammad to Bosra, told Khadijah that on the journey back to Mecca, two angels came and provided shade for Muhammad during the mid-day heat.

Muhammad's success as a merchant made Khadijah a large profit, double what she had expected, and shortly after his return in 595 she asked him through a friend, servant, or sister if he would marry her despite their fifteen-year age difference. Several writers have commented on Khadijah's independence in running a business, in hiring men, and in asking a man to marry her. In other words, women were freer before Islam than they were after it.

There are different versions of what happened next. Some claim Khadijah's father was dead and the marriage was approved by her uncle. Others claim her father was alive but disapproved of the marriage. Being a resourceful woman, Khadijah plied her father with alcohol until he was too drunk to object to the marriage.

As a wedding gift, Khadijah gave Muhammad a fifteen-year-old slave name Zeid (Zayd; Zaid) with whom Muhammad had developed a strong affection. And Muhammad set free a female slave he had inherited from his father.

The marriage between Muhammad and Khadijah produced four to seven children. There is general agreement the marriage produced four daughters: Zainab (Zaynab, Zeinab, Zeinale) (c. 600), Um Kalthum (Kulthum, Kolthum) (c.603), Ruqayya (Rockeya, Rokeiya, Ruqayya) (c. 604), and Fatima (Fatimah) (c.605), none of whom lived to be forty years of age. Writers generally agree that Zainab was the oldest, but the order of the last three is in dispute. Different accounts have the number of sons ranging from one to three, with two being the most frequently cited number. What is known is that the son(s) (Qasim, Tahir, Tayyib) died before adolescence. The son(s) appears to have been the first and/or last births in the marriage. Given her fertility during their marriage, some have speculated Khadijah must have been younger than forty when she married Muhammad, perhaps the same age or only a year or two older than him.

It was mentioned above that it is generally agreed the marriage produced four daughters. Some claim the marriage did not produce any daughters. Rather, the daughters were "created" so that certain individuals could falsely claim to have hereditary ties to Muhammad which would provide their heirs the right to be Muhammad's successor in Islam.

Although the date is uncertain, early in their marriage Zeid's father came to Mecca to purchase his son's freedom. Muhammad said he would let Zeid decide if he wanted freedom, in which case there would be no payment, or if he wanted to stay in Mecca with Muhammad. Zeid said he considered Muhammad to be a father from whom he had learned much and said he would accept slavery over freedom to stay close to him. Muhammad gave Zeid his freedom and proclaimed, "Zeid is my son, I am his heir and he is mine." As will be seen, this would later prove problematic for Muhammad when he decided he wanted to marry Zeid's attractive wife since it was prohibited for a father to marry his daughter-in-law.

When Muhammad was about thirty-five, his uncle, Abu Talib, was having difficulty supporting his family and, as was the tribal custom, Muhammad took Abu Talib's son, Ali, into his household. Ali was similar in age to Muhammad's daughters and was raised as a brother to the four girls. Some writers believe this occurred about the time Muhammad's last son by Khadijah died.

Earlier it was noted that wet-nurses were not immediately paid for their services, but could expect to ask those they had nursed for assistance. Because of a drought, Muhammad's wet-nurse came and ask for assistance. Khadijah gave her forty sheep and a camel.

Mecca

This was a time when there were many religions in Arabia, including Christianity and Judaism. In fact, it has been speculated that Khadijah was a Christian. Some have suggested it was from her Muhammad learned about Christianity and Judaism. Generally, Christians and Jews held the traditional Arabian religions in low regard because of their polytheistic beliefs.

Mecca was in a valley about a mile and half long and half a mile wide. It was a rocky and barren area, but it had developed into an important community of about five thousand residents for two reasons. First, the war between the Byzantine and Persian Empires had made the transportation of trade goods through disputed areas dangerous. For example, the Byzantine Empire wanted goods from the east, but Persia blocked most of the trade from the east unless it came from the north through the Caspian Sea or from the south through Arabia. Thus, many merchants transported their goods by sea to the tip of southern Yemen or further north up to the coastal city of Jeddah (Jedda, Jidda, Judda, Juddah). From Jeddah, the goods traveled forty-five to fifty miles northeast through Mecca and then finished the journey in Gaza or Syria. Other goods were transported through the Persian Gulf to the east coast of Arabia, where the route to Gaza or Syria again went through Mecca. And goods from Abyssinia (Ethiopia) went across the Red Sea to the west coast of Arabia and then east through Mecca to the Persian Empire or north to Gaza and Syria to the Byzantine Empire.

Mecca had developed into a place for the caravans to rest and obtain water from the numerous wells, and by Muhammad's time Meccan merchants were organizing many of the caravans. Although nearly surrounded by mountains, there were four gaps in the mountains that led into Mecca. Mecca also had items to export. For example, the leather of Mecca was in high demand in Syria. The caravans from Mecca generally went out and returned twice a year. In the fall, the caravans went south from Mecca to Yemen and west to Ethiopia. In the spring, they went north to Syria. The caravans would return laden with goods which would be sold to those traveling through Mecca. Caravans also returned with some of the goods those living in Mecca would need to survive since Mecca was not an agricultural center. These caravans were financially profitable for the Meccan merchants.

There was a second reason Mecca developed into an important community, namely its religious significance. In the center of Mecca was the *Kaaba*, which means "cube," that housed as many as three hundred and sixty idols worshiped by different Arab religions. The *Kaaba* included images of Jesus and the Virgin Mary. There was also a dry well into which pilgrims placed offerings. In fact, it was this structure and its idols that Abraha, the Yemen governor, was coming to destroy in 570, the year of Muhammad's birth.

It is not known when the *Kaaba* first took on religious significance. The *Kaaba* had an added sense of mystery since its origins were unknown although some believe it was built by Adam, and then after it was destroyed by the flood it was rebuilt by Abraham and his son Ishmael. While it was being rebuilt, the angel Gabriel brought them a black stone to incorporate into the wall. The black stone was about thirty to fifty centimeters in circumference (twelve to twenty inches) and was possibly a meteorite. It is the *Kaaba* toward which Muslim face during their daily prayers, and Muslims believe it is below the throne of the Islamic god.

During Muhammad's time, the *Kaaba* was constructed of stones loosely stacked on top of one another. It was probably slightly above the height of an average man, and it did not have a roof. It is not known how many different "religions" had idols in the *Kaaba*. What is apparent is this was a time in Mecca where there was tolerance of diverse religious beliefs.

There were also areas around Mecca that had long-standing religious significance, such as Mt. Arafat to the southeast. Because of the area's religious significance, many Arabs came to Mecca as pilgrims to perform religious rites. During these times, Mecca would hold fairs which would attract pilgrims. Pilgrims were a major source of revenue for Mecca since they had to pay a "visitor's tax." The merchants of Mecca also profited from the pilgrims, who purchased items they could not obtain elsewhere. Merchants in Mecca also made and sold religious idols to the pilgrims. Also of importance was the fact that, during the time for the religious pilgrimages, blood-feuds and attacks on caravans were prohibited. Some believe there were three sacred months in the fall and one in the winter, while others claim the area around Mecca was a sanctuary area year-round. Thus, it was a time when people could travel freely with less fear of being attacked.

After pointing out why Mecca was an important commercial and religious center during Muhammad's life, it now needs to be mentioned that some scholars do not believe Mecca was important as either a commercial or religious center. They list the silence of non-Muslim sources of the era on any mention of Mecca or other Arabian cities such as Medina or Taif while many other cities visited by caravans were mentioned. It is also noted that Mecca was not a "natural" crossroad or stopping place. It was an out-of-the-way barren land with few grazing areas for camels or other domestic animals, and nearby settlements such as Taif were more centrally located and less barren. Additionally, why would those from the east (for example, India) send trade goods to the southern peninsula of Arabia and then transfer the cargo to camels and transport it more than one thousand miles north across a desert to Syria? It would have made more sense to unload the cargo further north at the Gulf of Aqada or the Gulf of Suez. These scholars have also stated there simply was not enough "international" trade taking place in Arabia to support a city such as Mecca.

The belief that Mecca was an area with important religious idols attracting thousands of religious pilgrims has also been rejected by some writers. Again, part of the reason is because Mecca is not mentioned in the writings that exist from that time. Others claim Mecca may have had religious significance but that so did several other Arab cities. Therefore, they reject the idea Mecca held a major religious shrine to which thousands of pilgrims flocked.

Next?

The next chapter will continue examining Muhammad's life in Mecca. It will start with his call to prophecy and conclude with Muhammad and his followers leaving Mecca for Medina.

CHAPTER 7: MUHAMMAD: MECCA (PART II OF II)

The last chapter examined Muhammad's life in Mecca from his birth to shortly after his marriage. This chapter will start with Muhammad's call to prophecy and conclude with his leaving Mecca and going to Medina with his followers.

Muhammad: The Prophet Emerges

There were numerous indicators early in Muhammad's life suggesting he was a prophet. One example dealt with his pregnant mother hearing a voice stating she was carrying "the lord of his people." Another was when Muhammad's wet-nurse went from being dry to having an abundance of milk. The experiences with monks noting that Muhammad had a sign of prophecy, and the angels providing shade while he was returning to Mecca with a caravan are other examples that were cited earlier. Another experience mentioned previously was when two angels came and opened Muhammad's chest and took out "hatred and impurity." Muhammad also said that when traveling, the trees and stones greeted him.

Another incident on the road to becoming a prophet occurred in 605, when a serious dispute arose in Mecca concerning the *Kaaba.* As noted earlier, at this time the *Kaaba* was little more than a small area surrounded by a loosely-stacked stone wall the height of an average man with some openings for doorways. After the *Kaaba* was damaged by a flood, four of the local tribes decided it needed to be rebuilt. It was ripped down to the foundation and rebuilt with higher, thicker walls and with a roof. The roof had timbers from a Greek or Roman shipwreck near Jeddah and was crafted by a Christian or Jewish carpenter. Part of the reason for having higher walls and a roof was to make it more secure since a thief had recently stolen offerings placed in the dry well in the *Kaaba*. The thief was caught and his right hand was cut off.

After the reconstruction was completed, the various tribes each claimed the right to replace the black stone in the wall. The tension built over several days and with the threat of tribal war looming, it was decided the next man who entered from a certain doorway would make the decision as to which tribe had the right to replace the black stone. The decision fell to Muhammad since he was the next man to walk through the doorway and into the *Kaaba*. When he appeared, someone said, "He is the trustworthy one." Muhammad had the stone placed on a cloak—sometimes a piece of cloth or a rug—and a member of each of the four tribes held one corner of the cloak and lifted up the stone. Muhammad then pushed the stone from the cloak into the wall. Again, it is not known if this story is true or if it was developed later to demonstrate that Muhammad was a prophet who was guided through the doorway at just the right moment by a higher power.

Critics of Islam have suggested that Muhammad knew about the decision to select the next person to enter the *Kaaba*, and he timed his entrance accordingly.

The next incident clearly identified Muhammad as a prophet although there is some confusion over the details. The basic story is that Muhammad had the practice of going to a cave at the foot of Mt. Hira, about three miles north of Mecca, to escape the oppressive heat and to pray and meditate. Sometimes he went for several days and once a year for a month. While in the cave on a Monday in either July or August 610 or 611, Muhammad, who was about forty to forty-three years old, had a religious experience during the Arabic month of Ramadan. The angel Gabriel appeared before Muhammad and informed him he was "the prophet of the lord" and the "messenger of god." This is the same angel Gabriel who appeared before the Virgin Mary in Nazareth and announced the "coming of Jesus."

Those who have attempted to chronologically order the chapters in the *Koran* have pointed out that originally Muhammad may have thought the angel Gabriel was a different angel or even the Islamic god since the angel Gabriel was not mentioned for twelve years until the Medina period of his life. This is called the "night of power" or the "night of destiny."

The first revelation from the angel Gabriel either told him to "read" or "recite" and this first revelation is contained in verses 96:1-3 of the *Koran* (see B3, B4953, B4922). When Muhammad said he could not read, the angel "choked" or "pressed" him forcefully until he could not take it anymore. In fact, Muhammad thought he was going to die. The angel repeated the request to read and continued the choking and pressing. The angel Gabriel repeated this request three times to demonstrate to Muhammad the burden of being a prophet. Finally, the revelation was revealed, which was, "He has taught man that which he knew not" (96:5, B6982).

The initial meeting with the angel Gabriel was so traumatic that Muhammad became paralyzed with fear and did not return home when expected. Worried about his safety, Khadijah sent people out to look for him, and after they found him in the cave, they brought him home. In another version he was shaken by the experience but returned home unassisted. After either being returned home or returning home unassisted, he told Khadijah, "I am either a poet or a madman." Muhammad was concerned that the vision was a demon attempting to possess him. He asked to be covered or wrapped in a blanket or cloak for protection.

In some accounts, the angel, which only Muhammad could see, followed him into his home. To test if the vision was an angel or a demon, Khadijah either removed her veil—although this episode was before the veil had been imposed—or her shift. In another version, Muhammad climbed inside of Khadijah's shift. Out of modesty in response to Khadijah removing her veil or her shift, or by Muhammad getting inside of her shift, the angel left the house, and Khadijah declared it was an angel, not a demon. She also reassured Muhammad a god would not play tricks on him because of his trustworthiness, and therefore, he must be a prophet.

Khadijah then went to ask her cousin Waraqah (Waraka, Warakah, Waraqa, Warayah), a blind scholar who had knowledge of both Christian and Jewish Scriptures, about the vision. In some accounts, she went alone; in others, Muhammad went with her. Or, after Khadijah told Waraqah about Muhammad's vision, he went to see Muhammad at the *Kaaba*. Waraqah, who was probably a Christian, may have held a popular belief at the time. This belief was that a new prophet would soon be coming. After Waraqah felt a small lump about the size of a pigeon egg on Muhammad's back between his shoulder blades, he said Muhammad was "God's long-awaited messenger to the Arabs" and that Muhammad "would be the prophet of his people." He also told Muhammad his people would call him vile names, treat him badly, and eventually drive him out. This was a warning that his people would not readily accept his vision. Now Jews, Christians, and Arabs all had at least one prophet.

Some believe Muhammad had prior contact with Waraqah, from whom he learned about Christianity and Judaism. One account has this occurring after he returned from his first trip to Syria for Khadijah. Waraqah died a short time after the first revelation. However, Waraqah's support of Muhammad earned him the distinction of being the only non-Muslim allowed into paradise.

After the first revelation informing Muhammad he was a prophet and he was to read and recite, the revelations stopped for a few months to three years. Thus, Muhammad was a prophet with nothing to read or recite. Bitterly disappointed Muhammad thought of committing suicide by throwing himself off a mountain top; however, whenever he would start to the top of the mountain, the angel Gabriel would appear and announce once again that Muhammad was the prophet of the Islamic god.

Finally, the angel Gabriel reappeared with verses 93:1-11, which stated the Islamic god had not forsaken Muhammad. These verses ended with, "And proclaim the Grace of your Lord (i.e., the Prophethood and all other Graces)."

Initially, Muhammad did not tell many individuals about the revelations, probably keeping the knowledge limited to Khadijah and Waraqah. Later, the angel Gabriel would appear more frequently, telling Muhammad revelations from the Islamic god that would become part of the *Koran*. When the revelations came to Muhammad, he would fall into a "violent state of agitation." Others said he would foam at the mouth, roar like a camel, and snore. If he was in a public area, he would cover himself with a blanket or cloak. When he emerged his face, would be red and covered in sweat. He would then recite the revelation to his followers.

Early in his career as a prophet, Khadijah asked Muhammad if her non-believing parents were in hell. Muhammad answered "yes," noting that if she could see their true nature, she would detest them (see M203). She then asked if their son(s) was also in hell. Muhammad told her it depended on the strength of her beliefs. If her beliefs about Islam were true and strong, their son(s) was in paradise. If they were not true or not strong, the son(s) was in hell. This same question came up after Khadijah's death when he was asked about children who died before puberty. Muhammad replied that all children were born Muslim, and unless corrupted by their parents, they went to paradise (B1385). Other *hadith* reports are slightly contradictory and state that since the Islamic god created children, he knows what sort of deeds they would have done and treats them accordingly (B1383, B1384). Another *hadith* report states that Muslim parents who have had three children die before puberty are guaranteed admission into paradise (B1381). As noted earlier, Muhammad and Khadijah probably had from one to three sons die before puberty. More than a decade after Khadijah's death, Muhammad had another infant son die. A *hadith* report states he has a wet-nurse in paradise (B1382).

As with many new religious movements, Islam had a slow start, in part because the revelations were secretly disclosed only to close friends and family members. There is little question or controversy over his first convert being his wife, Khadijah, who would spend much, if not all, of her wealth supporting her husband's prophecy. There is, however, a question about the second convert. The answer to this question has consequences for the leadership of Islam after Muhammad's death, with some claiming the first male convert had a greater claim to be Muhammad's successor. Three males are generally mentioned as the first male to accept Islam. The first is Ali, the son of Muhammad's uncle, Abu-Talib. Ali was Muhammad's cousin. He was born about 599 to 600, and he went to live with Muhammad's family when he was five or six years old. Thus, he would have been ten to eleven years of age when he converted. Ali would marry Muhammad's daughter Fatima and become Muhammad's fourth successor. Many Muslims believe Ali should have succeeded Muhammad as the leader of Islam because he had a hereditary connection to Muhammad, he was one of the first to accept Islam, and he married one of Muhammad's daughters. Ali and Fatima had two sons. One produced an heir who provided a hereditary link to Muhammad and, some Muslims believe, a hereditary line to the leadership of Islam. This segment of Muslims is called Shites (Shi'a, Shi'ite, Shi'is), or the Party of Ali.

Two other males listed as the first to accept Islam are Zeid and Abu Bakr. Zeid was the former slave who Muhammad adopted as a son, while Abu Bakr was a businessman and Muhammad's friend. Abu Bakr was the most important of the three early male converts in the development of Islam. When they converted, Ali was still a child, and Zeid was a former slave who did not have any power or wealth. Abu Bakr, however, was an influential, respected, and wealthy man. As such, his conversion was most likely to influence others.

As will be seen after Khadijah's death, Abu Bakr became related to Muhammad through the marriage of his six-year-old daughter, Aisha, to Muhammad. Some claim the name Abu Bakr means "father of the maiden," in reference to his daughter, Aisha. After Muhammad died, Abu Bakr succeeded him as the leader of Islam.

Because the issue of the "first" convert is so important in Islam, some writers have tried to have more than one person being the "first" to accept Islam. This is done by claiming that Khadijah was the first woman, Ali was the first youth, and Abu Bakr was the first adult male.

Another early convert was Othman (Uthman), who may have initially been more interested in one of Muhammad's daughters than in his religion. After Abu Bakr's death Othman succeeded him as the leader of Islam. Two additional early converts were Bilal, a black slave who became Islam's first *muezzin*, or crier, and Omar, who succeeded Othman as the leader of Islam. Those who do not believe the leader of Islam needs to have a hereditary link to Muhammad but simply be a pious Muslim are called Sunni (Sunnite) since they are following in the *sunnah*, or path, of Muhammad.

More revelations started coming to Muhammad, letting him know the Islamic god was revealing to him a "Weighty Word," or important laws and obligations (73:5). Also, Muhammad was to devote himself completely to the Islamic god (73:8), and only the Islamic god had the right to be worshiped (73:9).

By 613, the number of Muhammad's followers was small, probably around fifteen to forty. As mentioned earlier, this was because his early work was conducted privately and unobtrusively among close friends, family members, and those who came voluntarily to him. His early converts were from diverse groups. Some were family members such as Ali, Khadijah, and Zeid. There were also friends such as Abu Bakr. From outside the circle of family and friends there were a few young men from prominent families who themselves had little power or wealth. But the largest group consisted of young men who did not have tribal connections or who came from tribes with little power. There were also some slaves and ex-slaves who were attracted to his preaching. The slaves may have originated from areas where Christianity and Judaism flourished, and therefore, they were familiar with some of Muhammad's views, especially monotheism. Thus, it was a movement comprised primarily of young men who recognized they did not have and were not likely to have what those at the top of society possessed, or of slaves or ex-slaves who had nothing to lose in adopting a new religion. Several writers have observed his early followers were primarily strong young males.

In 613, he received a revelation telling him to "proclaim openly (Allah's Message of Islamic Monotheism)..." (15:94) and to "warn your tribe (Muhammad)..." (26:214). One of his first public meetings was the "declaration at Mt. Sira," where he invited non-Muslims to convert to Islam. From this he gained few converts, so he stood on the roads coming into Mecca to preach to those coming into the city. Also, the pilgrims on religious retreats would set up their tents outside of Mecca, where Muhammad would visit them to talk about Islam.

There is an account of Muhammad going into the *Kaaba* and ordering those present to repeat, "There is no god but Allah." Those assembled considered the order to be blasphemous and attacked him. One of Khadijah's sons rushed to assist his step-father and was killed defending him. Some claim he was the first martyr in Islam.

Many of the businessmen in Mecca, especially the influential Abu Sufyan, were concerned with Muhammad's religious pronouncements. The first concern was why would a god select Muhammad as a prophet rather than one of the current religious or political leaders of Mecca? After all, although Muhammad was a member of the powerful *Quraysh* tribe, he was an orphan from a humble family, and certainly god would have selected someone of noble birth. They compared Muhammad to a palm tree growing out of a dung heap. A second concern was more practical, namely that Muhammad's emphasis on only one god might decrease the number of religious pilgrims coming to Mecca. Meccan merchants made money from the religious pilgrims who visited the *Kaaba* to worship their idols. These pilgrims did not want to listen to Muhammad vilify their idols. After all, hadn't their idols defeated the army coming from Yemen in 570? Additionally, since Islam had prohibitions on the sale or use of certain items, the merchants' profits would be further reduced. A third reason for opposing Muhammad, especially later on, was that some of the revelations were in vast contrast to the existing standards of the time, so much so that they must have seemed shocking even to the pagan Arabs.

One example deals with replacing clan, family, and tribal ties with religious ties. This was a time when an attack on an individual was also an attack on that individual's clan, family, and tribe. Thus, hereditary connections were an important source of identity and security. With Islam, these hereditary connections were negated. In Islam, what mattered was the individual's religion.

Early in his prophecy, those in power in Mecca probably ignored Muhammad. He may have been an amusing figure since at this time there were many healers, magicians, or poets who claimed divine inspiration. In addition, many of the powerful individuals in Mecca had traveled to other areas where they had been exposed to some of Muhammad's religious beliefs, especially that of monotheism. Also, those in power in Mecca had a great deal of religious tolerance, in part from their travels and in part from the *Kaaba's* housing idols for many religions.

However, at some point the *Quraysh* leaders in Mecca must have started to worry about the number of converts he was attracting or about his negative impact on religious pilgrims. To prevent Muhammad from gaining additional converts or power, those coming into Mecca were told to avoid him since he was a dangerous magician. Although many did avoid Muhammad, others were probably curious of the magician who believed he was a prophet, and they returned home and told others about Muhammad and his teachings.

Although his number of followers was still relatively small, there is little doubt Muhammad was becoming a source of conflict in Mecca. If one member in a family converted to Islam, there was conflict since this challenged the existing clan, family, and tribal traditions. Arranged marriages were cancelled if one of the parties converted to Islam, again placing strain on families that should have been united and strengthened by the marriage. One example is with Muhammad's daughters, Ruqayya and Umm Kalthum, who were either engaged or married to Abu Lahab's sons. Because of Abu Lahab's hatred of Muhammad and Islam, the engagements or the marriages were cancelled.

Another example of the increasing level of hostility toward Muhammad concerns Omar, who was on his way to kill Muhammad when he was told his sister and her husband had converted to Islam. Omar did not believe she had converted, and he diverted to his sister's house, where she confessed she had converted to Islam. Upon learning this, he either hit or sliced his sister with his sword, after which he felt a certain amount of guilt and he allowed her to read him a passage that would become part of the *Koran*. Omar was so moved by what she read that he went to Muhammad and converted to Islam. There are several variations of the story on Omar's conversion to Islam. Omar would become the second leader of Islam after Muhammad's death. He was somewhat typical of those joining Islam in that he was a young Arab male who was strong and an excellent horseman. Muhammad was alleged to have said, "If Satan met Omar, Satan would get out of Omar's way."

Another example of the increasing tension was when some Muslims were praying outside of Mecca and some non-Muslims came by and started to mock them. One of the Muslims picked up the jawbone of a camel and hit one of the mockers. Some claim this was the first blood shed for Islam, although, as mentioned earlier, it may have been Muhammad's stepson. Muhammad told his followers to be patient and to give violence a respite, at least temporarily (73:10).

Medina Comes Calling: First Visit

The oasis of Medina was two hundred and fifty to two hundred and seventy miles north of Mecca. It had two large Arab tribes, the *Aus* (*Aws*) and the *Khazraj* (*Kjazraj*), who had engaged in three non-decisive but bloody battles which had ended in a truce. A fourth battle was imminent since there was still tension and occasional conflicts, mostly in the form of assassinations which further increased the tension. The cause of the conflict probably resulted from the rapid transformation of nomadic groups accustomed to wandering the land to settling, living, and working in an agricultural and urban society. There were also disputes over land. Previously, the land was something everyone could use. Now, with agriculture expanding, there was ownership of land with disputes over ownership rights. Some have suggested the Arabs in Medina were worried that continued violence would weaken them to the point where they would become vulnerable to conquest by the three largest Jewish tribes who lived in Medina. This was unlikely since the three Jewish tribes did not form an alliance. In fact, two of the Jewish tribes formed an alliance with the *Aus* and the third with the *Khazraj*.

Fearing a fourth battle, members from the Aus went to Mecca to seek assistance from the powerful *Quraysh* tribe, which was refused. Muhammad went to the Aus and asked if they would like something better than what they had come for. They asked what was better, and he said Islam. He then recited verses from the *Koran*. The leader of the Aus said they had come for something "other than this."

Muhammad's Mannerisms

Physically, Muhammad has been described as of middle height, with broad shoulders and a large head. Muhammad's hands, joints, and mouth have also been described as large. His skin had a bluish tint, although it is noted his face had a whitish tint. Or his face had a reddish tint. His beard was thick, and he generally wore his hair to his shoulders. He had long chest hair.

Muhammad, as might be expected, started to adopt mannerisms he felt were appropriate and representative of a prophet. For example, he wore a veil over his face. He would not be the first to withdraw his hand from a handshake, and when staring at someone he would not be the first to divert his eyes. He was somewhat obsessive with dental hygiene and frequently used a tooth-stick, which was made from the root of a tree. He made excessive use of perfumes. When his hair started to turn grey, he either used dye (B166) or he didn't use dye (B3550). When he visited a home, he would knock three times before entering. He also repeated a sentence three times to make certain it was understood (B94, B95). Absolution included placing water in his nose and blowing it out (B161). There are also accounts of Muhammad having lice (B7001). In one account, he went to visit the wife of a friend who provided him with food, and while he ate she searched his hair for lice (B2788, B2789).

Mecca Worried

Initially, Muhammad may have been amusing to the *Quraysh* leaders in Mecca. Then he became an annoyance. Finally, he became a threat. Initially, they tolerated Muhammad, believing he would either regain his senses or leave Mecca. Some believe his followers would tire of him and return to their families and religions. Then when Muhammad's revelations became less tolerant of other religions, the *Quraysh* leaders went on the offensive. They told Muhammad that if he were a prophet, he should be able to perform miracles (13:27, 17:90). Muhammad received a revelation noting that miracles were only performed by prophets when the Islamic god willed it (13:38).

The *Quraysh* leaders in Mecca then sent a delegation to Medina to ask some of the rabbis if Muhammad was a prophet. They gave the delegation three questions to ask him, stating if he answered them correctly that he was a prophet and they should follow him. When given the questions, Muhammad said he would provide the answers the next day. He was apparently waiting for a revelation with the answers. This went on for more than two weeks until the revelation finally came. Muhammad displayed more knowledge in answering the questions than the rabbis had expected, although they still did not recognize him as a prophet. This resulted in some converts to Islam by those who were impressed with Muhammad's ability to receive the answers to the questions (18:23-24).

Many believe it was about this time the first negative revelations about Jews were revealed. It may have been because Jews failed to accept him as a prophet or because they had provided the leaders in Mecca with the questions with which to test him.

Emigration to Ethiopia

As concern increased among Mecca's leaders over Muhammad's increase in converts and power, anger and irritation also increased against him and his followers. As a result of increasing hostility, some of Muhammad's followers fled to Abyssinia (Ethiopia), a Christian kingdom on the west side of the Red Sea. Accounts differ as to the specific reasons for the emigrations, the number of emigrations and emigrants, the dates of the emigrations, and when the emigrants returned to Mecca. Some believe that about ten adult males and their families left in 615. Others claim about eighty-three left. They left in small groups so their absences were less likely to be noticed, and thus, it was less likely family members would attempt to prevent them from leaving. The *Quraysh* sent a delegation to bribe the Abyssinian king to force the emigrants to return to Mecca. Although the governor considered Muslims heathens, he was tolerant of their religious beliefs and refused the request, especially after one of the emigrants read him a section of the *Koran* (19:16-21). It is reported that the governor wept after listening to the reading and stated, "They shall not be betrayed." They returned to

Mecca after about three months, describing their stay in Abyssinia as "miserable."

It is also believed that in 616 another emigration took place to Abyssinia, this time with about eighty adult males and their families. One of the emigrants was Muhammad's daughter, Ruqayya, who was considered the most beautiful of his daughters, and her husband, Othman, who was not only handsome and wealthy but also her cousin. It has been suggested that these emigrants did not leave because of religious persecution but to establish trade routes. Or Muhammad may have sent them away because he feared the pressure on them to renounce Islam was becoming too great.

In about 617, the *Quraysh* leaders in Mecca organized a boycott against Muhammad and his followers. This included avoiding Muslims both commercially and socially. They were mocked during their prayers. Additionally, some Muslims may have been placed under "house arrest" by family members and prevented from attending Islamic religious meetings. Arranged marriages between Muslim and non-Muslim families were cancelled or delayed. Generally, the boycott consisted of mild sanctions. This was primarily because it would have been dangerous for a member of one clan, family, or tribe to inflict an injury on the member of another. The exception was, of course, for slaves. The most notable example was the early Muslim convert Bilal, whose owner subjected him to intense torture in an attempt to have him renounce Islam. For example, Bilal was forced to lie on the scorching sand with heavy rocks placed on his chest while his owner shouted for him to renounce Islam, which he refused to do. Abu Bakr either purchased Bilal or traded another slave for his freedom.

Most writers believe the boycott had little or no impact on the lives of most Muslims and resulted in few, if any, hardships. After all, Mecca was an area where there was commercial activity and most merchants would not enforce a boycott if it meant a loss of revenue. Also, many believed it was wrong to boycott clan, family, or tribal members. The "boycott" lasted until 619.

In 619 or 620, Muhammad's uncle, Abu Talib, died. Abu Talib had raised Muhammad after the deaths of his mother and grandfather. And when Abu Talib had financial difficulties, Muhammad had raised his son, Ali. Although Abu Talib was not a Muslim, he had the power to provide Muhammad with protection through his *Quraysh* tribal ties. An attack on Muhammad would have been an attack on the *Quraysh* and would have resulted in a blood-feud. After Abu Talib died, his brother, Abu Lahab, initially agreed to provide the same level of protection to Muhammad as had his brother. However, Abu Lahab changed his mind after Muhammad said Abu Talib resided in hell, although in a shallow part (M209). In fact, Muhammad told Abu Lahab that while most of those in hell were in a lake of fire, Abu Talib was in a puddle. The split between the two must have been bitter because verses 111:1-5 are devoted to Abu Lahab and his wife. It states they will burn in the fires of hell.

About two months later, Khadijah died after twenty-five years of marriage. She had been the first to accept Muhammad as the messenger of the Islamic god and one of his biggest supporters, both emotionally and financially. Muhammad said she lived in paradise next to a river in a house made of reeds, and there was no noise or hardship for her. Some authors reverse the deaths and believe they occurred a few weeks apart.

Enter Satan—The Satanic Verses

Shortly after Khadijah died, it is believed Muhammad received the controversial "Satanic Verses," although some claim it was before she died, perhaps as early as the first emigration to Ethiopia. Recent knowledge of the Satanic Verses was prompted by the book, *The Satanic Verses*, by Salman Rushdie, who, in 1989, had a death warrant placed on him by Iran's Ayatollah Khomeini for daring to publicize a taboo issue in Islam. This issue was resurrected by Rushdie's knighthood in 2007, when there were more demands for his death.

As noted above, this is a controversial and taboo area within Islam. Having the Islamic god put words in your mouth is one thing, but having Satan do so without the prophet or his followers knowing the difference is something very odd. Although some apologists try and downplay the Satanic Verses, it needs to be stressed that this episode is accepted as authentic by most, if not all, of the early

Muslim biographers such as Ishaq, Sa'd, and Tabari. As mentioned earlier, at least one biographer knew about the verses and accepted them as authentic but omitted them because they "were disgraceful to discuss" and they "would distress certain people."

The context of the Satanic Verses is as follows. With the conflict and tension increasing, the *Quraysh* leaders of Mecca offered Muhammad what some have referred to as the "Mecca Bargain." Essentially, they would make him a partner in the *Kaaba*, which would provide him with power, wealth, and as many wives as he wanted. In exchange, Muhammad would stop criticizing the idols in the *Kaaba*. In addition, if Muhammad worshiped some of their idols, they would worship his god.

Rather than saying "no" to the offer, Muhammad said he would wait to see what revelations came to him. Based on the next revelation, Muhammad rejected the offer (109:1-6). There was then another revelation where again the offer was rejected (39:64-66). The next revelation reads, "Have you then considered *Al-Lat* and *Al-Uzza* and *Manat...*" (53:19-20). It was at this point Satan "cast" the following words on Muhammad's tongue: "These are the exalted *Gharaniq* [a high flying crane] whose intercession is approved [or hoped for]." *Al-Lat*, *al-Uzza*, and *Manat* were three widely worshiped female idols. The *gharaniq* were cranes believed to fly so high that they were close to the heavens and could intervene with the gods and idols on behalf of worshipers. After Muhammad recited the revelation, his followers, the polytheistic Quraysh, pagans, and idolaters, held a joint prayer session (B4862). Soon, rumors were rampant with some claiming Muhammad had reverted back to polytheism while others claimed the *Quraysh* had converted to Islam.

For Muhammad, the "revelation" of the Satanic Verses resolved some problems. Muhammad's early biographers explained it was easy for him to be deceived by Satan since the Satanic Verses brought reconciliation with his clan, family, and tribe. The Satanic Verses also meant his relatives, who were currently non-Muslim, would accept his religion and would reside in paradise rather than hell.

For the *Quraysh* leaders in Mecca, the Satanic Verses also appeared at an opportune time since they were becoming concerned over Muhammad's increase in followers and power. As noted earlier, with more than three hundred and sixty idols in the *Kaaba,* Mecca was a site for religious pilgrimages, and the leaders in Mecca feared Muhammad's monotheistic views might reduce the number of religious pilgrims coming to Mecca. There were few religious pilgrims who wanted to travel to Mecca to be told by Muhammad and his followers they were worshiping false idols. If this occurred, there were other cities with similar religious shrines the religious pilgrims could visit and at which they would not be harassed.

The length of time between Muhammad's acceptance of the Satanic Verses and the revelation rejecting them is unclear, with some having it arrive the same day, while others saying it was several months later. What is known is that the revelation rejecting the Satanic Verses, which is not in the *Koran*, has the angel Gabriel asking, "What have you done Muhammad? You have read to these people something I did not bring you from God, and you have said what He did not say to you." The angel Gabriel then provided a new series of revelations. In the first revelation, it was noted that Satan had influenced all prophets by throwing in falsehoods, and the Islamic god had also intervened on their behalf. In other words, Muhammad was not the first prophet to be fooled by Satan. Additionally, the Islamic god would abolish or cancel what Satan had said and then reveal his revelation (22:52). There was also another revelation noting, "Verily, they were about to tempt you away from that which We have revealed (the *Koran*) unto you (Muhammad), to fabricate something other than it against Us... And had We not make you stand firm, you would nearly have inclined to them a little" (17:73-74). The next revelation replaced the Satanic Verses and followed the mention of the three female idols in verse 53:19. The verses (53:21-27) state,

> Is it for you the males and for Him the females? That indeed is a division most unfair. They are but names which you have named - you and your fathers - for which Allah has sent down no authority. They follow but a guess and that which they themselves desire, whereas there has surely come to them the guidance from their Lord. Or shall man have what he wishes. But to Allah belongs the Last (Hereafter) and the

first (the world). And there are many angels in the heavens, whose intercession will avail nothing except after Allah has given leave for whom He will and is pleased with. Verily, those who believe not in the Hereafter, name the angels with female names.

The new revelations stated it was impossible for pagan idols to have any intercession with the Islamic god. In fact, the Islamic god must give permission before intercession is allowed (2:255, 34:23). Also, it is foolish to believe the Islamic god would be given three daughters in society where males were more valuable than females since this would be "a division most unfair." Additionally, the names of the three idols are just meaningless names given by forefathers who had previously taken the wrong path while Muslims had been sent a prophet.

Verses 17:72-75 were then revealed, and they were a warning to Muhammad. They start by saying that those who are blind to the Islamic god's signs in this world will be blind in the next. It continues by stating Muhammad was being led away from what had been revealed to him, the *Koran*, and that he would have become an "intimate friend" of those who were leading him astray had the Islamic god not intervened to make him "stand firm." And, had Muhammad continued going astray, he would have suffered double the punishment in this life and after death. After these revelations, Muhammad then went back to rejecting the idols in the *Kaaba*.

The Satanic Verses are only one of many controversial aspects of Muhammad's life. As has already been noted, there are many aspects of the life of Muhammad where serious questions can be raised in terms of whether something is an accurate portrayal of his life or if it was developed as needed to justify his behavior, to provide him with the characteristics of a prophet, or to fill in missing gaps in his life. It has also been mentioned that there are alternative versions of almost every "fact" of Muhammad's life, such as the year of his birth, the number and ordering of his wives, and the number of his children. However, the Satanic Verses are different from other aspects of his life in two ways. First, this story is consistently presented in the early Muslim sources. In fact, it is mentioned in the

Koran (22:52), so even the Islamic god accepted the story as true. In fact, it is incomprehensible the Satanic Verses would be accepted as true if the story came from less than credible sources. Second, unlike the other stories about Muhammad which stressed his positive characteristics, this story is damaging to him as a prophet. For example, why didn't Muhammad recognize the ideological differences between a "revelation" from Satan and a "revelation" from the Islamic god? In fact, Muhammad appeared ready to accept the money, power, and women provided by the "Mecca Bargain" until his followers, who recognized the obvious inconsistencies between Muhammad's teachings and the Satanic Verses, started to rebel. Also, if Satan could send and have Muhammad accept one set of revelations, then why not others? Or is it Satan, not the Islamic god, who was sending all of the revelations?

Some believe it was about this time the revelation started to include "Jewish lore," probably indicating he had contact with an individual or individuals familiar with Jewish Scriptures and history.

The *Quraysh* were upset with Muhammad's rejection of their agreement. They felt betrayed and tricked, and it exacerbated an already tense situation.

Protection Gone

Khadijah was Muhammad's only wife when she was alive. After her death he had many wives, although scholars disagree on the number and the order. One month after Khadijah's death, Muhammad married the portly Sauda (Sau'da, Saudah, Sawda, Sawdah). She was thirty to fifty years old at the time and the widow of one of his followers who had fled to Abyssinia. The marriage was probably the fulfillment of an obligation to a follower, to prevent her from marrying out of Islam, or to provide someone to help with household tasks such as raising his daughters. Accounts claim she was a heavy woman of good disposition.

He also married Aisha, the six-year-old daughter of Abu Bakr, who was one of his closest followers and someone whose business dealings provided him extensive knowledge of the nomadic tribes.

The consummation of the marriage, or the rape of Aisha, would not take place for three years. Apologists claim Abu Bakr offered Aisha to Muhammad, although again the *hadith* reports support the view it was Muhammad who asked for Aisha in marriage (B5078, B5125). It appears that Abu Bakr had already arranged a marriage for Aisha which was not to Muhammad. Muhammad's claim to Aisha came from two dreams. In the first, a man was carrying a body wrapped in silk. The man held out the silk-wrapped body and told Muhammad to uncover his wife. When he did, he saw Aisha. The second dream was basically the same, only an angel was carrying the silk-wrapped body. Again, Muhammad was told to uncover his wife, and again it was Aisha. Muhammad then said, "If it is from Allah, then it will surely be accomplished," or "He will cause it to come true," or "If this be from God, He will bring it to pass."

Although Muhammad and Abu Bakr were good friends, apparently Aisha had not had much contact with Muhammad. After her marriage to Muhammad, Aisha was given a basket of dates to take to him, and upon seeing him, she was filled with alarm and aversion. Other accounts claim she was familiar with Muhammad since he visited her father at his home almost daily.

Within Arab societies at this time, males who had formed close bonds of friendship considered one another brothers, and thus when Muhammad approached Abu Bakr about marrying Aisha, he said it would be improper for Muhammad to marry her because she was, in essence, his niece. Muhammad replied that they were only brothers in religion, and therefore, the marriage was proper (B5081). It is reported that Aisha became a very beautiful woman. In 656, twenty-four years after Muhammad's death, she briefly wielded power that challenged the leadership of Islam and she was responsible for about two thousand *hadith* reports.

Around this time, Muhammad had a vision of a place with water and date palms that were between two black rocks. This was a reference to Medina.

With his wife and uncle both dead, in 620 Muhammad started to look for another settlement where he could move with his followers, one which might be more receptive to his religion. Muhammad and Zeid, or Muhammad and a servant, went to a small commercial area known as Taif (Ta'if) that was about forty to sixty miles east of Mecca. Taif, like Mecca, was also on the caravan route, and it had a religious shrine like the *Kaaba*. Unlike Mecca, it had a better climate and fertile land which produced cereals, dates, and grapes. In fact, it was said the grapes in Taif were so pure they looked like flasks of purified honey. Writers have been curious over the selection of Taif because many of those in Mecca who rejected Muhammad and Islam had summer homes and property in Taif. Although Taif was only two days from Mecca and Muhammad had been active as a prophet for almost a decade, few in Taif seemed to be aware of him or Islam. After Muhammad explained he wanted to move himself and his followers from Mecca to Taif, the leaders of the settlement who did not want a conflict with Mecca rejected his proposal. In fact, they chased Muhammad and his companion out of the city by throwing rocks at them.

Night Journey

On his way back to Mecca, another important event took place in Muhammad's life, namely the *miraj*, or the "ascension to the heavens," although some accounts have this occurring at a different time and place. This event is also known as the "night journey." It is also the event which provides Islam with a connection to Jerusalem. The story is that Muhammad was visited by the angel Gabriel and sometimes also by the angel Michael and taken to "the furthest mosque," allegedly in Jerusalem, by a *Buraq*, which was a white, winged, horse-like animal. Here he met the prophets of the past such as Abraham, Adam, and Jesus. He then toured heaven, or paradise. Based on this experience, Muhammad instituted the five daily prayers for Muslims. Originally, the Islamic god, who was veiled, ordered followers to pray fifty times a day. Muhammad went back and said this was too many times, so it was reduced to forty times a day. Muhammad continued to bargain until the Islamic god reduced the number to five times per day. Muhammad claimed to have proof of the journey, including his ability to describe a mosque he had not previously been to, of stopping along the way to tell members of a caravan where to find a lost camel, and by describing a caravan on its way to Mecca (B3207, B3239, B3887, B5576, M162). Verse 17:1 briefly mentions the "journey by night."

Many have noted there was no mosque for Muhammad to visit in Jerusalem at the time. Basically, at the time Muhammad claimed to visit a mosque in Jerusalem there was a garbage dump on the site.

Medina Comes Calling—Again and Again

After leaving Taif and experiencing the night journey, Muhammad went back to Mecca, where he continued to preach to groups in public areas. Then, in 620, a group of about six to twelve Arab men arrived from Medina on a pilgrimage to the *Kaaba*. The men were from the *Khazraj* tribe, had heard about Muhammad, and had sought him out. There had been a fourth bloody battle between the two Arab tribes in Medina, the *Aus* and the *Khazraj*, and they were looking for a way to resolve the fighting. Unlike the *Aus*, who had come to Mecca earlier to seek assistance against the *Khazraj*, this time the *Khazraj* were looking for a way to unite the two Arab tribes against the three Jewish tribes. The hostility toward the Jewish tribes was because two of the Jewish tribes had allied with *Aus*, which had aided in the defeat of the *Khazraj* in the last battle. And there was speculation that the Arabs in Medina had heard the Jews were awaiting the arrival of a new prophet, and this may have been an attempt to ally the prophet with the Arabs rather than the Jews. After talking with Muhammad, they all converted to Islam, and they pledged to go back to Medina and unite the Arab tribes through Islam.

The following year, in 621, about five of the *Khazraj* who had earlier converted to Islam and seven others, including two from the *Aus* tribe, came to Mecca and converted to Islam with the Pledge of al-Aqabah (Accaba, Akaba). Aqabah was a village near Mecca where the new converts took the pledge and agreed to follow Muhammad and Islam. They were looking for a leader who would unite the Arabs just as a leader had united the *Quraysh* decades earlier. Some reports claim Muhammad had some of his followers go to Medina with the converts to teach them about Islam. Others believe the followers went to Medina to access the political situation so there would not be a repeat of the fiasco at Taif.

Some accounts have the "night journey" occurring after the Pledge of al-Aqabah.

In March of 622, about seventy-five pilgrims, including two women, came to Mecca from Medina. They also wanted Muhammad to come to Medina and put an end to the war between the two Arab tribes. Muhammad accepted the offer, and the pilgrims took a Second Pledge of Aqabah to accept Islam and obey and fight for Allah and Muhammad as they would members of their own tribes.

Muhammad's decision to move to Medina was motivated by several factors. First, hostility against Muslims had increased since the deaths of Khadijah, who had been a supporter with close family ties to Mecca, and of Abu Talib, who although not Muslim had been a powerful tribal member who provided Muhammad some level of protection. Second, Muhammad must have realized that by moving to Medina his position would go from that of a religious leader with a small group of persecuted followers to the *de facto* military, political, and religious leader of two Arab tribes, which would give him greater power to win converts to Islam. He would do this by replacing the allegiance to clan, family, or tribe with an allegiance with religion. In fact, after the Second Pledge, one man noted the Arabs in Medina were "men of war" who were willing to sever ties with the Jews of Medina. Third, the presence of the three Jewish tribes must have been an incentive to Muhammad. These three tribes belonged to an established religion which recognized one god, and if these tribes would recognize him as the new prophet, then other Jewish tribes might follow them, and he would have thousands of followers. Fourth, the large Jewish presence in Medina, with its emphasis on monotheism, made Islam seem more acceptable to the idolatrous and polytheistic pagan Arabs. Fifth, Muhammad must have realized Medina was the place of his earlier vision, which had water and date palms surrounded by two black rocks. These were the lava fields surrounding Medina.

Asking an outsider such as Muhammad to come as an arbitrator was evidently a common practice among warring Arab tribes. In fact, it was Abu Sufyan's role in Mecca to arbitrate disputes among the various clans, families, and tribes in an attempt to prevent violence. Medina also offered Muhammad and his followers a safe sanctuary. The Jewish tribes had not been consulted on this matter but thought that with his emphasis on monotheism, Muhammad might be their anticipated prophet.

The Jewish tribes in Medina were successful in both agricultural and commercial areas, which attracted many Arabs as customers and workers. It is not known if the Jewish tribes were Arabs who had adopted Islam or if they were part of the Hebrew Diaspora after the Roman destruction of Jerusalem. It is fairly certain the Jewish population of Medina first settled the area to which the nomadic Arabs gradually migrated as workers. The population of the city and surrounding area was probably between ten thousand and forty thousand individuals. The two Arab tribes were jealous of the success of the Jewish tribes.

Medina was very different, both geographically and commercially, from Mecca. Mecca was located in a barren sandy valley surrounded by mountains to the west, south, and east. Although Mecca had many wells, the soil was not suitable for agriculture. To the west of Mecca was the Red Sea, and to the east was one of the largest continuous deserts in the world. Mecca was hot, often reaching more than one hundred and twenty degrees Fahrenheit in the summer. It was ravaged by strong winds that produced dust and sandstorms, and rainfall was infrequent, but when it came it could be heavy. Although nearly surrounded by mountains and lava formations, Medina was a twenty-square mile oasis with orchards and fields of grains. Rather than a central city, Medina consisted of a series of tribal settlements with many surrounded by groves of date trees and fields. Each settlement had a fort where people could go for protection if attacked. It is estimated that at this time there were two hundred settlements in Medina.

Some believe two revelations were received about this time or shortly after arriving in Medina. The first is verse 2:190-193, which is the first or one of the first *jihad* verses. It starts by saying, "And fight in the way of Allah." It continues by saying, "And kill them wherever you find them, and turn them out from where they have turned you out." The last verse is, "And fight them until there is no more

Fitnah (disbelief and worshiping of others along with Allah) and (all and every kind of) worship is for Allah (Alone)." Verse 22:39 may also have been received. This starts by saying, "Permission to fight (against disbelievers) is given to those (believers) who are fought against because they have been wronged; and surely, Allah is Able to give them (believers) victor..."

Time to Go!

Shortly after the Second Pledge of Aqabah starting in April 622 and over the next few months, Muhammad and his followers, which estimates place at a number of anywhere from seventy to two hundred, started to plan and organize the ten-day, two hundred and fifty- to two hundred and seventy-mile journey north to Medina. This move was called the *hegira* (*hijra, hijrah*), or the flight, although some claim there was literally no opposition to their leaving, no attempt to stop them from leaving, and no attempt to follow or pursue them. Additionally, there had been no new boycotts or persecutions of Muslims. Thus, the correct word for the "flight" would be "emigration." Others, however, saw it as a "breaking of ties." That is, by leaving Mecca, Muhammad's followers were leaving behind ties to their clans, families, and tribes and joining the Muslim community. After they arrived in Medina, they were known as the refugees, or *muhajirin*. The Muslims already in Medina were known as the allies, citizens, helpers, or *ansar*.

Whether it was a breaking of ties, emigration, or flight, small groups of Muslims started leaving Mecca for Medina on different days and at different times. This might have been an attempt to make the emigration less noticeable, and thus, non-Muslims had less opportunity to try and prevent clan, family, or tribal members who were Muslim from leaving. A simpler explanation is that it took some longer to prepare to move than others. Certainly the *Quraysh* leaders in Mecca must have realized what was happening and had discussions over what to do. In some ways, Muhammad leaving of his own accord seemed a perfect solution to the problematic prophet. Still, however, they must have been distressed that some of their clan, family, and tribal members were also leaving. However, at least those who remained in Mecca would be free from his influence. There might have been discussion about assassinating Muhammad with a member from each tribe taking part in the assassination to prevent any blood feuds from occurring. If necessary, Muhammad's tribe might have even be paid "blood money" to prevent it from taking revenge.

Muhammad and Abu Bakr were among the last to leave. Their reason for leaving last may have been to make certain that those who said they were leaving actually left. This event is considered so important in Islamic history that it marks the start of the Islamic calendar. Thus, 622 is the first year which could be loosely stated as 1 AH, or the year of the *hegira.* It has been noted the calendar starts with Muhammad assuming a more military-political role than a religious role. Why, for example, didn't the calendar start with Muhammad's birth, his death, or with his first revelation (see B3934)?

It is not known when the Islamic calendar system came into existence. Some have Muhammad instituting the calendar shortly after arriving in Medina. Others have it being implemented shortly after Muhammad's death by one of his successors who used the date because it was "definite" and "well-known."

There are stories that a group from Mecca was planning to assassinate, exile, or lock up (place in irons) Muhammad. In fact, the *Koran* (8:30) states, "And (remember) when the disbelievers plotted against you (Muhammad) to imprison you, or to kill you..." One story claims that after Muhammad left Mecca, Ali stayed in his house and slept in his bed to deceive the assassins into believing Muhammad was still there. Some versions of the story have the angel Gabriel telling Muhammad not to sleep in his bed as well as telling him when to leave, although these "revelations" did not make it into the *Koran.* Thus, if there were any assassins, they were peering through a window in Muhammad's house watching Ali sleep under Muhammad's green cloak while Muhammad was making his escape. Most believe the high drama of the "flight" may have been embellished. Within Mecca, Muhammad would have had protection from his tribe, and furthermore, Mecca was a sanctuary. For Muhammad, the most dangerous time would have been on the road between Mecca and Medina after he had left the protection of his clan, family, tribe, and the sanctuary around Mecca.

After escaping, leaving, or sneaking out of Mecca on a Monday, Muhammad and Abu Bakr hid in a cave on Mount Thur (Thaur, Thawr) about six miles south of Mecca for one to four days. Abu Bakr's son and daughter brought them food and water as well as information about what was happening in Mecca and when it was safe to continue on their journey to Medina. There are stories that assassins looking for Muhammad approached the cave he was hiding in but a spider wove a web covering the cave opening. A similar story is that a bush or a tree sprouted and hid the cave opening as the assassins approached. Also, birds waited in trees and sang to distract the attention of assassins who approached the cave. And wild doves built a nest in the branches of a tree or bush that covered the cave opening, and the assassins reasoned that the doves would not nest where there was danger (see 9:40).

When they felt safe, Muhammad and Abu Bakr left for Medina with a guide. They went west to the Red Sea and then north. They finally turned east and reached Medina after about twelve days. Ali stayed behind in Mecca for three days to take care of some of the property issues concerning those who had left Mecca for Medina. Muhammad's wife, Sauda, and two of his daughters, Um Kalthum and Fatima, also remained behind in Mecca. Abu Bakr's family—including his daughters, one of whom was Aisha, who was married to Muhammad; his son; and his wife—also remained in Mecca. All were all left unmolested and none was taken hostage, which seems to suggest Muhammad was seen as more of a nuisance than as a threat.

Those who have ordered the *suras* in the *Koran* have noticed that during Muhammad's last three years in Mecca there were about thirty *suras*, many of which were very long. During this time, many of the *suras* contained information on Christianity which has been called "meager and deceptive." It has been speculated that he may have acquired this knowledge from Christian slaves who may have been captured when fairly young, which would explain their distorted and fragmentary knowledge.

What Happens in Medina?

The next two chapters will examine Muhammad's life in Medina. It will be seen that he went from preaching nonviolence and tolerance to a handful of followers to preaching intolerance and violence to thousands of bandits.

CHAPTER 8: MUHAMMAD: MEDINA (PART I OF II)

After more than twelve years of preaching in Mecca, Muhammad and his followers voluntarily left and moved to Medina without incident. It cannot help but be noticed that after more than twelve years of attempting to convert the citizens of Mecca to Islam, Muhammad left with a handful of followers, a couple hundred at most. With the exception of his family and close friends, most of his followers were from the fringe element of society and were those with nothing to lose by adhering to a new religion. It also cannot help but be noticed that for its time, Mecca appeared to be a prosperous and successful city. Although in a barren area, the resourcefulness of the merchants of Mecca had apparently turned it into a thriving city. In a remote and lawless area, they had helped to establish sanctuary areas in and around the city, as well as ways to handle the violence that took place other than through revenge, which simply created a cycle of violence. And there was religious tolerance. Christianity, Judaism, idolatry, and polytheism were accepted and tolerated.

Islam could not gain a foothold in a relatively lawful, prosperous, and tolerant city such as Mecca. Instead, Muhammad had to take his followers to a city racked by a civil war between two Arab tribes, a city where there was tension and unrest not only between the two major Arab tribes but also between the Arabs and the Jews. Medina was a city of chaos and violence, and it was where Muhammad went to bring about peace. Muhammad ultimately brought about peace in Medina through the expulsion and genocide of the Jewish tribes, and by turning his followers into bandits, rapists, and robbers who brought slaughter and violence to the surrounding area.

Arriving in Medina

In the last chapter, Muhammad's followers left Mecca and started on the journey to Medina. Muhammad and Abu Bakr were among the last to leave, and out of fear there might be an attempt to kill Muhammad, they hid in a cave until they deemed it safe to leave for Medina.

After leaving the cave, they traveled for twelve days until they arrived at an oasis on the outskirts of Medina where they stayed for a few days on a Monday on either September 12, 20, 24, or 27 in 622. It was here Muhammad laid the foundation of the "first mosque to be built in Islam." After a few days, Muhammad and Abu Bakr rode into Medina at either at noon in the afternoon or during the evening. Since Muhammad needed to find a location for his home and mosque as he rode into the city, he dropped the reins of his camel, allowing it to roam freely or, according to Muhammad, to be guided by the Islamic god. This meant the land where the camel finally stopped would be hallowed, and it would be the site of his home and mosque. It also meant Muhammad did not have to choose the land of one tribe over another. The camel finally knelt down on a piece of land either used for drying dates or in an orchard of palm trees and pagan graves.

Medina would become the second holy city of Islam. It was the site of Muhammad's mosque and home and is currently the site of the Mosque of the Prophet, where Muhammad and some of his followers are buried. As noted earlier, Medina was named Yathrib at this time. It was not until shortly after Muhammad's death it was renamed Medina, which means "City of the Prophet of God" or "City of the Messenger of God."

At the time of his arrival, there was no common government in Medina and Muhammad either wrote or drafted the Constitution of Medina or the Charter of Medina which, depending on how they are numbered, has between forty-seven and fifty-two provisions. The original document has been lost and scholars disagree as to when it was created. They also disagree on whether it was a single document created at one point in time or if it was composed of multiple documents created at different periods of time. Since the *Koran* had not been fully revealed at the time the Constitution of Medina was created, there are some tribal customs and traditions within the document.

There are several important provisions of the constitution which will be mentioned. One is that it attempted to unify the Arab clans, families, and tribes in Medina into an Islamic community. In an attempt to prevent inter-tribal warfare, the constitution stated that all disputes among the tribes in Medina, regardless of religion, were to be settled by Muhammad. This provision was similar to what already existed in Mecca. Another provision stated the newly converted Muslims were no longer to fight among themselves. This was because all Muslims are supposed to be friends to other Muslims but not to non-Muslims, and Muslims are not supposed to slay Muslims. Preventing inter-tribal warfare facilitated the creation of a unified community based on religious rather than clan, family, or tribal ties. This reduced the internal threats to the Islamic community.

The constitution also provided for the common defense of Medina. Rather than each tribe being seen as a separate tribal community responsible for its own defense, the constitution mandated that an attack against one tribe was treated as an attack against all the tribes in Medina. Rather than being a series of tribal communities often warring with each other, Medina now became a unified community with a unified military force. This was a way of dealing with external threats to the Islamic community.

The constitution also stated there was no peace as long as the Muslims were fighting in the path of the Islamic god. It is not known if the Jewish or the polytheist tribes signed the constitution. Since Muhammad had become the most powerful figure in Medina, they may have felt compelled to sign it. One of the provisions states, "To Jews who follow us belong help and equality. He shall not be wronged nor shall his enemies be aided." The words *follow us* referred to following Muhammad into Islam and only applied to Jews who converted to Islam. The constitution was probably created at least in part shortly after Muhammad arrived in Medina. This was when he was still hoping the Jewish tribes would recognize him as their long-awaited prophet.

This was a constitution that primarily benefitted the Muslim community. For example, the Jewish tribes could not go to war without Muhammad's permission. While the constitution did not immediately eliminate clan, family, and tribal connections, it started the creation of one community united by Islam. For the present, it provided for the uniting of Muhammad's followers from Mecca with those in Medina and for the two warring Arab tribes in Medina. This uniting of Muslims was necessary since they were from different towns and often different clans, families, and tribes.

Apologists for Islam often note this document came years before similar constitutions appeared in England or the United States. What they fail to mention is it lacked originality since it mimicked what existed in Mecca. It also appeared to allow for some religious freedom, something not currently allowed in Muslim countries or by the *Koran*. The apologists also claim the constitution provided one of the first provisions to protect women, which is not true. Basically, it stated women would be given protection if their families consented. The constitution provided Muhammad with another role, namely that of a military and political leader.

Either shortly before leaving Mecca or shortly after arriving in Medina, Muhammad started to receive *jihad* verses. One was mentioned in the last chapter and reads, "Permission to fight (against disbelievers) is given to those (believers) who are fought against, because they have been wronged; and surely, Allah is Able to give them (believers) victory" (22:39-40). The revelation continues by saying, "Those who have been expelled from their homes unjustly only because they said 'Our Lord is Allah.'" (22:41). We can see in this revelation that Muhammad and his followers were given permission by the Islamic god to fight disbelievers. This relates especially to the Muslims who left their homes and possessions in Mecca when they immigrated to Medina.

In verses 2:2-5, it is revealed that the rightly-guided, those who follow the Islamic god's commands, will be rewarded with paradise. Verses 2:6-7 read that some are not going to heed Muhammad's message because the Islamic god prevents them from seeing or hearing the message. These individuals will have tremendous torment. And in verses 2:8-10, hypocrites are mentioned. The hypocrites are those who pretend to believe "while in fact they believe not."

While Muhammad's mosque and home were being prepared, he stayed with two of his daughters and his wife, Sauda, at the home of a new convert. Although Muhammad only had one wife living with him at this time, eventually he had several wives and an apartment was added for each. After he had more than one wife, Muhammad rotated nightly among them since he did not have an apartment of his own. The "apartments" for his wives were very modest, only twelve by fourteen feet, with thatched palm leaf roofs and low ceilings which one follower noted he could touch when seated on the ground.

Child Bride - Oops, Problem with the Legacy

In the last chapter it was mentioned that Muhammad married Abu Bakr's daughter, Aisha, in Mecca when she was six years old. The marriage came about because Muhammad claimed he had dreams in which he was shown something covered by a silken cloth. When he removed the cloth, he saw it had been covering Aisha. Muhammad said, "If this is from Allah, then it must happen" (B3895, B3896, B5078, B5125, B5133, B5134, B5158, B7011, B7012, D2116).

In May 623, the now nine-year-old Aisha arrived from Mecca. She was described as having "remarkable beauty," which is a perverted attribute for a child. In June 623, the fifty-three-year-old Muhammad consummated the marriage with the nine-year-old Aisha. Sexual intercourse with a nine-year-old child has certainly tarnished Muhammad's legacy. Islamic apologists claim she was older than nine, that she was nine but had an early puberty, or that Muhammad should not be criticized since this was the custom of the time. Given the amount of Muslim literature devoted to defending Muhammad's statutory rape of Aisha, there is little doubt about her age being nine. In the *hadith* reports, Aisha said she was on a swing, or a see-saw, playing with some of her girlfriends when her mother or nurse came to her. After playing with her friends, Aisha was somewhat "disheveled" and her mother or nurse washed her face. Some other women or her mother dressed her and took her into a bedroom where she was told to sit on Muhammad's lap. The women left the room and Muhammad consummated the marriage (B3894, B3896, D2116, M1422, M1422R1). There are some variations of the story, such as who came to get her, who washed her face, who took her into the room, and who was in the room other than lecherous Muhammad. After the marriage, Aisha continued to play with her friends, her dolls, and her toys in her new home (B3894, B3895, B3896, B5133, B5134, B5158, B5160, D4915).

It is difficult for Islamic apologists to say Aisha was older than nine when the consummation or rape took place since she stated in several *hadith* reports she was nine. Claiming Aisha made an error on her age would cast doubt on the thousands of other *hadith* reports attributed to her. To claim Muhammad was simply a man of the times who was following tradition also has some problems. After all, because of divine inspiration prophets are supposed to break from barbaric traditions and establish a higher example for their followers. The sexual arousal of a fifty three-year-old man by a child and the consummation of the marriage does not establish a higher example. Additionally, Muhammad's followers are compelled to follow his behavior, which now includes sex with a nine-year-old. The *Koran* states very clearly, in more than one place, that Muslims should follow Muhammad's behavior and his example. One verse claims, "And verily, you (Muhammad) are on an exalted (standard of) character" (68:29). Another informs Muslims that "indeed in the Messenger of Allah (Muhammad) you have a good example to follow for him who hoped for (the meeting with) Allah and the last Day, and remember Allah much" (33:21).

Aisha appears to have become Muhammad's favorite wife. After his death, she noted she had special features that none of his other wives had: (1) the Islamic god brought her image to Muhammad in his dreams, (2) she was married when she was six, (3) the marriage was consummated when she was nine, (4) she was a virgin when the marriage was consummated, (5) Muhammad received a revelation from the Islamic god when they were "in a single blanket," (6) she was dear to him, (7) there was a revelation from the Islamic god about her, (8) she saw the angel Gabriel and he sent his greeting to her, (9) she was with him when he died, (10) she was the only one he married whose parents had made the migration from Mecca to Medina, (11) they took baths from the same vessel, (12) Muhammad prayed with Aisha stretched out in front of him, (13) he died with her on her day and in her apartment, and (14) Muhammad was buried in her apartment. Although Aisha did not mention this as one of her "special features," some believe she was the first child born into Islam, although this does not seem likely.

One of Muhammad's early biographers said it was well-known among his followers that if someone wanted a favor from Muhammad, it was best to wait until he was staying with Aisha. It was during the time he stayed with her that he was the happiest and was the most likely to grant the favor.

Above it was stated that Aisha was probably Muhammad's favorite wife. It is better to say Aisha was Muhammad's favorite wife after Khadijah. Even Aisha said she felt jealous over Muhammad's first wife, Khadijah (B3816, B3817, B3818, B5229, B6004, B7484, M2435).

For men with more than one wife there was supposed to be equality in terms of what each wife received. Thus, Muhammad rotated between his two wives, spending one night with Aisha and the next with Sauda. Shortly after his marriage to Aisha, the portly Sauda gave up her "night" to Aisha (B2688, B5212). Some authors claim Sauda did this because she feared Muhammad was going to divorce her (D2130). Although this seems unlikely, verse 4:128 states if a wife thought her husband was going to desert her, it was better to "make terms of peace between themselves." This may be what happened in this case.

To justify what would become multiple marriages after Khadijah's death, apologists claim most of Muhammad's marriages and those of his daughters were for political reasons. As will be seen, this claim is weak. Aisha, for example, was the daughter of Abu Bakr, who was Muhammad's closest supporter. Muhammad did not need to marry Aisha for political reasons. Other than lust, Muhammad may have had another reason for marrying Aisha, namely to separate himself and his religion from Christian and Jewish practices where polygamy was not allowed.

Why Can't We All Get Along?

After moving to Medina, Muhammad encountered some new problems. One problem was the difference in the environment and weather from Mecca. Summers had more dampness, and the nights and winters were cooler than in Mecca. Also, the water was considered brackish. As a result, many of those from Mecca became ill from what was known as "Medina fever." In addition, many in Medina did not welcome the arrival of Muhammad and his followers.

Among those who did not welcome Muhammad and his followers were the twenty Jewish tribes. Of the twenty Jewish tribes, there were three major tribes: *Banu-Kainuka* (*Bani Qainuqa, Qaynuga, Banu Qaynuqa*), *Banu-Nadhir* (*Bani-an-Nadir*), and the *Banu-Kuraiza* (*Qoreiga, Banu Quraiza*). Although the Jewish tribes must have welcomed someone they thought could bring about an end of the violence, they soon realized Muhammad was not their long-awaited prophet even though he tried to convince them he was by adopting certain Jewish customs "as he understood them." For example, Muhammad claimed Abraham was a Muslim (3:67), he had his followers face Jerusalem when saying their prayers, he ordered a fast during Yom Kippur, and he adopted certain Jewish dietary practices. Muhammad also claimed that both the *Torah* and *Bible* predicted his coming. There were even some revelations that were positive toward Judaism which were probably included to make Islam more attractive to Jews (2:47, 2:62, 5:20, 5:44, 28:4).

However, Muhammad's inability to speak Hebrew and answer basic questions about Judaism were factors in the Jews' rejection of him. The Jews even used their limited knowledge of the *Old Testament* to demonstrate the angel Gabriel's revelations were not from God and that Muhammad was not a prophet of God. For example, Muhammad thought Abraham took Ishmael to be sacrificed, when it was Isaac. In some cases the Jews ridiculed him and may have said he was a madman or that he was possessed, which are terms used in the *Torah* for false prophets. Muhammad's lack of performing miracles also indicated he was not a prophet, although Muslims would later claim the *Koran* was his miracle. In fact, every verse in each *sura*, or chapter, is known as an *aya*, or miracle. Others claimed Muhammad had no need to produce miracles. Although the *Koran* does not mention any miracles by Muhammad, the *hadith* reports include several.

When he realized the Jews were not going to accept him, Muhammad had another revelation telling him and his followers not to pray facing Jerusalem but toward his birthplace of Mecca (2:142-144, B7252). He was ridiculed by the Jews when he made this change since they claimed the Arabs' prophet did not even know in which direction to worship. And they asked why he was praying toward the *Kaaba*, which was representative of pagan polytheism. The Jewish criticisms are addressed in the *Koran* (16:101-102), where Jews are told to accept what the Islamic god gives them. Later, he dismissed or eliminated other Jewish practices he had adopted. To separate Islam from Judaism and Christianity, Muhammad decided to call worshipers to prayer by having Bilal, the former slave and early convert, use his loud voice rather than the trumpet used in Judaism or the bell in Christianity. There was the claim that if followers did not come to prayer, Muhammad had their houses burnt down.

After only a few Jews had converted to Islam, Muhammad received more revelations which cancelled out the earlier positive revelations about Jews. Verse 4:46 notes Allah cursed the Jews for their disbelief. Rather than being Allah's chosen people (2:47), they were now cursed because of their transgressions (5:78). There are even verses where Allah transformed them into monkeys and pigs for their transgressions (2:63-65, 5:60, 7:166). Jews were also criticized for murdering earlier prophets, such as Christ (2:91), and for corrupting the *Torah*, which foretold that Muhammad was the messenger from the Islamic god (2:41-42). He also told Christians and Jews that since Islam was the final religion, they had to convert (3:85).

In Mecca, Muhammad had been mocked for his religious views. But mocking was all his critics could do since they did not have the knowledge to challenge his religious beliefs. However, in Medina he was confronted by a more educated and literate group capable of challenging his religious beliefs. In fact, the Jewish tribes had established schools where the students learned the *Torah*.

When he thought the Jewish tribes would accept him as a prophet, he imitated and mimicked some of their customs. After he was rejected, he forbade his followers from following Jewish customs. For example, earlier Muhammad told his followers to wear their hair like the Jews—basically hanging loose. Now he told his followers to wear it like the pagans—parted in the middle. Where the Jews sat at funerals, Muhammad had his followers stand.

In addition to Muhammad's problem with the Jewish tribes, he was also experiencing problems with the Arab tribes. The problems between the two major Arab tribes, who constituted the majority of the population of Medina, were more difficult to resolve than he had anticipated. Also, many of the Muslim emigrants from Mecca were unable to support themselves and had to rely on assistance from those in Medina. Although Mecca had ample water from its numerous wells, the soil was too rocky for farming. It prospered as a commercial center, as a crossroad for caravans, and as a site for religious pilgrims. Medina was an oasis that supported farming, and one of the Jewish tribes there engaged in metalwork such as making jewelry and weapons. Both farming and metalworking required skills that few, if any, of Muhammad's followers from Mecca possessed. Other than Abu Bakr, most of Muhammad's followers from Mecca were from the fringe elements of Meccan society and, therefore, possessed few skills. Those who lived in Medina who had converted to Islam were growing tired of providing support to the emigrants from Mecca. The accounts suggest that life was difficult for the Muslim emigrants in Medina, with one account stating Muhammad existed on dates and water. There were other reports indicating this was a difficult time financially for Muhammad and his followers. For example, Aisha noted that after her marriage there was no wedding feast. Another example of Muhammad's poverty was cited in the *hadith* reports when Aisha claimed Muhammad had to mortgage his armor to a Jew to buy grain to feed his family (B2068, B2069, B2096, B2251, B2252, B2509, B2513). Muhammad must have been angry over being rejected by the Jewish tribes as well as jealous of their success.

The First *Jihad*

As will be the case many times during Muhammad's life, revelations provided a solution to his problems. Basically, he used a revelation giving him permission to fight and plunder non-Muslims to receive compensation for the homes his followers left in Mecca (22:39-40). The Islamic god told Muhammad that not only could he raid caravans going into and coming out of Mecca, but also that the Islamic god would assist him. This revelation came at just the right moment for a man who had accomplished little since arriving in Medina and who was probably in danger of losing power. There are even claims there was a plot to murder him because of his failure as a leader. Medina was in the right location as a raiding center against caravans to and from Mecca since it was near the trade route between Mecca and Syria. Even if the caravans went as far west as they could along the shore of the Red Sea, they would only be seventy-five to eighty miles from Medina but more than two hundred and fifty miles from the protection of Mecca. Muhammad had been a caravan member and had knowledge of the best places, times, and ways of attacking them. And although his followers from Mecca were too few in number to constitute a raiding force when combined with his followers in Medina, he had the numbers needed to be an efficient and effective bandit. These revelations marked the transformation of Muhammad from a prophet and peacemaker into a bandit and warlord.

Initially, the banditry consisted of little more than an ineffective and undeclared war against Mecca and its citizens. It was being waged in part for loot and in part for revenge against the way Muhammad and other Muslims had been treated. Some claim the banditry was to compensate Muslims for what they had voluntarily left behind in Mecca.

There are two important points to remember concerning this banditry. First, although this was somewhat of a lawless area where there were also non-Muslim gangs of bandits, the *Quraysh* leaders in Mecca had brought some semblance of security for the caravans traveling from, to, or through Mecca. For example, when Khadijah hired Muhammad to take her caravan to Syria, there was only one other person with him, a slave who was characterized as a "lad." Second, through this banditry Muhammad was literally transforming the social structure of the Arab world. This was a time when loyalty was to one's clan, family, and tribe. These ties provided individuals with protection and security since an attack on an individual was also an attack on that person's clan, family, and tribe. The raids by Muhammad's bandits were unprecedented because Muslim bandits were now attacking their own clan, family, and tribal members. For Muslims, the Islamic community replaced the clan, family, and tribe in providing protection and security. Even the *Koran* has revelations that negate clan, family, and tribal ties and replace them with Islam (see 9:10).

The raids were designed to obtain booty, loot, and slaves. They were also designed to capture non-Muslims for conversion, execution, or ransom. The raids were believed to have been common among the nomadic Arabs, with one tribe raiding another for items such as camels, goats, or women. What made these raids unique was that a religious leader was authorizing, encouraging, justifying, leading, planning, and sanctioning the raids. Some have noted Muhammad used religion to justify murder, rape, robbery, slavery, and torture.

For some writers, this is where the concept of *jihad* first entered into Islam since the raids were religiously justified because Muslims were attacking non-Muslims. The attacks were no longer clan, family, or tribal affairs but those of one religion against all non-Muslims.

Muhammad put the angel Gabriel's revelations into use soon after arriving in Medina. By some accounts, the first raid occurred in March 623 about seven months after arriving in Medina, with thirty emigrants from Mecca participating. On the first raid there were not any Muslim converts from Medina. Muhammad did not lead a raid until the summer or fall of 623. Although the early raids did not produce any booty, loot, plunder, or prisoners, they did attract converts. For many new converts, especially males, the decision over whether to herd goats for a living or engage in god-sanctioned raids that could produce booty, loot, plunder, prisoners, and women was not a difficult one. The initial lack of success with banditry may have been due to the inexperience of Muslims with banditry or because spies in Medina were taking information about the raids to Mecca. Meccan spies may have been using carrier pigeons. This is probably why Muhammad started sending the leader of the raids out with sealed instructions which were not to be opened for two or three days.

Converts were also coming because Muhammad was challenging the most powerful city in the area without consequence. Previously, they might have feared the wrath of Mecca if they converted to Islam. Now they feared the wrath of Muhammad if they did not convert. With more converts and with the Muslim converts in Medina participating, the size of the Muslim raiding parties kept increasing. Muhammad also secured treaties or alliances with several tribes which allowed the raiding parties safe passage as well as information on caravans.

Success—Finally!

After several unsuccessful raids, the first "successful" raid took place in November or December 623, although not without controversy. A *Quraysh* caravan from Mecca, which was carrying leather, raisins, and other merchandise, was attacked and captured by one of Muhammad's raiding parties. One of the men with the caravan became the first—of millions—to be killed in the Islamic *jihad.* Two others were captured and one escaped. After returning to Medina with their loot, controversy erupted when some claimed the raid had taken place during the sacred month and within the sacred land surrounding Mecca. Thus, bloodshed had taken place at a time and place where it was prohibited. Initially Muhammad refused to take his share of the loot from the caravan, waiting perhaps to gauge the reaction of his followers because of the violations. Among his followers there were no rejections of Islam. In fact, his followers seemed more concerned about getting their share of the loot than about prior clan, family, or tribal beliefs relating to sacred places and times. By this time, his followers had discarded so many of their former beliefs that discarding another did not seem to matter. And perhaps the type of followers Muhammad was attracting were never bound by clan, family, or tribal beliefs about morality. Fortunately for any followers who may have had lingering doubts about the place and time of the raid, another revelation made the raid acceptable. The revelation stated that violations during the sacred month were serious, but the offense of the non-Muslims against Islam was more serious (2:217). Therefore, the raid was justified and Muhammad and his bandits were provided the right to kill and plunder on sacred land and during sacred periods. This was an important revelation in that it justified any activity that would benefit Islam. Muhammad quickly took his share of the loot, as did his followers.

As more converts joined Islam and Muhammad became more powerful, the revelations he received became more violent in nature. The compassionate, spiritual, and tolerant preacher from Mecca who lived off the generosity of others transformed into an intolerant, merciless bandit living off what his bandits and robbers stole from others. Gone were centuries of clan, family, and tribal customs and laws. Non-Muslims were now the enemy, and stealing their property was justified and legal, according to the Islamic god (48: 20-21). Killing non-Muslims was also sanctioned, as was killing those who left Islam (4:89).

By attacking the caravans coming into or out of Mecca, Muhammad was not just cutting into the profits of the caravan owners, but he was also literally stealing the items the citizens of Mecca needed to survive. As noted earlier, Mecca was not an agricultural community. Rather, it imported much of the food and other necessities needed for survival. Even though Muhammad and his followers were threatening the lives of those in Mecca, the Muslims living in Mecca remained unmolested although they may have been passing information to Muhammad about caravan departure times and planned routes via carrier pigeons.

The Raid That Changed the World

By now, it is believed Muhammad had about fifteen hundred followers in Medina, of whom about three hundred and eighty were from Mecca and the remainder converts were from Medina.

In January or March 624, Muhammad's spies reported that a large caravan would be going through Badr (Bedr), which was about twenty miles south of Medina. Badr was an oasis and a resting area for caravans traveling to and from Mecca. Muhammad organized a raiding party of about three hundred men and between one thousand and five thousand angels in white turbans to attack the caravan on its way to Mecca (8:9). The angels reaffirmed to the Muslim bandits that they were engaging in banditry, murder, plunder, and theft on the side of the Islamic god and with god's approval. Muhammad did not know the Meccan merchants had received news of his plan and had reinforced the caravan with nine hundred to one thousand men.

Just prior to the raid, Muhammad told his followers that those who died fighting in *jihad* immediately entered paradise. One of his soldiers threw down the dates he was eating and rushed into the Meccan forces. He was killed, but his status in paradise remains undetermined. Muhammad was asked by another follower, "What makes god laugh?" Muhammad told him the Islamic god laughed upon seeing men plunge into battle without armor. The man removed his armor and made the Islamic god laugh a short time later. It was not recorded how many Muslims were willing to die to make the Islamic god laugh.

What started as a raid soon turned into a battle, and there were several factors that weighted the battle in Muhammad's favor. First, Muhammad's followers were united behind him. Those from Mecca were not united as one force. Rather, they were businessmen who were individually watching over their goods, often with family members and friends who had come to assist them. Thus, the Meccan businessmen were not united behind one leader who provided a battle plan or strategy. Perhaps because of the lack of leadership, some of the Meccan men returned home before the battle.

Second, for Muhammad's followers there was no downside to going to war or into battle. If they won, there was loot. If they were killed, they went to paradise, where they were dressed in silk and were seated on thrones with gold and precious stones. There were rivers of honey, water, and wine which would not produce the aching head or intoxication (56:19). There was also ample food and shade. They would have a harem with full-breasted maidens who were perpetual virgins (38:51, 44:53-55, 55:58-77, 56:15-37, 78:33). They would also be served by "immortal boys" (56:17). It is important to remember paradise is not immediately promised to

Muslims who die, but to Muslims who die fighting in *jihad* for the Islamic god.

Third, those from Mecca still believed in the old values that taught loyalty to one's clan, family, and tribe. These values stressed that you protected your clan, family, and tribal members; you did not kill them. In fact, there was disagreement among the Meccans before the battle over whether they could fight clan, family, and tribal members who were Muslim. Thus, some of those from Mecca may not have fought as aggressively as Muhammad's bandits. One example deals with Abu Bakr, Muhammad's loyal supporter and Aisha's father, and his son, who were on opposite sides at the battle. After converting to Islam, Abu Bakr's son told his father that during the battle he had twice come "under his sword," but he had allowed his father to live. Abu Bakr replied to his son that if he had come under his sword once, he would have killed him. This is supported in the *Koran* and the *hadith* reports, which command followers to love Muhammad more than any member of their family, including their children (3:28, 9:23, M44).

Fourth, the Muslims had blocked up the wells and positioned themselves on firm ground with the sun to their backs. Those from Mecca had run low on water and had to advance through soft sand with the sun in their eyes.

Fifth, most of those from Mecca were middle-aged merchants who were concerned about their merchandise rather than seasoned soldiers. In contrast, the Muslim bandits from Medina were younger and probably in better physical condition than the middle-aged merchants from Mecca. Additionally, the recent tribal wars in Medina had better prepared the Muslim bandits from Medina for fighting. The last war in Mecca had been over for thirty years. Muhammad's men also had armor made by the Jews in Medina that protected their heads and bodies, leaving only their legs exposed.

Sixth, prior to the main battle, there were several contests between champions where one member from each side fought each other. The single contests were all won by Muhammad's bandits, which did not bode well for the merchants from Mecca.

Seventh, other than to protect their merchandise, the merchants from Mecca had little enthusiasm for or interest in fighting. However,

Muhammad's men were eager to fight. There were no clan, family, or tribal ties holding them back. Through this battle they could make up for the boycotts, the emigration, and the ridicule they had suffered in Mecca.

Eighth, just prior to both sides going into battle, the Muslims arranged themselves in lines for prayers, much as they did when in a mosque. This created somewhat of a battle formation which assisted them when the battle started. Some believe a sandstorm blinded the Meccans.

The Battle at Badr rapidly changed from a battle between two forces into a flight for survival for those from Mecca. It was during this flight that many from Mecca were either killed or captured. Early in the battle Muhammad returned to his tent and fainted.

The battle was a military victory for Muhammad since fifty to seventy men from Mecca were killed, including some irreplaceable leaders, and another seventy were captured. In all of Mecca, there were probably no more than a dozen men with the leadership abilities of those who had been killed. Additionally, there was the loss of prestige. The once mighty Mecca had been defeated by the man who had been publically ridiculed, scorned, and who had to sneak out of the city only a few years earlier. One survivor of the battle, Abu Sufyan, had a son killed in the battle and made it his mission in life to kill Muhammad. After returning to Mecca, he would not allow any public show of grief over those who had been killed in the battle since it would allow the Muslims to gloat over their victory. Also, grief simply drained their energy and time, both of which were needed for revenge. Given the deaths of Mecca's leaders at Badr, Abu Sufyan became the new leader of the city.

In contrast, the Muslims suffered fourteen losses. Additionally, there was some loot from the caravan, although most of it made its way back to Mecca. And one of Muhammad's enemies was either captured or killed in the battle, and his severed head soon rolled at Muhammad's feet, to which Muhammad proclaimed, "It is more acceptable to me than the choicest camel in all Arabia" and "Praise be to Allah." Thus, this was an important victory for Muhammad, and most of *Sura* 8 (The Spoils of War) is devoted to the battle.

In *Sura* 8, in addition to being told the Islamic god will send angels to help them (8:9), it was also revealed Muslims would go to hell if they retreated in a battle unless it was a strategy (8:16). *Sura* 8 also instructs Muslims to fight until there are no more disbelievers (8:39) and to enjoy the booty because it is good and lawful (8:69).

After the battle, there was a discussion over the distribution of the loot. Some of the bandits felt they had fought harder or longer, or captured or killed in a greater number than others and were, therefore, deserving of a greater share of loot. In what might have become a contentious issue, there were more revelations, perhaps, in an attempt to bring harmony and peace among the bandits, murderers, and thieves. First, the Islamic god made it apparent he had done all the work since, "You killed them not, but Allah killed them" (8:17). Because Allah did all the work, the "spoils [of war] are for Allah and his Messenger" (8:1). For a brief moment there must have been a very confused group of bandits wondering if they had just looted a caravan but were going to go home empty-handed. Fortunately, Allah decided to give Muhammad twenty percent of the loot (8:41), with the remainder going to the bandits. They were told to enjoy it since the stolen property was both lawful and good (8:69, B335).

The victory came at a critical time for Muhammad. He had not resolved the conflict between the Arab tribes. There was growing friction between the emigrants from Mecca and the converts from Medina. Also, the Jewish tribes had rejected him. This victory became a sign of the Islamic god's faith in Muhammad and his claim to be a prophet. In fact, the victory was seen as a miracle of the Islamic god. After all, the Muslims had been outnumbered and still won the battle, not with military strength but with the help of the angels and of the Islamic god. The *Koran* states, "And Allah has already made you victorious at Badr, when you were a weak little force. So fear Allah much that you may be grateful" (3:123).

As noted earlier, the leadership in Mecca had been largely destroyed, which eliminated any military threat from Mecca at least temporarily. The victory must also have been satisfying for Muhammad and the emigrants from Mecca in that those who had earlier persecuted them were now either captive, dead, fleeing, or scared. It also alleviated Muhammad's financial problems which had plagued him since arriving in Medina. As noted earlier, according to some accounts, before Badr, Muhammad was so short of money that his meals consisted of dates and water. Now Muhammad and his followers had the loot from the caravan. Additionally, there were prisoners, and those they did not butcher could be ransomed for more loot.

There are two accounts on discussions about the fate of the prisoners. In one account, Muhammad said killing them would have been pleasing to the Islamic god. Also, a revelation stated, "It is not for a Prophet that he should have prisoners of war (and free them with ransom) until he had made a great slaughter (among his enemies) in the land" (8:67). However, another account has Muhammad and Abu Bakr suggesting the prisoners not be killed because they might convert to Islam (see 8:70).

After hearing about the Muslim victory at Badr and the loot, there were many new converts to Islam. This battle is called the "Day of Deliverance" since prior to the battle Islam was seen as weak and after the battle it became strong.

Muhammad had the bodies of the Meccan dead thrown into a dry well, a depression, or a pit. After the battle, he called those from Mecca the "people of the pit." The overwhelming rejection of clan, family, and tribal connections by Muslims was shown earlier with the example of Abu Bakr and his son. Another was a young Muslim who watched his father's body being dragged into the pit. The son noted he had been a good, kind, and loving father, but he was not a Muslim and would forever reside in hell (B3976).

Some of the captives were murdered shortly after the battle. Two of those murdered were a father and son who had abused the former slave and Muslim convert Bilal. Another was a Meccan poet who had been critical of Muhammad. Knowing his fate, he said insightfully, "Islam hath rent all bonds asunder." When Muhammad saw the bound man, he shouted, "Cut off his head." Muhammad's order was quickly obeyed. Two days later, another Meccan poet who had been critical of Muhammad was also beheaded.

It is believed that shortly after the battle Muhammad used the terms "Islam" and "Muslim" for the first time. Previously, his followers were known simply as "believers." Early in the development of Islam, followers needed ways to identify one another. Initially, the end of the turban was allowed to hang down the back. This separated Muslims from non-Muslims, who tucked in the ends of the turban. Then once they identified each other, they would say, "Peace upon you." However, Muhammad's followers still did not have a name, either for the religion or for themselves. Some believe the term "Muslim" loosely translated at the time as "traitor" and was imposed on Muhammad and his followers for being traitors to their clans, families, and tribes. Muhammad may have changed the meaning from something negative—that is, turning a friend over to the enemy—to something positive—that is, turning a friend over to the Islamic god.

Also, shortly after the battle, Muhammad received more revelations about disbelievers. They were the "worst of moving (living) creatures" (8:55), and "they are the worst of creatures" (98:6). After the battle, Muhammad received the news his daughter, Ruqayya, who was married to Othman, had died.

One of the captives was Abul As, his daughter Zainab's husband. Zainab, who was still in Mecca, sent an onyx necklace Khadijah had given her at her marriage for his ransom. Perhaps moved by seeing the necklace or by the fact that Abul As had rejected offers to divorce Zainab by those in Mecca, Muhammad requested Abul As be released and the necklace returned to Zainab. Muhammad's followers agreed with his request under the conditions Zainab would leave Mecca and come to live in Medina. These conditions were approved. After returning to Mecca, Abul As sent Zainab away on a camel litter under the protection of his brother. However, not far out of Mecca, some men stopped Zainab and prevented her from leaving. Perhaps they thought she could be used as a hostage to prevent Muhammad from attacking Mecca, perhaps they feared allowing her to leave showed their weakness, or perhaps they were angry about what had happened at Badr. Abu Sufyan came upon the scene and told the Meccan men they had no right to keep a daughter from her father or to retaliate against her. He told Zainab to return to Mecca and to secretly leave in a few days. A few days later, Muhammad's adopted son, Zeid, took her to Medina, where the stress of men waving spears and swords at her resulted in a miscarriage. She had already had a son die in infancy. In some accounts, the miscarriage took place in Mecca when men, angry about the defeat at Badr, broke into her house and knocked her down.

The treatment of Zainab was considered reprehensible by most of the citizens of Mecca. In addition to Abu Sufyan, most Meccan citizens rebuked those who had tried to prevent Zainab from leaving. Even Abu Sufyan's wife, Hind, who vowed to eat the liver of the man who killed her son at Badr, vented her indignation at what had happened to Zainab.

The victory at Badr increased Muhammad's prestige and power in the eyes of many who lived in and around Medina. It also attracted many new followers who realized that a better living was available through looting and pillaging rather than in farming and herding. Also, some of the surrounding tribes started to send him gifts notifying Muhammad they were his allies. Muhammad would only accept the gifts if they converted to Islam, which many did. Muhammad also used some of his share of the loot to bribe tribes to join Islam and to inform him of passing caravans he could loot.

Still, some did not like Muhammad, especially after learning some of their relatives had been killed at Badr. They also did not like watching relatives being marched into Medina in chains as prisoners after the battle. Many of these individuals must have privately and selectively expressed their disgust at the many changes brought by the prophet and his religion.

Murdered Poets' Society

Two poets did more than express their disgust in private or to selective individuals. Rather, they publically criticized Muhammad and Islam. In a largely non-literate society, poetry was an important and powerful way of communicating information. Poets, by reading their poetry in public areas, expressed their opinions and thoughts much as a journalist would in contemporary society. A good poet, through techniques such as humor or sarcasm, could have others repeating thoughts or lines from the poetry, which in a society with limited sources of information would often make the views of the poet the prevailing views.

After the Battle of Badr, Muhammad must have felt a new sense of power. He had won a decisive victory at Badr and had murdered two poets from Mecca who had publically mocked him. He now turned his wrath on poets in Medina. In March 624, he turned his wrath on the Jewish poetess, Asma bint Marwan, the mother of five children. She wrote a poem noting the foolishness of trusting a stranger who had risen against his own clan, family, and tribe; who encouraged others do the same; and who killed his own people in battle. She also suggested the people of Medina rise up against him. After hearing one of her poems, Muhammad asked his followers, "Who will rid me of her?" One of Muhammad's followers quickly offered his services and went into her home at night when she was sleeping, removed a sucking child from her breast, and drove his sword so forcefully through her body he could not pull it out. Muhammad, who knew about the plan to murder Asma, asked the next day if she was dead. The murderer said she was. Muhammad said the murderer had assisted the Islamic god and his prophet. When asked if there would be repercussions over the murder, Muhammad said, "A couple of goats will hardly knock their heads together for it." The murderer openly bragged about what he had done and challenged those who opposed the murder to do something about it. No one, including her widowed husband, dared to do anything to bring the murderer to justice. In the past there would have been demands for revenge against the murderer by her clan, family, and tribe, or as a minimum he would have been required to compensate her family via blood money for what he had done. The lack of public action and outrage demonstrated how powerful Muhammad had become.

In April 624, Abu Afak, a Jewish poet who was said to be between ninety and one hundred and twenty years of age, was singled out by Muhammad after he composed poetry critical of Muhammad and Islam. Muhammad asked, "Who will rid me of this pestilent fellow?" or "Who will deal with the rascal for me?" There seemed to be no shortage of Muslims willing to commit murder at Muhammad's request, and Abu Afak was dead by morning. Although the identity of the murderer was again known, he also escaped punishment. To the non-Muslims in Medina, especially the Jews, the lawlessness must have been shocking and a frightening indicator of what was coming.

Some sources reverse these two assassinations. An old man and a nursing mother hardly represented a physical threat to Muhammad. They did, however, represent a threat to his credibility, and for that Muhammad proclaimed they were to be murdered. Some writers have noted this changed the nature of Islam from conversion through the power of ideas to conversion through fear.

We need to remember that in Islam, Muhammad is the ideal man whose behavior is to be followed. These two examples establish how Muslims at all times are to deal with those who criticize Islam.

Jewish Tribe Number One

As Muhammad grew more powerful, he also grew bolder and would soon find reasons to attack the three largest Jewish tribes in Medina. His major reason was probably nothing more than the recognition they knew more than him about religion, a subject over which, as a prophet, he claimed exclusive knowledge. Additionally, he saw the Jewish tribes as a threat to his power because of their denial of his prophecy and their refusal to join Islam. He probably also wanted their wealth. There is little doubt the Jews in Medina criticized and opposed Muhammad on religious grounds. There is no mention they ever posed a physical threat to him or his followers. Thus, Muhammad must have been waiting for a reason to attack the Jewish tribes and put an end to their threat to his credibility and his power. Additionally, the Muslims from Medina probably resented the prosperity of the Jewish tribes and were willing allies of Muhammad.

Some believe Muhammad received additional revelations at this time about the Jewish tribes. One said the Jewish tribes would try and corrupt and harm Muhammad, and that the hatred in their hearts was far worse than what came from their mouths (3:118).

The first Jewish tribe to feel Muhammad's rage was the *Banu-Kainuka*, which consisted of about fifteen hundred members, many of whom were goldsmiths. This tribe was the weakest of the three tribes and had about three hundred men who could be considered "soldiers." There are different versions of the pretext used to attack the *Banu-Kainuka*, and there are slight differences in the most widely told version. The basic story is that without her knowledge, a Jewish boy used a nail or thorn to pin the bottom edge of the dress of a Muslim girl or woman to her upper dress while she was sitting in a goldsmith's shop. When she rose to leave, she found her lower anatomy exposed. She screamed at her exposure, and a Muslim man came and killed the boy. The Muslim murderer was then killed by the murdered Jewish boy's brothers. Some claim Muhammad then received a revelation to attack the Jewish tribe (3:13; 8:58). Muhammad laid siege to the *Banu-Kainuka* Jews, who finally surrendered after about two weeks. The other two large Jewish tribes did not come to the assistance of the *Banu-Kainuka*. Initially, Muhammad was going to execute them, but he relented and made them leave Medina. They had to leave behind most of their possessions including their metalworking tools. They owned little, if any, agricultural property. Some accounts have the *Banu-Kainuka* moving to Syria, where they vanished from the historical record, while another account has them moving to the oasis of Khaibar (Khaybar, Kheibar, Khybar) which Muhammad would attack and conquer a few years later.

Others claim the reason for attacking the *Banu-Kainuka* was that Ali wanted to marry Muhammad's youngest daughter, Fatima, who was between ten and twenty years of age, but needed something of value as a bride price. Although Ali's father did not have much wealth when he died, what he did have Ali could not inherit since his father was not a Muslim. Ali's booty after the Battle of Badr included two camels, which some believe he planned to use as a bride price for Fatima. Others believe Ali was going to use the two camels to start an import/export business which, if successful, would provide him the financial resources to marry Fatima. Most of what he exported would be from the Jewish tribes. The camel story then converges with the story of some drunks killing, butchering, and eating the camels (B3091). Thus, Ali still needed something of value to give Muhammad so he could marry Fatima. This may have been why Muhammad contrived the attack on the *Banu-Kainuka*—so that Ali's share of the booty provided him the financial resources to marry Fatima in 624. They had a son, Hasan, in March of 625. Some have the marriage and birth taking place earlier. At the time, Hasan was Muhammad's only living grandchild, and his name means "beautiful" or "handsome" in Arabic. He was said to resemble Muhammad in appearance (B3543, B3753, B4003, B5579, B5580, B5581).

There are three related events to the attack on the *Banu-Kainuka* and Ali's marriage to Fatima. First, two of Muhammad's closest friends and strongest allies, Abu Bakr and Omar, had earlier asked Muhammad for permission to marry Fatima. Although Muhammad was married to Abu Bakr's daughter, Aisha, and would eventually marry Omar's daughter, Hafsa (Hafsah, Haifsa, Haifsah), he denied their requests. Second, after Muhammad and Ali confronted the drunks who had killed the camels, they insulted Muhammad, but he could not retaliate because they had been at the Battle of Badr. Muhammad's opposition to alcohol and later revelations prohibiting it may have come partly from this event. Third, if Ali had planned to go into the import/export business, Muhammad was quietly pleased that the camels had been killed. Ali was an excellent soldier, and Muhammad needed him in Medina, not traveling with caravans.

Whatever the reason for the attack on the *Banu-Kainuka*, the financial circumstances of Muhammad and his followers again improved significantly after their surrender. Muhammad had his twenty percent of the loot, Ali could marry Fatima, and the other followers had loot and the homes of the exiled *Banu-Kainuka* (see B2089).

Several have commented that it was odd Muhammad came to Medina to mediate disputes between the tribes in a peaceful manner, even creating the Constitution of Medina to address issues such as those in this dispute. However, in this case he chose the threat of violence to solve the problem, even to the point of almost massacring an entire tribe over what had started as an innocent joke and then had escalated into murder by one of Muhammad's followers.

Othman, who had been widowed when Muhammad's daughter, Ruqayya, died during or shortly after the Battle of Badr, married Um-Kalthum, another of Muhammad's daughters. Thus, he was given the title "the owner of two lights" or the "possessor of two lights."

Mecca Comes Calling

About a month after the exile of the *Banu-Kainuka*, Abu-Sufyan made an ineffective raid on Medina, perhaps in an attempt to build Meccan morale or to demonstrate that Mecca was still a force to be reckoned with. The force of two hundred men attacked the northeast outskirts of Medina two to three miles from the center of the city, where they destroyed some fields, burned some houses, and killed two agricultural workers. They then loaded their horses with barley meal as their loot. However, when either confronted by a force from Medina or afraid they were being followed and about to be overtaken by a force from Medina, they threw away sacks of barley meal to lighten their loads and travel faster. This "petty" raid became known as the barley meal raid.

Muhammad the Bandit

Meanwhile, Muhammad was authorizing additional raids on tribes to the west, east, and south. He was after booty, converts, taxes, and for the tribes to sever contact with Mecca. He was probably also attempting to demonstrate to the tribes that Muslims and Medina were powerful and that any attacks on Muslims or assistance to Mecca would be dealt with harshly.

About this time Muhammad's adopted son, Zeid, captured a rich caravan from Mecca.

Another Murdered Poet

Although the dates differ, it was probably in September 624 that another poet, Kab Ashraf, who had written poetry critical of Muslim women, would soon be dead. As Muhammad had done previously, once he heard about the sarcastic poetry, he asked his followers, "Who will rid me of he who has hurt Allah and his Prophet?" Four men from the poet's tribe, including the poet's foster brother, offered to kill him. Muhammad gave them his permission to kill him and to use lies to get the poet out of his house. After luring him out of his house under the pretense of friendship, the men turned on Kab, yelling, "Slay him! Slay the enemy of god!" When the men returned to Muhammad, they threw Kab's head at his feet and Muhammad praised the Islamic god for what had been done (B4037).

The day after Kab was murdered, Muhammad told his followers, "Whoever of the Jews falls into your hands, kill him!" One of Muhammad's followers soon killed a Jewish merchant. When the murderer's brother rebuked him for the crime, the murderer replied that if Muhammad had ordered him to kill his brother, he would have done so unquestionably. The non-Muslim brother was either inspired by his brother's commitment to Islam, fearful of being murdered on a whim by his Muslim brother, or sensed the futility or resisting Islam. He quickly converted, saying, "By god any religion that would so affect you is truly wonderful."

There are at least three passages in the *Koran* which deal directly or indirectly with poets. Verse 6:93 states that individuals should not tell lies "against Allah." In this verse, the torment for telling lies against Allah is brought about by angels either during the dying process or after death. In later verses there is a warning not to annoy the Islamic god (33:57) and not to spread false news (33:61). The next passage reads, "Accursed, they shall be seized wherever found, and killed with a (terrible) slaughter" (33:61). As can be seen, the penalty for offending the Islamic god or Muhammad was to take place immediately, and the instrument of death was no longer by angels but by mad Muslims.

The murder of the three poets in Medina illustrates the power Muhammad had achieved. At will, Muhammad could order his followers to murder innocent citizens, and he would be obeyed without question. Also, his actions and those of his followers were without the threat of punishment or sanction by others. In the past, these murders would have called for revenge by the clan, family, or tribe. At a minimum, some type of blood money would have been paid by the murderer. Now these murders were treated as legal executions authorized by a legitimate authority. It must also have created apprehension and fear among the two remaining Jewish tribes.

Medina 1, Mecca 1

After losing the Battle of Badr and having more caravans hijacked, those in Mecca must have realized Mecca's position as a wealthy commercial center was in jeopardy. Thus, if it was going to survive, it needed to neutralize Muhammad. In the spring of 625, Abu Sufyan raised an army of about three thousand men, including some of the exiled *Banu-Kainuka*. With his army, he marched out of Mecca to do battle with Muhammad and to put an end to his banditry. When Muhammad learned about the advancing army, he wanted to retreat to the fortified houses in Medina. However, many in Medina feared the Meccan army would destroy their fields and groves and insisted on marching out to meet it. Others, still confident after the Battle of Badr, claimed they would be laughed at throughout Arabia if they did not confront the Meccan army. Muhammad reluctantly agreed to leave the fortified housed in Medina and marched north-west four to five miles out of Medina to a hill near the mountain of Uhud (Ohod). He had about one thousand bandits with him. However, about three hundred of the bandits left before the battle started and returned to their fortified homes in Medina. The battle started off well for Muhammad, but when the Meccan army appeared to be in retreat, some of Muhammad's archers stopped fighting and ran to loot the Meccan camp. This gave the Meccan cavalry, led by Khalid, the opportunity to attack the rear of Muhammad's army. Now Muhammad's army was in disarray and retreated. Some of the Meccan cavalry attacked Muhammad's position, attempting to kill him. Several of Muhammad's followers were killed protecting him, and he was injured in the battle when a front tooth (or teeth) was broken (or knocked out) and a strong blow literally drove his helmet into his cheek (B2903, B2911, B4073, B4075, B4076, M19). A Meccan soldier cried out that he had killed Muhammad. Those in the Meccan army believed Muhammad was dead and that their goal had been accomplished. Additionally, most had no grievance against his followers, many of whom were related by clan, family, or tribe. Thus, instead of pursuing and killing the retreating Muslims, Abu Sufyan considered the battle over. Before taking his victorious army back to Mecca, the bodies of the dead Muslims were mutilated by the women who had accompanied the Meccan army. They made ornaments from the body parts of the dead Muslim bandits. And, as she had promised she would do after the death of her son at Badr, Abu Sufyan's wife, Hind, cut out the liver from one of the bodies and ate part of it.

Muhammad was taken to a ravine or cave and hidden by Ali and some others. He was apparently not easy to move since he had become "heavy with age." He was even provided with a new set of armor so he would not be recognized. Muhammad returned to the battlefield after the Meccan army left. Upon seeing the mutilation that had taken place on his followers, he swore to mutilate the Meccans killed in the next battle. He then changed his mind and forbade mutilation after a battle. He had his followers bury two to three to a grave, with those who could recite the most revelations buried first.

It seemed a victory for Abu Sufyan. His soldiers had killed seventy-five Muslims, seventy of whom were from Medina and five of whom were from Mecca. In addition, seventy Muslims—including Muhammad—were wounded. The Meccan army suffered fourteen to twenty-two losses.

After burying their dead, Muhammad and his army then started back to Medina. Then, in a show of defiance, Muhammad started to follow the Meccan army. This was to demonstrate that the deaths had not weakened the power of Medina. At one point, the Meccans considered turning back and "finishing" the battle but were deterred when they overestimated the size of Muhammad's army. In fact, they believed all of Medina was following them because Muhammad exaggerated the size of his army by having his followers light more than five hundred campfires that night.

The mood of Muhammad's followers was bleak after returning to Medina, and at least one prisoner from the battle at Badr was beheaded. Although Abu Sufyan and the Meccan army had technically "won" the Battle of Uhud, some considered it a draw since Muhammad was not killed and his army of bandits was not destroyed. The purpose of the battle had been to kill Muhammad and, regardless of the number of deaths on each side, this goal was not achieved. Muhammad was now faced with explaining the loss.

After all, the Muslim victory at the Battle of Badr had been seen as a positive sign from the Islamic god. At Badr, there had been angels who had helped Muslims win the battle, and Muhammad had received a revelation that twenty "steadfast men" could overcome two hundred, and that one hundred could overcome one thousand (8:65). The problem for Muhammad was how to explain the Battle of Uhud with the loss of so many, including some of his most loyal followers. There was another revelation, one of the longest in the *Koran*, where the blame for the loss was placed on the Muslims who were more intent on looting than on fighting. Basically, the loss was permitted because the Muslims had disobeyed the Islamic god. Muhammad did, however, forgive them. It was also explained that the Islamic god was using this to "test" the believers (3:140-141, 3:152-155).

One additional event after the battle demonstrated Muhammad's absolute power. During the battle, one of Muhammad's followers had used the confusion of the battle to kill another Muslim to settle a blood feud from something that had happed before Muhammad had arrived in Medina. When Muhammad found out about this, he had the man beheaded. The message was clear. Muhammad settled disputes.

It was probably shortly after this battle Muhammad received more revelations. The revelations said that for those who died in a *jihad*, or holy war, there was a special reward (55:72, 74, 76), and that "*Jihad* (holy fighting in Allah's cause) is ordained for you (Muslims) though you dislike it, and it may be that you dislike a thing which is good for you and that you like a thing which is bad for you. Allah knows but you do not know" (2:216).

One tribe associated with the *Quraysh* in Mecca believed the Battle of Uhud had weakened Medina to the point where it could be attacked and looted. Thus, the bandits in the tribe set out in pursuit of easy loot. Muhammad found out about the impending attack and sent a force of about two hundred men to confront it. The surprised attackers quickly retreated.

Jewish Tribe # 2

After Muhammad recovered from his wounds at the Battle of Uhud, he laid siege in August 625 to another of the Jewish tribes, the *Banu-Nadhir* (*Nadir*). Certainly his motives for the siege were mixed. He wanted to rid the city of those who rejected his religion and who openly mocked him. He also wanted their property. Additionally, after Uhud he probably wanted to demonstrate he was still a powerful military figure who needed to be feared and respected.

The *Banu-Nadhir* had some productive fields, many with date palms. It was claimed they grew a date so clear and pure the pit could be seen. They had continued commercial activities with Mecca, and they may have provided information to Abu Sufyan which assisted him on the barley meal raid. Also, there were some reports, although they may have been planted by Muhammad to justify the siege, that the *Banu-Nadhir* Jews were going to drop a large stone on him from a roof and kill him. Some accounts have the angel Gabriel revealing to Muhammad the plot to kill him, although this revelation is not in the *Koran*. Muhammad's forces surrounded the Jewish community. Initially, the Jewish farmers resisted the siege, but when Muhammad's soldiers started cutting down their palm trees as sanctioned by a revelation (59:5), they surrendered. The siege lasted two weeks. Muhammad allowed each family to leave with what one camel could carry. Some accounts have the Jews leaving Medina reciting psalms, letting Muhammad know they stood behind their God.

The one large remaining Jewish tribe did not come to the assistance of the *Banu-Nadhir*.

Since there was no actual fighting involved, Muhammad said he had received a revelation that the goods and property could be apportioned at his discretion (59:1-10). He took some of the land for his family, set aside some for relief for the poor, and divided the rest among his followers. Some believe the *Banu-Nadhir* moved to the oasis of Khaibar, about seventy miles north of Medina, where some had estates and where the previously exiled *Banu-Kainuka* may have gone. Other accounts have them moving to Syria.

Sura 59, "The Gathering," describes the siege and expulsion of the *Banu-Nadhir* Jews.

Since the *Banu-Nadhir* Jews left their homes and fields behind, this alleviated another problem for Muhammad, namely providing for those who had moved from Mecca. Muhammad turned over the homes and fields of the *Banu-Nadhir* Jews mostly to those who had emigrated with him from Mecca.

Some believe it was during or shortly after the siege of the *Banu-Nadhir* Jews that the prohibition of alcohol was revealed. When some followers started attending the services drunk, there was a revelation about the evil of wine. When this was not enough, another revelation banned the consumption of wine.

The leaders of Mecca tried to demonstrate to the nomadic tribes that they were still the major power in the area by claiming they had decisively won the Battle of Uhud and that Muhammad and his army had been neutralized. Still, however, many of the Arab tribes remained loyal to Muhammad, perhaps waiting to see what would happen between the two opposing forces. In 625 and 626, Muhammad sent raiding parties to crush tribes he learned had anti-Islamic activity taking place or which might be considering an attack on Medina. One of the raiding parties went five hundred miles north of Medina. For Muhammad to receive information there was anti-Islamic activity taking place five hundred miles away and then quickly mount a raiding party to crush the activity seemed to indicate his power and influence were growing. These raids were less about booty and more about demonstrating Muhammad and Islam were the new power in the area. In addition to the raids, Muhammad also had his bandits assassinate those making anti-Islamic or anti-Muhammad comments in nomadic tribes.

About this time Muhammad sent one of his followers to murder Abu Sufyan. The plot failed and, on his return to Medina, the failed murderer met a one-eyed shepherd who said he would never become a Muslim. After the shepherd went to sleep, the assassin pushed one end of his bow into the shepherd's good eye, killing him. After describing the murder, Muhammad blessed the murderer.

Next?

After preaching for more than a decade and gaining few followers in Mecca, Muhammad's fortunes changed dramatically in Medina. Here in the space of a few years he gained thousands of converts. He became powerful as a military, political, and religious leader. And he became wealthy. The next chapter will cover the last years of Muhammad's life as well as the expansion of Islam.

CHAPTER 9: MUHAMMAD: MEDINA (PART II)

In 622, Muhammad left Mecca for Medina. After thirteen years of preaching in Mecca, he had very few followers, little power, and little wealth. Over the next few years in Medina he obtained thousands of followers. His power extended over much of Arabia, and he had become wealthy via banditry, robbery, theft, and slavery.

Two is Never Enough

When Muhammad came to Medina, he had two wives. The first was the portly Sauda, whom he probably married to take care of household duties and to help raise his younger children. Sauda was probably also responsible for looking after Muhammad's child-bride, Aisha, who came to live with him as a wife when she was nine (B5158, B5160, B5133, B5134).

Muhammad married several more women, although the number of wives, the dates of the marriages, and the ordering of the marriages differ from author to author. He also had a harem with slave-concubines. Muhammad's critics perceive him as a sex-maniac because of his multiple marriages and his concubines. However, apologists for Islam have offered several explanations for his multiple marriages—although they are silent on his concubines. One is that this was an era where marriages were arranged to create or strengthen clan, family, or tribal bonds. Another justification for his multiple marriages was that some of them were out of compassion to older widows who had few prospects of remarriage. Some claim the marriages gave Muhammad connections to tribes living along caravan routes who informed him of passing caravans he could plunder. Apologists for Islam also state the marriages provided Muhammad with new tribal connections where he might find bandits, converts, robbers, or at a minimum make it difficult for these tribes to resist him since he was, through marriage, a tribal member.

Even though the number of his wives would soon reach double figures, Muhammad did not marry anyone from Medina. This was because he had been brought to Medina to act as an arbitrator between two warring tribes, and a marriage to a member from one tribe would have changed his status from that of an impartial and objective arbitrator to someone who would be seen as biased.

Muhammad's critics claim the justification of political motivations behind his multiple marriages is used to dismiss claims of hyper-sexuality or deviant passion on his part. After Khadijah's death, he quickly married the widowed and portly Sauda. There is no mention of new tribal connections being forged with this marriage. He married Aisha in Mecca when she was six and consummated the marriage in Medina when she was nine. Thus, she was hardly married because she was old or widowed. She was also the daughter of his best friend and strongest supporter, Abu Bakr.

Muhammad's next marriage was in January or February 625 to Hafsa (Hafsah, Haifsa, Haifsah), who was eighteen to twenty years old and, reportedly, very beautiful. She was also very "accomplished," which included the ability to read and write. It is reported she had a "violent temper." Her husband had been killed at Badr, and she was the daughter of his supporter and second successor, Omar. Aisha welcomed someone into the household closer to her age.

One of his next marriages was to Salam (Salamah), who was twenty-nine, and again, the widow of one of his supporters. As can be seen from this still incomplete list of Muhammad's wives, Aisha, Hafsa, and Salam were the daughters of his strongest supporters with whom he did not need to create an alliance.

The next marriage was to Habibah, Abu Sufyan's daughter. She had migrated to Ethiopia with her husband during one of the Muslim emigrations. Her husband had left Islam and converted to

Christianity before he died. Another marriage took place to Zaynab (Zainab, Zeinab), whose husband had been killed at Badr. She was thirty and died eight months after they were married. Both of these women met the "widowed" category, and through his marriage to Habibah, Muhammad was now Abu Sufyan's son-in-law.

While apologists and critics offer self-serving explanations for Muhammad's multiple marriages, the reason may be nothing more complex than he wanted a wife who would provide him with a son.

Oops, Another Problem With the Legacy

Earlier it was mentioned that Muhammad's marriage to the child-bride Aisha has created some problems with his legacy. Another wife, Zaynab (Zainab), has also caused his legacy some problems, in part because she was his cousin, and in part because she was divorced from his adopted son, Zeid. Although their names are similar, Zaynab is different from Zainab, who was mentioned above as the wife who died shortly after marrying Muhammad.

Muhammad arranged the marriage between Zaynab and Zeid. Initially, Zaynab had not approved of the marriage, perhaps because she belonged to the high status *Quraysh* tribe while Zeid was a former slave. For Zaynab, Islam had not erased the importance of clan, family, and tribal status, and marrying someone like Zeid was still seen as disgraceful. It is reported that Zeid also objected to the marriage, perhaps recognizing the status inequities would create interesting power conflicts within the marriage. The marriage finally took place after Muhammad received a revelation, which is not in the *Koran*, that it should take place. After the marriage, Muhammad went to Zaynab and Zeid's home. He saw Zaynab in a "light house dress," "thin shift," or "scanty underdress," which was then moved by a light wind, exposing more of her than she had intended. Muhammad left mumbling something about Allah and her body causing men's hearts to turn. Although Zaynab was by some accounts thirty to thirty-five years of age, she was by all accounts very beautiful. When Zeid returned home, Zaynab told him what Muhammad had seen and said. Zeid quickly went to Muhammad and told him that since Zaynab had excited him, he would divorce her, which he did.

Fortunately, any problems Muhammad had about marrying his first cousin and adopted son's former wife were soon vanquished by a revelation he had while lying with Aisha. She recalled he fainted while the revelation was being received. Basically, the revelation approved of his marriage to Zaynab (33:37-38). In fact, in the revelation Muhammad is chastised for his hesitation to marry Zaynab. Also, those who considered the marriage unlawful, scandalous, or just plain tacky were wrong since adopted sons were not real sons (33:4-5, B4782, B5088). To cease all controversy on the matter, the verse states that "Allah's Command must be fulfilled" (33:37) and that "there is no blame on the Prophet in that which Allah has made legal for him" (33:38). After he awoke, he told Aisha Allah had blessed his marriage to Zaynab. He then asked Aisha, "Who will go and tell Zaynab the good news?" Aisha evidently did not believe the news was "good" enough to go, so she sent a servant. Zaynab was then allowed a short period of sexual abstinence to ascertain she was not pregnant before she married Muhammad.

Zaynab would often brag to Muhammad's other wives that she was the most honored of his wives since the others were given in marriage by their brothers, fathers, or guardians, while she was given by the Islamic god (B4787).

This marriage must have been scandalous for the Muslim community. In a short time, Muslims had changed their religious beliefs and acquired the occupation of bandits, murderers, rapists, robbers, and thieves of those who belonged to their clans, families, and tribes. However, this marriage must have pushed the limits for even the morally-challenged Muslims. Thus, there was the need for more revelations to quell the building outrage and to establish more liberal sexual guidelines. Fortunately, they were received in a timely manner and stated that the Islamic god gave Zaynab to Muhammad in marriage and that Muhammad should not forbid himself that which the Islamic god had made legal (33:47-48). Nor should Muhammad fear what others would say about him. Instead, he should fear not obeying the Islamic god. Just in case there was still doubt about the legality or uniqueness of the marriage, Muslims also learned this had been the Islamic god's way with other prophets. If there was any lingering doubt about the marriage, one last verse (33:40) reminded Muslims that "Muhammad is not the father of any of your men, but he is the Messenger of Allah and the last (end) of the Prophets." In other words, Muhammad did not have any sons, so he could not be marrying his ex-adopted son's ex-wife.

In the past, Zeid would have been Muhammad's son, adopted or not. As was mentioned earlier, prior to having a sexy wife, Muhammad considered Zeid his son and proclaimed, "Zeid is my son, I am his heir and he is mine." Fortunately for Muhammad, another revelation ended any controversy over this issue. Verse 4:23 provided a list of females men were not allowed to marry, such as daughters, mothers, and sisters. And it specified that men were not allowed to marry the wife of a son who came from their loins. Since Zeid was an adopted son, Muhammad's marriage to Zaynab was legal. Some apologists have suggested Zaynab was not satisfied being married to the adopted son of the prophet and, knowing Muhammad's "weakness" for attractive women, may have schemed to entice him into marriage. Other Islamic apologists defend Muhammad's marriage to Zaynab by claiming she divorced Zeid because they did not get along. In an era when marriages were arranged and not based on "getting along," this explanation seems flawed. Other apologists state that Allah made Zaynab "unattractive" to Zeid. But this explanation is also flawed, since marriages were not based on attractiveness. There are those who claim Zaynab was "old," and thus, it was not her beauty that moved Muhammad. However, Aisha noted she felt uneasy about the marriage because of Zaynab's beauty (B2661). Also, to claim she was "old" and "unattractive," some writers have cited her age at death, which occurred after Muhammad died, not her age when she married Muhammad. Apologists also claim Muhammad had a political motivation for the marriage since Zaynab was related to Abu Sufyan, the powerful political figure in Mecca, and Muhammad wanted to create a "family" relationship with him. But by Zaynab being married to his son, Muhammad already had the "family" relationship, and Muhammad was already married to his daughter, Habibah. Also, it needs to be remembered that the goal of Islam was to eliminate clan, family, and tribal connections.

The marriage of a father to a son's wife was prohibited by the pre-Islamic religious beliefs. As he had in other areas, Muhammad may have been further increasing the tolerance of his believers into accepting what would have previously been intolerable. All he needed to do was produce a revelation which justified the behavior.

After the marriage to Zaynab, there were several revelations concerning his wives, who were called the "Mothers of the Faithful." In verse 33:50, we learn, "O wives of the Prophet! Whoever of you commits an open illegal sexual intercourse, the torment for her will be doubled, and that is ever easy for Allah." And if Muhammad's wives were obedient to the Islamic god and Muhammad, they would receive double the reward in paradise (33:31). Obedience meant they were also to stay in their homes and not go outside like in the "time of ignorance" (33:33). When others visited their homes, they had to speak from behind a curtain (33:53). They also were forbidden to marry after Muhammad's death (33:53).

Also, it appears that the wedding feast for Zaynab went longer than Muhammad anticipated (B6238, B6239), so verse 33:53 was revealed. In it, Muslims were instructed that if they were invited to Muhammad's home as a guest for a meal, they were to eat and leave. In fact, guests were to "disperse without sitting for a talk." This behavior "annoys the Prophet," but Muhammad was too shy to ask the annoying guests to leave.

It is about this time some believe the veil was imposed on all Muslim women; in fact, the revelation was probably received during or after the wedding of Muhammad and Zaynab (24:31, 33:55, 33:56, 33:59, B4790, B4791, B4793, B4794, B5166, B5170, B5171, B5466, B6238, B6239, B7421). This revelation required women to completely cover their bodies with the exception of their eyes (24:31, 33:55, 33:59, B4758, B4759, B4790). At this time, Muhammad had several wives, some of whom were young and attractive, and with followers continually coming and going, Muhammad may have been worried that his followers, who were obligated to follow his behavior and example, may be subject to the same temptation he had been subject to when he saw Zaynab.

With an increasing number of wives, Muhammad rotated nightly among the women so each would have a night with him (B5068,

B5215). As noted earlier, Sauda had given her night to Aisha. Muslims claim Muhammad's sexual powers were such that he could "visit" all of his wives in one night (B268, B270, B284, B5068, B5215). Aisha, however, said that "magic was worked on Allah's Messenger so that he used to think that he had sexual relations with his wives while actually he had not" (B5765, B5766, B6063). She also noted Muhammad "began to fancy that he was doing a thing which he was not actually doing" (B3268).

It was about this time that his grandson by his deceased daughter, Ruqayya, and her husband, Othman, died. However, his daughter Fatima had another son, Husayn, by her husband Ali. Their first son was named Hasan, and Muhammad liked the name and decided their second child should be named Husayn, which means "little Hasan." Ali and Fatima would have three more children, two daughters and a stillborn son.

Muhammad's increasing list of wives created some additional problems. One of the revelations from the angel Gabriel was that men should have no more than four wives. Muhammad was beyond four and counting. Again, the angel Gabriel intervened, stating that it was lawful for Muhammad to have as many wives as he wanted as long as a proper dowry was involved. In fact, this verse states this is a privilege only for Muhammad and not for other Muslim men (33:50).

More Raids

There were more raids, some of which were for loot, but an increasing number were a demonstration of force to quell anti-Islamic activity and rhetoric. One of these raids had more than five hundred bandits, which was an impressive number for the era. Also, as more tribes pledged themselves to Islam and since fighting between Muslims was prohibited, some of these raids were searching for other areas to raid for booty, loot, and slaves.

With fewer Arab tribes to raid because of their conversion to Islam, Muhammad decided to raid a Jewish tribe called *Banu Mustalia* (*Banu al-Mustaliq*, *Banu Mustalik*, *Beni-Mustalik*), which was located near the Red Sea between Jeddah and Rabigh. He justified the raid by claiming the small Jewish farming community was going to attack Medina. The bandits rode into the small community screaming, "O Conqueror! Kill! Kill!" It was a quick victory for Muhammad, and the loot included two thousand camels, five thousand sheep, and two hundred women. One of the captives was Juwayriqa (Juwairiah, Juwairiyah, Juwariyah, Juwayriyya, Juwayriyah, Juwayriyyah, Juweira), the beautiful seventeen- to twenty-year-old daughter of the tribe's chief. Aisha described her as "a sweet, beautiful woman, who captivated anyone who looked at her." Either Muhammad was so taken by her beauty that he asked her to marry him or she considered her option of being gang raped and sold into slavery and she asked Muhammad to marry her. She must also have considered the consequences of her actions for her family and tribe. She chose to become one of his wives, which meant her family and tribe were now related to Muhammad, so he had forty to one hundred of the captives freed. Although some accounts have Muhammad marrying her out of compassion and pity, this seems unlikely given his lack of concern for other captives. It may have been nothing more than a demonstration of total conquest and domination of the tribe by the forced conversion and sexual domination of a member of the ruling family. Some place this raid two years later, in 628.

Bad News for Rape Victims

It was Muhammad's practice to take at least one wife on each of the raids he personally led, and they drew lots to see who would accompany him (B2688). For the raid on the *Banu Mustalia*, he took Aisha, who was about fourteen at the time. Some accounts have his wife, Salam, also accompanying Muhammad on this raid. As the Muslim bandits were leaving with their booty and Muhammad with his "new" wife, Aisha was accidently left behind when she went to look for an onyx necklace she had lost. Aisha's mother had given her the necklace when she married Muhammad, and it was her most valuable possession. Aisha was left behind because she traveled in an enclosed basket which hung from the side of a camel. Given the secrecy surrounding Muhammad's wives and because at the time she was "slight," those leading her camel assumed she was inside the basket. After finding the necklace and realizing the caravan had left for Medina, she waited for someone from the caravan to notice her absence and to come back and find her. Finally, a young, handsome Muslim bandit who had lagged behind the caravan found her and took her back to Muhammad in Medina. For weeks there was gossip about Aisha. Rumors were rampant on whether she had planned to be left behind to meet the handsome bandit and if the young bandit had seen her without her veil. This must have been a fairly stressful time for all involved. Because of the stress, Aisha became sick and with Muhammad's approval, she went to live with her parents. Muhammad became distant from her, which caused her considerable distress and resulted in some of her hair falling out. As Muhammad's "favorite" wife, Aisha had many rivals among Muhammad's other wives and concubines, and many of them used this event against her. To save Muhammad's reputation, Ali told him to divorce Aisha since women were plentiful. A divorce, however, would have signified that something had taken place and reflect badly on both Muhammad and Aisha's father, Abu Bakr. Also, acknowledging that Aisha had committed adultery would have resulted in her being stoned to death. Fortunately, Muhammad received revelations from the angel Gabriel which proclaimed Aisha's innocence (24:11-20). During this revelation, sweat ran down his face "like silver beads on a day of hail" and he announced, "Rejoice, Aisha! Allah has revealed your innocence." The episode was thereafter called "the affair of the lie." Aisha's depression was lifted by the intervention of the Islamic god, and her marriage and reputation remained intact (B3388, B4141, B4750, B7369, B7545). Aisha stated she always knew the Islamic god would reveal her innocence (B7545).

Muhammad was so enraged by this episode that after the revelation of Aisha's innocence, he recommended the gossips be killed (B6662) or receive a flogging of eighty lashes (24:4). *Sharia* demands, "As for someone who accuses the Mother of the Faithful Aisha of adultery after the revelation from heaven of her innocence (24:11-12), such a person is an unbeliever (*kafir*) denying the *Koran* and must be killed" (p18.3).

Perhaps it was at this time the revelation came which said, "O wives off the Prophet! Whoever of you commits an open illegal sexual intercourse, the torment for her will be doubled, and that is ever easy for Allah" (33:30).

This episode provides insight into the daily lives of Muhammad's wives. Aisha noted she first heard about the gossip when she was "attending to her needs" one night. It appears that at night Muhammad's wives would go into the fields and "attend to their needs" or "answer the call of nature." The *hadith* reports state Muhammad gave his wives permission to attend to their needs at night (B5237). In other words, they were largely housebound during the day. Also, Omar thought they should be veiled when going out at night, but Muhammad did not. Some believe it was at this time, not during his marriage to Zaynab, the verse of the veil was revealed (B146).

The title of this section implies Aisha's scandal created problems for women. Verse 24:4 states, "And those who accuse chaste women, and produce not four witnesses, flog them with 80 stripes, and reject their testimony forever." This is also in the *sharia*, which has a section on "the penalty for accusing a person of adultery without proof" (o13.0). Basically, to prove adultery it is required that four Muslim males testify they witnessed the penis being inserted into the vagina (o24.9). Making the accusation without the requisite four Muslim males means there is no proof, and the accuser is scourged with eighty lashes. If a married woman accuses a man of rape and if there are not four witnesses as a minimum, the woman is guilty of false accusations, and she is scourged. Or, by admitting she is a married woman who had sexual intercourse outside of marriage, she may be stoned to death. If an unmarried woman accuses four men of gang rape and the men do not confess, the woman is guilty at a minimum of false accusations and at a maximum of admitting to adultery or fornication and being stoned to death.

Mecca Back Again: The Trench

In February, March, or April 626 or 627, Abu Sufyan returned to Medina to kill Muhammad, destroy Islam, and end the threat to

Mecca and its caravans. Some claim he had assistance from the two Jewish tribes exiled from Medina who wanted to reclaim their possessions. There are reports he had ten thousand soldiers, although this number may have become exaggerated over time. At the time, there were perhaps three thousand Muslim defenders in Medina. However, knowledge of the impending attack allowed Muhammad six to eight days to prepare for the attack. Evidently, three sides of the area that was most likely to be attacked were protected by buildings that created a "fort" type of defense. There was one area where the buildings were not close enough to provide an adequate defense, especially against a cavalry attack. Thus, Muhammad had a wide, deep trench dug along this area, which was a defensive method not previously used in Arabia, but which one of Muhammad's followers had seen used by the Persians. The trench was dug using picks and shovels, the dirt being removed by date baskets. For those who were not working hard enough or who left without permission, there was a revelation stating the Islamic god knew who was slipping away (24:63-64). The trench changed the Meccan battle plan from one of a cavalry attack and a quick victory to one of a siege. Knowledge of the impending attack also allowed those in Medina to harvest their crops, especially the grain Abu Sufyan needed for his camels and horses. The siege provided Muhammad time to contact some of the tribes that had come to destroy him and bribe them to leave Abu Sufyan's army.

In what is called the "Battle of the Trench" or the "Battle of Khandaq," Abu Sufyan's army was hampered by heavy rain, strong winds, and cold conditions and was unable to cross the trench and penetrate Medina. Additionally, there was no grain for their camels and horses. Although ten thousand men seem like a large army, most were only there because of the prospect of quick and easy booty. They did not have an allegiance to Abu Sufyan or a desire to rid the world of Muhammad. Although some writers have criticized Abu Sufyan for the lack of a plan or strategy, in his defense it must be noted that there was little unity or coordination in his "army." Siege warfare was also something with which he did not have experience. Additionally, rather than attacking in force, at this time "battles" were often between champions or small groups, rather than large segments of the army. The death toll for the battle is estimated to be about ten, six Muslims and four from Abu Sufyan's army. After two weeks it was apparent that Medina was not going to be taken, and the different segments of Abu Sufyan's army went their separate ways. Again, Muhammad had defeated Mecca. During the march back to Mecca Abu Sufyan must have realized that Mecca's days were numbered. Muhammad had defeated the coalition Meccan army with a much smaller force. Muhammad had prevented the Meccan army from penetrating Medina. And, Muhammad controlled the trade routes into and out of Mecca. The lingering question was, "Would Muhammad now try to destroy Mecca, as Mecca had tried to destroy Medina?"

Many defenders of Muhammad claim that he only used violence in self-defense. Of the almost eighty raids and battles Muhammad authorized and participated in, this was one of the few that was defensive. The *Koran* has numerous verses which authorize Muslims to initiate aggression against non-Muslims. As noted in Chapter 1, for Muslims the world is separated into the House of Islam, which is territory under Islamic rule, and the House of War, which is territory not under Islamic control. Territory not under Islamic control, the House of War, is seen as a threat of Islam. Therefore, attacking these territories is seen as an act of self-defense. There are more than one hundred verses in the *Koran* that call for and allow Muslims to attack non-Muslims.

Jewish Tribe # 3

Perhaps seeing what had happened to the other Jewish tribes, the remaining Jewish tribe, *Banu-Kuraiza*, either refused to assist Muhammad during the Battle of the Trench, hoping he would be defeated, or provided minimal aid to Abu Sufyan. As Abu Sufyan was withdrawing his forces, the angel Gabriel, who was wearing a turban heavy with gold and silver and riding a mule, approached Muhammad and told him the Islamic god commanded him to laid siege to the last Jewish tribe in Medina since they had conspired against him (B2813, B4117). This revelation does not appear in the *Koran*. Muhammad apparently did not feel threatened by the last

Jewish tribe since he was taking a bath when the angel Gabriel came with the revelation.

After a twenty-five-day siege, the Jewish tribe of two thousand individuals surrendered. The men were given the option of converting to Islam or death, and the women and children had the option of converting to Islam or slavery. All but four of the men chose death. Muhammad had all males who had reached puberty beheaded in the public marketplace in Medina. Their bodies were then dumped in a large pit the Jewish men had been forced to dig before they were executed. The number executed varies from six hundred to nine hundred, and the executions started early in the morning and continued into the night. Muhammad watched the mass slaughter with Aisha sitting next to him. Muhammad had some of the Jews killed by members from each of the Arab tribes in Medina. This would prevent blood-feuds and further desensitize them to murder and theft. Some accounts have Muhammad severing the first few heads, including that of a woman. More than one thousand children and women became the booty of war and were divided up according to custom, with twenty percent going to Muhammad. Many of the captives were ransomed to the *Bani Nadir*, who had fled to the oasis of Khaibar. Those who were not ransomed were sold into slavery. The money bought more camels, horses, and weapons.

After the executions, some accounts have Muhammad dragging Reihana (Rainah, Raihana, Rayhana, Rayhanah), the beautiful teenage widow of one of the men who had been beheaded, into an apartment and raping her. Or we can assume that after watching her father, brothers, and husband having their heads chopped off and her friends, mother, and sisters being distributed as the profits of war, she willingly jumped into bed with Muhammad. He found her so pleasing that he asked her to become one of his wives. Some accounts list her as one of his wives, although some claim she did not become his wife until shortly before his death. Other accounts have her refusing to "take the veil" and of showing a "repugnance toward Islam," preferring to become a part of his harem as a concubine. As noted earlier with the *Banu Mustalia*, the rape of a conquered enemy's daughters and wives was the display of total victory and domination.

The *Koran* deals with this event in verses 33:25-27. In this section, the Islamic god approved of the theft, enslavement, and mass murder of Jews.

The New "Improved" Ethnically Cleansed Medina

Muhammad had completed his genocidal ethnic cleansing of Medina. He had eliminated a Jewish community which had roots going back more than two thousand years. He started by attempting to convince the Jewish community he was their long-awaited prophet. When that did not work, he started to preach against them. Then there were attacks on individual Jews, the forced expulsion of two Jewish tribes, and finally the massacre and enslavement of the third tribe. Since the *Koran* is not in chronological order, it is difficult to know when certain passages were written. However, there are a number of derogatory passages about Jews, one describing Jews as the enemy of the Islamic god and another describing them as the enemy of the believers.

The booty and loot from the *Banu-Kuraiza* was vast and greatly increased the wealth of Muhammad and his followers. The opportunity to acquire booty, loot, and women must have made Islam attractive to many men who had few skills, which limited their economic opportunities, and poor body and dental hygiene, which limited their romantic prospects.

Making Use of the New Loot

In late 627, Muhammad sent two expeditions north. One of the expeditions was led by his ex-adopted son, Zeid, in an attempt to divert the trade route from Mecca to Medina. He was also looking for converts, and those in the north had been influenced by the monotheism of both Christians and Jews and might be receptive to Islam.

With more camels and horses purchased from banditry and robbery, Muhammad could send out more raiding parties. As a result, soon Muhammad's non-Muslim son-in-law, Abul As, was captured once again, although there are different versions of the story. Abul

As was returning to Mecca with a caravan laden with goods when it was attacked and captured by Muhammad's bandits, robbers, and thieves. He was either captured or escaped to Medina where he was reunited with his wife, Zainab. Muhammad requested his followers return the loot from the caravan to Abul As, which they did. Abul As was so moved by this action that after taking the caravan to its owners in Mecca, he returned to Medina and embraced Islam. The reunion of Abul As and Zainab was short-lived since she would die within the year; some say it was from the harsh treatment she received years earlier when attempting to leave Mecca to join her father in Medina.

Around this time, eight men came to Medina and accepted Islam. After a short time, they claimed the climate in Medina did not agree with them and that they were sick. Muhammad told them to go live with a shepherd who was guarding a herd of camels until they regained their health. The men did what Muhammad told them to do, but after a short period they cruelly tortured and killed the shepherd, scattered the camels, and fled the area. Muhammad sent a force after the men, who were quickly captured and brought before him. He ordered their hands and feet cut off and their eyes gouged out. He then ordered the men to be taken outside of the city and left until they died (B3018). Muhammad then received another revelation telling him death was to be simple, either by beheading or crucifixion. This revelation is not in the *Koran.*

During this time, Muhammad also continued to make contact and treaties with the tribes around Medina. If the tribes would not embrace Islam, Muhammad, at least, persuaded them to remain neutral.

Back to Mecca

In March of 628, as the result of a dream, Muhammad decided to lead a group of religious pilgrims to Mecca during one of the minor religious pilgrimages. He selected the time of a minor pilgrimage because there was less probability of meeting a hostile tribe along the way or at Mecca. Although technically on a religious pilgrimage, Muhammad probably had other reasons for the trip. A minor reason was that some of his followers from Mecca wanted to see their families. However, his major reason must have been the realization his former powerful enemy was no longer a threat to him, his followers, or his religion. Thus, he must have thought it better to convert them rather than fight them. He had already changed the focus of the daily prayers from Jerusalem to Mecca, demonstrating its importance in Islam. This minor pilgrimage to the *Kaaba* in Mecca was another attempt to illustrate Mecca's importance in Islam.

Whatever Muhammad's reasons for the religious pilgrimage, he initially encountered a problem. Basically, while there was no shortage of Muslims willing to participate in raids where there was the prospect of booty, loot, and women, there were few who wanted to go on a religious pilgrimage where there was only religious booty. This provides an indicator of the motivations of many of the early converts to Islam.

Finally, Muhammad obtained between fourteen hundred and sixteen hundred followers to accompany him to Mecca. He also took one hundred sacrificial camels. When the citizens of Mecca heard Muhammad was approaching, they assumed he was coming to attack the city since Muslims had been known to violate the rule against fighting in a sacred place during a sacred time. Thus, a cavalry troop of two hundred men wearing panther skins to illustrate they were beasts of prey was sent to block his entry into Mecca. Muhammad and his followers stopped eight to ten miles northwest of Mecca near the village of Hudaibiya (Hudaybiyah, Hudabeya). After a conference, Muhammad offered Mecca a ten-year truce in which he would stop raiding Meccan caravans if his followers could make the annual pilgrimage to Mecca. He also agreed not to accept any converts from Mecca unless their guardians gave permission. Muhammad was given permission to make alliances with other Arab tribes even if the tribe had an alliance with Mecca. Both sides signed the "Treaty of Hudaibiya," which would go into effect after one year of peace. After facing the camels toward Mecca and tying garlands around their necks, they were sacrificed, and Muhammad and his followers returned to Medina. Muhammad's status increased to that of an independent political power worthy of forming a treaty with Mecca.

The angel Gabriel came and revealed several revelations about this time. Verse 48:1 revealed that as a result of the treaty, Muhammad had been given a "manifest victory," and verse 60:7 revealed the Islamic god would make "friendships between you and those whom you hold as enemies."

Some believe the "Treaty of Hudaibiya" occurred earlier, shortly after the Battle of the Trench. Islamic apologists believe the treaty initiated a diplomatic period within Islam during which Muhammad tried to bring about the unity of Arab tribes. In addition, in April or May 628 he sent letters to six foreign rulers inviting them to join Islam. A *hadith* report (B65) claims Muhammad may have written the letters. He was told the rulers would not read them unless they were sealed, so he had a silver ring crafted and engraved with "Muhammad, the Messenger of Allah."

The envoy Muhammad sent to Egypt with a letter was met by the Roman governor, who rejected the offer to join Islam but gave Muhammad four slaves, including two Coptic slave girls who were sisters. Muhammad would keep the beautiful, curly-haired, light-skinned, twenty-year-old Mary (Maimuna, Maria, Mariah, Mariyah, Maryah) for his harem.

It was about this time that a Jewish sorcerer and his daughter attempted to kill Muhammad. They obtained a hair from his head and tied it into eleven knots. The daughter then placed a curse on the hair and dropped it into a well. The only way to undo the curse was to untie the knots. As a result of the curse, Muhammad became weak, suffered memory loss, and believed he had done things which he had not done. The angel Gabriel came with several revelations which are in the *Koran* (114:1-6; 115:1-5). Ali recited these *suras* over the well, and Muhammad recovered. These two *suras* are called "the two takings of refuge" and are recited by Muslims to protect them against evil.

Not Again!

The treaty with Mecca prevented Muhammad from attacking its caravans. Thus, twenty days after returning from Mecca, Muhammad sought out additional Jewish victims, this time at the oasis of

Khaibar. Khaibar, which means "community" in Hebrew, was a wealthy Jewish farming and commerce settlement about ninety-five miles and six days northeast of Medina. It was also where some of the Jews expelled from Medina, especially the *Banu Nadir*, had settled. Additionally, some of the captive children and women from the *Banu-Kuraiza* had been ransomed by relatives and were now living in Khaibar.

The Jews living in Khaibar belonged to several tribes, each having its own land with a castle or fortress for protection. As with the three Jewish tribes in Medina, the tribes in Khaibar were not united. When the leaders of Khaibar saw Muhammad and his bandits approaching, they decided to fight as individual tribes rather than as a unified army. Thus, they retreated to their individual forts, a mistake they would later regret since Muhammad had a relatively small army which would have been unable to defeat the combined strength of the men of Khaibar. Muhammad laid siege to the forts one by one, and it is reported that initially both sides suffered heavy losses. Later in the battle, the capture of the forts was facilitated when two men from Khaibar provided information on the vulnerable areas of each fort.

The "battle" appears to have lasted at least two months. Some believe it was during this battle where the Islamic concept of "temporary marriage" emerged. Temporary marriage allowed Muslim bandits to unilaterally "marry" captive women for the purpose of sex. Thus, it was not technically adultery or rape. When it was convenient, the Muslim rapists could dissolve the marriage. Others believe it was at Khaibar where temporary marriage was prohibited while still others believe it was prohibited under Omar, the second leader of Islam after Muhammad.

The various accounts of the attack on Khaibar are confusing. As noted earlier, the conquest of the first few forts involved savage fighting. Thus, when each fort fell, Muhammad took loot and prisoners. When there were only a few forts left to conquer, the Jewish leaders asked Muhammad if, instead of killing or enslaving them, he would allow them to continue living and farming the rich oasis. They pleaded that they knew how to farm and if he allowed them to stay, he could have half of what they produced every year. Muhammad agreed to the proposal, adding that they could not conceal any of their treasure, which was reported to be substantial, and he had the right to expel them whenever he wanted, which one of his successors did in less than a decade.

Thus, some of the Jewish farmers became tenants on what had been their land, with half of their produce going to Muhammad. Since they were now working for Muhammad, he provided them protection from raiding bands of Arabs. The Jews of Khaibar became the first of many to be placed under *dhimminitude*. *Dhimmintude* is imposed on non-Muslims in conquered territories. Although it varied in form over time and territory, basically the Muslim conqueror placed the *dhimmis* in an inferior legal status where they were heavily taxed, dominated, treated with contempt, and humiliated. Those accorded the status were generally Christians and Jews or "people of the book." Generally, they could not touch a Muslim woman, build religious structures higher than nearby Mosques, say anything critical of Islam, hold public office, or have military equipment. Additionally, they often had to wear distinctive clothing. They could not own or ride horses. Instead, they had to ride donkeys, often facing backward. And, if riding a donkey, they had to dismount and bow if a Muslim passed by.

After their surrender, Kinana, one of the Jewish leaders of Khaibar, was brought before Muhammad since he allegedly knew the location of the treasure of the Jewish tribes of Arabia. Part of this treasure had been seen when the *Banu Nadir* had been forcibly marched out of Medina. Kinana said the treasure had been used to pay for the ransom of Jewish captives and for weapons. Muhammad did not believe him and ordered that Kinana be tortured until he revealed the location of the treasure. After being tortured, which included a fire on Kinana's chest, he still refused to reveal the location of the treasure. As Kinana approached death, Muhammad ordered him to be beheaded, an order which was rapidly carried out. Muhammad's men did find a small amount of treasure.

There were revelations about Khaibar. One verse, 59:14, said the Jews of Khaibar would not fight as a unified force because "their hearts are divided." Verse 2:249 is also thought to have been revealed at this time and deals with a small force, Muhammad's band of bandits and robbers, overcoming a larger force, the Jews at Khaibar.

Earlier it was noted the details about the raid on Khaibar are confusing. Apparently the Jewish farmers who surrendered later in the battle were initially given their "freedom" and allowed to continue farming. But those whose forts were taken by force in the savage fighting remained prisoners. Additionally, because the location of the treasure was not revealed, some Jews lost their freedom.

One captive taken early in the fighting was Kinana's teenage widow, Safiya (Safiyah, Safiyyah, Sophia). It is believed she was about fifteen to seventeen, and her beauty was widely known. Muhammad might have known about her since she was part of the *Banu Nadir* tribe he had earlier expelled from Medina. Some accounts have Muhammad throwing a blanket over Safiya after her capture, indicating his intention to marry her. Prior to the consummation of the marriage, the two had to wait in Khaibar because she was "unclean." After an appropriate period of time, the two of them left Khaibar with Muhammad eagerly looking for a place where the consummation of the marriage could take place. Safiya found the first spot Muhammad selected unsuitable, and they had to continue on the journey a few more miles before the consummation could finally take place (B2235, B2893, B5085, B5159, B5169, B2893, B5387). One of Muhammad's men spent the night outside the "honeymooners'" tent with his sword drawn because he feared Safiya might attempt to kill Muhammad since he was responsible for the death of her husband and other relatives. It may have been her agreement to marry Muhammad that swayed him to allow some of the Jewish farmers to stay in Khaibar under *dhimmitude* (B371).

What is clear is that Muhammad did not observe the traditional waiting period before consummating this "marriage." In this era, divorced or widowed women were required to have two or three menstrual periods before remarriage to prevent disputes about paternity. The *Koran* states that women who were widowed should wait four months and ten days before remarrying (2:234).

It is at Khaibar that many Islamic scholars believe a Jewish woman poisoned the food she prepared for Muhammad and his companions. Upon his first bite, Muhammad realized the food was poisoned and spit it out. However, two of his companions did not have such discriminating and sensitive taste buds and died as a result of eating the poisoned food. The woman admitted to poisoning the food and was killed in some accounts and spared in others. Some claim Muhammad suffered daily from the effects of the poison for the remainder of his life, and it was this poison that finally killed him (B4428). The poison did not seem to affect his sex drive and his need to consummate his marriage with Safiya.

Khaibar is significant for several reasons. First, after the surrounding tribes heard what had happened to the *Banu Mustalia* and to those at Khaibar, they capitulated before Muhammad attacked them. They agreed to live under *dhimmitude* and give him fifty percent of their produce. In return, he would protect them from marauding groups of non-Muslim bandits. Thus, Khaibar made Muhammad a wealthy man. Aisha said she had never eaten her fill of dates until the conquest of Khaibar. Second, it was in leaving Khaibar that Muhammad must have started to realize how powerful he had become and that more than just the area around Medina was within his grasp. As a result, there would be many more raids some for revenge, some simply to demonstrate Muhammad was the power in the area, and some to seek out new tribes to conquer, convert, and loot. This was necessary since the treaty with Mecca, as well as other cities and tribes, meant Muhammad's regional source of wealth from banditry and robbery no longer existed. His only alternative was to expand to areas where there were no treaties to violate and no Muslims to fight against. Third, on the way to Khaibar, Ali asked why he was going to fight a peaceful tribe. Muhammad answered it was because of the booty, but more importantly, it was because they were not Muslims and they had to be made to adhere to the rules of Islam. Fourth, Muhammad must have recognized his power was not only spiritual, but also military. Fifth, Muhammad is claimed to have stated after the "battle" that the only religion in Arabia would be Islam.

Back to Mecca

In early 629, Muhammad and about two thousand followers started on the minor pilgrimage to Mecca, as allowed by the "Treaty of Hudaibiya." In fear of their arrival, most of the citizens of Mecca left the city and went into hiding in the nearby mountains. Muhammad rode into Mecca on the same camel he had ridden when he left Mecca in 622. Muhammad entered the *Kaaba* and touched the black stone, yelling, "There is no god but Allah alone!" There was no violence or looting and he acquired many converts from Mecca who were impressed by the orderly, religious behavior of Muhammad and his followers, including Khalid, the leader of the Meccan cavalry at Uhud. It was Khalid who had secured victory for Mecca at the battle.

Unusual: A Battle for Revenge, Not Loot

In 629, another battle took place, but this time it was for revenge, not loot. As noted earlier, after the treaty with Mecca, Muhammad had letters sent to several foreign leaders asking them to join Islam. For example, the king of Iran, the sultan of Byzantine, the king of Abyssinia (Ethiopia), the emperor of Rome, the Roman governor of Egypt, the king of Syria, the king of Yemen, and the king of Oman were all sent similar letters. The envoy Muhammad sent to the Byzantine Empire was murdered. Muhammad was outraged and quickly organized an army of about three thousand bandits to avenge the murder. The army of bandits was commanded by his ex-adopted son, Zeid. The Byzantine army heard about the advancing Muslim army and sent between ten thousand and two hundred thousand soldiers to defend its territory. The two forces confronted each other near the village of Mutah, which is south of Amman in Jordan. Most accounts say the battle was costly for Islam, with as many as two thousand Muslim bandits, including Zeid, being slaughtered by the experienced and professional Byzantine army. A few apologists claim it was a minor skirmish in which fewer than ten Muslims, including Zeid, were killed. Either way, it was a defeat for Muhammad since his force was either slaughtered or the engagement was minor, and he did not obtain revenge for the murder of his envoy. However, what emerged from this engagement was a new Muslim commander named Khalid, who had only recently converted to Islam. During the battle, he broke nine swords in combat and became known as the "Sword of Allah." Given that he broke nine swords, the minor skirmish explanation does not seem satisfactory.

Back to Mecca—This Time Not in Peace

As he often did after a defeat such as the one at Mutah, Muhammad sought to redeem himself and Islam through a quick victory. Muhammad must have realized his power had grown strong enough to capture Mecca. In either late 629 or early 630, he claimed the "Truce of Hudaibiya" had been violated. One alleged violation was that a tribe allied with Mecca had attacked a Muslim tribe. A second violation was when a non-Muslim killed a Muslim in a personal dispute.

In response, Muhammad assembled an army of ten thousand bandits—not pilgrims—and led them toward Mecca in early January 630. There was a minor skirmish in which thirteen to twenty-eight Meccan soldiers were killed. Soon those from Mecca realized that fighting was useless, and Abu Sufyan allowed Muhammad and his forces to enter Mecca unchallenged. With a few exceptions, all minor members of Mecca, Muhammad granted an amnesty to the residents of Mecca. One who was not granted amnesty and who was quickly killed was the man who had attacked Muhammad's daughter, Zainab, when she tried to leave Mecca to join her family in Medina. Another was a scribe who Muhammad claimed had falsified revelations dictated to him. Plus, he had left Islam. Some authors claim the scribe re-converted to Islam and was spared. With the exception of the black stone, Muhammad had all the religious symbols of the Arab religions destroyed in and around the *Kaaba*, including those dealing with Christianity. Muhammad also declared Mecca the Holy City of Islam and stated that those who did not believe in Islam should not come onto its sacred land.

Abu Sufyan soon converted to Islam, stating that Muhammad's god had defeated his god(s) and he, therefore, owed his former god(s) no allegiance. Muhammad also married Maymona (Maymūnah), who was between twenty-seven and thirty-six and was a widow. She was related to a powerful figure in Mecca. Muhammad was sixty at the time of this marriage. Some have his marriage to Habibah, Abu Sufyan's daughter, occurring after his conquest of Mecca.

Even a Prophet Has Domestic Problems

Muhammad had the practice of rotating nightly among his wives, except for Sauda, who had given her night to Aisha. At some point he started to violate the practice by spending too many nights with Mary, one of his concubines, who was known for her beauty, curly hair, and light complexion. His other wives, especially Aisha and Haifsa, became angry and confronted him, causing Muhammad some anguish and embarrassment. Thus, to resolve the situation, Muhammad needed another revelation from the angel Gabriel, which he received in a timely manner. The revelation started with the angel Gabriel asking Muhammad why he was denying himself something the Islamic god had made lawful to him, which was sex with Mary. The message continued by stating that if Muhammad divorced his troublesome wives, the Islamic god would give him better wives, ones who were more compliant and loyal. The revelation also told him since the relationship with Mary was lawful, Muhammad did not have to restrain himself (66:1-12). Additionally, if his wives stayed married to him it would be on his terms, and if they stayed married to him, they could not remarry after he died. Muhammad offered his wives the opportunity for divorce (33:28-29), and some accounts have one or two of his new wives choosing divorce (B4913, B5191).

Not only was his relationship with Mary lawful, but another revelation (33:51) also told Muhammad he could "postpone" his scheduled turns with his wives and "receive whom you will." Verse 33:52 suggests Muhammad may have pushed the limit too far, with two to three times the number of wives allowed to other Muslims, and it reads, "It is not lawful for you (to marry other) women after this, nor to change them for other wives even though their beauty attracts you, except those (slaves) whom your right hand possesses."

In other words, Muhammad could not take any more wives, but the number of women for his harem was unlimited (B4788, B4789).

For followers such as Abu Bakr and Omar, whose daughters were married to Muhammad, it must have been difficult seeing their daughters deserted for a concubine. Apparently, during this time Muhammad took an oath to not visit his wives for one month. In twenty-nine days he was back, and when his followers said it had not been a month, he told them this month had twenty nine days (B5201, B5202, B5203).

After Khadijah, all of Muhammad's numerous wives and concubines were childless until Mary bore the light-skinned Ibrahim (Abraham), who Muhammad proclaimed as his own. Even the angel Gabriel came and offered a revelation, which is not in the *Koran*, addressing Muhammad as "O Father of Ibrahim." A slave who bore a child to her owner obtained the status of wife, which also gave her freedom. It is not known if Mary continued to be a concubine or became on of Muhammad's wives. Ibrahim died one to two years after birth. The child, especially since he was a son, caused some envy and jealousy among his many childless wives, and some have suggested that the child's death may not have been "natural." The *hadith* reports note that Ibrahim has a wet-nurse in paradise (B1382, B3255).

Muhammad may have had as many as thirteen to fifteen additional wives, but the record is not clear. Some of the "wives" may have been short-lived relationships that ended in death or divorce. And some of the claims may be nothing more than clan, family, or tribal attempts to claim a connection to Muhammad.

Although Muhammad may have been able to control his wives through revelations, this did not mean they were without power. Aisha narrated several *hadith* reports illustrating where Muhammad's wives conspired against him (see B4912, B4914, B4915, B4916, B5267, B6691, B6972). In one report, Aisha and Haifsa thought Muhammad was spending too much time with Zaynab, and when asked about it, Muhammad replied that she had honey and he liked sweet things. Aisha told Haifsa the next time she saw Muhammad she was to ask, "What is that bad smell?" When he said he had been drinking honey, she was to say, "The bees must have gotten it from a foul-smelling flower." Aisha would do the same, as would Safiya. Aisha's planned worked, and soon Muhammad was declining Zaynab's offer of honey. Sauda seemed delighted and said, "We have deprived him of honey," resulting in Aisha telling her to be quiet. Some accounts claim Haifsa provided the honey and Aisha and Sauda engaged in the plot.

Another of Muhammad's daughters, Um Kalthum, died in 630 or 631.

More Conquests

Early in 630, the *Hawazin* and *Thaqueef* (*Thaqif*) tribes who lived three days outside of Mecca started organizing a large army of nomadic tribes to attack Mecca for two reasons. First, the tribal leaders believed there was going to be a violent conflict between Mecca and Medina and the two forces would exhaust each other. This would allow them to loot the cities and become the new trade center for the area. Second, they wanted to attack Muhammad before he gained more power and attacked them. It is estimated the Muslim bandits consisted of between ten thousand and twelve thousand men and the tribal army consisted of between four thousand men and twenty thousand women and children. The *Hawazin* and *Thaqueef* tribes brought their women and children with them, believing the men would fight harder and would not flee if they knew there was no escape for their families. Prior to the battle, Muhammad told his followers, "Whoever kills an unbeliever shall own the booty from him."

The Muslim army won what became known as the Battle of Hunayn (Hunain). In addition to the loot, it is estimated there were six thousand captives, twenty-four thousand camels, and forty thousand sheep. Muhammad's foster sister from his wet-nurse was among the captives. He gave her freedom and two slaves.

After his victory at Hunayn, Muhammad decided to attack Taif, which he had visited and been chased out of when he was still preaching in Mecca. It was located at an oasis with water and fertile soil and was famous for its fourteen types of fruit trees and its grains. The city was surrounded by a wall. After his arrival, Muhammad found the typical siege that had worked against Jewish tribes was ineffective. Thus, some siege equipment was built and used against the walled city. This proved ineffective, and after twenty to forty days, Muhammad received another revelation that this was not the time to attack Taif. Again, this revelation does not appear in the *Koran.* Muhammad and his troops soon left for Medina.

After arriving back in Medina, Muhammad had to decide what to do with the spoils from the battle at Hunayn. However, the captives from the battle announced their decision to convert to Islam and requested their goods and family members be returned. This presented a problem since his bandits expected their share of the loot. Thus, Muhammad told them they could have either their families or their goods. They chose their families. Still, however, many of Muhammad's followers did not want to give up their captives, who could be sold as slaves or ransomed to family members. Thus, he had to promise them more loot in the future.

By 630, Muhammad had become powerful enough to bring more of the Arabian Peninsula under his control. He sent his bandits and robbers out to subdue and convert numerous tribes to Islam. The tribes also had to pay taxes to Mecca. For many of the tribes in the north, Islam had some appeal, if not as a religion then as a protector. Many of the small communities had depended on the Persian and Byzantine Empires to provide them protection. As these empires declined, they looked to Islam for protection from marauding Arab tribes. Initially, Muhammad probably provided protection without demanding they convert to Islam.

In summer or fall of 630, Muhammad led a force of thirty thousand bandits to Tabuk (Tabouk, Tebuk) in what is now northwestern Saudi Arabia. At the time, this was probably the largest army assembled in Arabia. Tabuk was on the Byzantine border and was a stopping point on the caravan route between Medina and Damascus. This is sometimes called the "Battle of Tabuk" but is more correctly labeled the "Expedition to Tabuk." Muhammad's reason for the expedition was that he heard the Byzantine army was going to invade Arabia, and his army went to prevent the invasion. After marching his army of bandits to Tabuk, Muhammad found there was no Byzantine army waiting to invade Arabia. After spending ten days searching in vain for the Byzantine army, Muhammad marched his bandits back to Medina. Some claim that the Byzantine army retreated in fear, but most believe the reports of the massing army were false. Although no battle took place, it demonstrated Muhammad's ability to raise a large force of armed bandits. In his absence, Muhammad placed Ali in charge of Medina, with some believing this meant Ali should be his successor.

While looking for the Byzantine army, some of Muhammad's robbers went north to the head of the Gulf of Aqaba. This is one of two gulfs separated by the Sinai Peninsula at the northern end of the Red Sea. To the west is the Gulf of Suez and to the east is the Gulf of Aqaba. Because of its location along a trading route, it had roots going back more than four thousand years. The governor of the city was forced to pay tribute to Muhammad. This city would become a stepping stone for the Islamic invasion and conquest of Egypt, which would start within a decade.

In an area where the tribes were accustomed to fighting small, limited tribal skirmishes, Muhammad changed the rules by creating a large "military force" which was far superior to what any one tribe could resist. The numerous raids on caravans and the various wars against the bandits from Mecca had turned many in Muhammad's army into experienced and seasoned soldiers. Those in the other tribes were generally farmers or herders and only fought when their freedom and lives and freedom depended on it. Additionally, the booty and loot stolen from others meant Muhammad's bandits purchased camels and horses which gave them mobility and speed, as well as the most modern military equipment of the era. In contrast, the tribes they attacked often used their farming tools as weapons. When Muhammad attempted to bring some of the tribes under his control, some refused and Muhammad's bandits fought and won battles against them. Soon word of Muhammad's power grew, and the surrounding tribes sent delegates requesting his protection and support. Protection and support were offered to those tribes that would accept Islam and agree to pay taxes. Even the citizens of Taif finally capitulated. Muhammad also acquired more men from among those who decided that banditry, looting, pillaging, and raping were a better way of life than herding goats or tending a date orchard.

Those who did not convert were either killed or converted to *dhimmitude* status.

In 631, Muhammad made another pilgrimage from Medina to Mecca. This was Muhammad's first pilgrimage to Mecca after it was ruled by a Muslim. While in Mecca, he received a revelation which stated non-Muslims would be allowed to take part in future pilgrimages to Mecca or approach the *Kaaba* (9:28). It was also ordered that Christian churches and Jewish synagogues in Mecca be destroyed and that mosques be built in their place. Additionally, those tribes who had not accepted Islam were told they had four months to accept Islam or be attacked. Ambassadors from numerous tribes came to Medina informing Muhammad their chiefs were willing to accept Islam.

Muhammad was still unhappy about the reverse at the Battle of Mutah and ordered Osama, the son of Zeid, who had been killed during the battle, to lead a force back to the Syrian front to "wipe out the memory of the disaster."

Death Becomes Him...Finally!

Muhammad claimed the angel Gabriel visited him once a year and had him recite the revelations to make certain he had not forgotten any. In 632, the angel Gabriel had him recite the revelations twice. Muhammad told one of his followers this was a sign that "my time has come."

In February or March of 632, Muhammad made his last pilgrimage to Mecca, the "Farewell Pilgrimage," with between forty thousand and one hundred and twenty thousand followers. Here he made a speech before his followers which is known as the Sermon on Mount Arafat. In the speech, he told his followers the religion was complete, all the revelations had been revealed, and no prophets would come after him. He told them not to fight, murder, or steal among themselves since all Muslims were brothers. He said that if they followed the *Koran* and his example, they would not go astray. He also told them how to deal with non-Muslims, namely fight them with the sword until they submitted to Islam. Specifically, he said, "I was ordered by Allah to fight against the people till they testify that none has the right to be worshiped but Allah, and that Muhammad is the messenger of Allah."

Either while returning to or shortly after returning to Medina, Muhammad came down with a fever and a short, painful illness followed. As his illness intensified, Muhammad asked Abu Bakr to lead the prayers, which he did (B679, B3384). One *hadith* report (B467) has Muhammad coming to a prayer session and saying, "There is no one who had done more favor to me with his life than Abu Bakr." Some assume this meant that Abu Bakr, not Ali, was to succeed him as the leader of Islam. At some point Muhammad called his wives together and noted his illness would prevent him from visiting each wife according to her turn. He asked their permission to stay in Aisha's house until he recovered. His wives granted his wish (B3099, B5217). It appears he was dragged rather than carried into Aisha's house since the *hadith* reports note his legs dragged on the ground as he was moved (B198, B4442). As noted earlier, this may have been because he had become too heavy to carry.

A *hadith* report states he asked for paper to write a statement so his followers would not go astray (B114). This is either an indication he was not an "illiterate prophet," he had learned to write, or he was delusional (B4431, B4432, B7366). There are *hadith* reports which suggest he did know how to write (B65, D2993, D3021 D3056, M1774R1).

At some point in the illness he asked to see his only surviving daughter, Fatima. He told her the meaning of the angel Gabriel visiting him and of having him twice recite the revelations. He also told Fatima she would be the first in his family to follow him. When she started to cry, he told her, "Don't you like to be chief of all the ladies of Paradise?" or "Don't you like to be chief of all the lady-believers?" She then smiled (B3624, B3716, B4433, B4434).

At one point Aisha thought he had died. However, he awoke and told her, "No prophet is taken by death until he has been shown his place in paradise and then offered the choice to live or die."

The illness intensified and became very painful. After twenty days, on a Monday, either June 7 or 8 of 632, Muhammad died in Aisha's house. His last words were, "May Allah curse the Jews and Christians, for they built the places of worship at the graves of their

Prophets" (B435, B436, B3453, B3454, B4441). Aisha claimed he died with his head either on her breast or in her lap. Others believe he died with his head on Ali's chest. Aisha noted that after his death there was almost no food in her house, only some barley which was soon gone (B3097). Aisha also stated that when Muhammad died his armor was mortgaged to a Jew (B2916), although this is hard to believe. Other *hadith* reports claims his estate consisted of his arms, a white mule, and a piece of land that was to be given to charity (B2739, B2873). Although all Muslims were ordered to make a will, Muhammad did not have one; he claimed he was exempt since he had bequeathed the *Koran* (B2740).

Muhammad was buried under the bed in Aisha's house where he died. According to the *hadith* reports, all prophets are alive in the grave and can hear what is taking place among the living (D1042). Aisha lived in the apartment until she died almost half a century later. She lived in a room next to the area known as the "Prophet's Cemetery." Her father would later be buried in the same room, which she visited unveiled. After Omar was also buried in the room, she would only visit it veiled.

During his time in Medina, Muhammad had authorized at least eighty-six expeditions or raids, of which he personally led twenty-seven.

What Does It Mean?

The earlier chapter examined the ideological foundations of Islam to understand why all Muslims are obligated to fight until non-Muslims have converted to Islam, have been subjugated by Islam, or have been killed. The behavior of Muhammad was also examined since Muslims are compelled to follow his behavior. As was seen, Muhammad authorized attacks on non-Muslims and told his followers they were to continue until all worshiped the Islamic god and admitted Muhammad was his prophet.

The following chapters will examine the more recent attacks by Muslims on non-Muslims.

CHAPTER 10: RECENT WAKE-UP ALARMS

The earlier chapters examined the ideological beliefs of Islam as presented in its holiest religious documents. In addition, the behavior of its prophet, Muhammad, which Muslims are obligated to follow, was also examined. The chapters on Muhammad also included a survey of Islam's early bloody and intolerant history. The purpose of these chapters was to alert or awaken non-Muslims that—like it or not—they are engaged in a life and death struggle with Islam. The struggle is not with extreme Islam, Islamofascism, radical Islam, or a hijacked Islam, but with Islam.

This chapter will examine the recent "wake-up" alarms which should have alerted non-Muslims to the dangers they confront. The following two chapters will examine second attacks and describe why many who are under attack have returned to a pre-9/11 mentality. The last chapter will illustrate the Islamic infestation of the West.

The Sound of Alarms Going Off

9/11 was a series of four wake-up alarms for the United States to the danger of Islam. The first alarm went off at 8:44 a.m. when Flight 11 crashed into the north side of the North Tower of the WTC. The second was at 9:03 a.m. when Flight 175 crashed into the south side of the South Tower of the WTC. The third was at 9:37 a.m. when Flight 77 crashed into the western side of the Pentagon. And the fourth was at about 10:03 a.m. when Flight 93 crashed into a field in Pennsylvania. In a little more than an hour, Americans heard the collective screams and cries of almost three thousand innocent, terrified individuals being incinerated, being crushed in collapsing buildings or crashing airplanes, or plunging to their deaths from the WTC. At 8:30 p.m. on 9/11, President Bush addressed a shocked nation:

> Today, our fellow citizens, our way of life, our very freedom came under attack in a series of deliberate and deadly terrorist acts. The victims were in airplanes, or in their offices: secretaries, businessmen and women, military and federal workers, moms and dads, friends and neighbors. Thousands of lives were suddenly ended by evil, despicable acts of terror... These acts of mass murder were intended to frighten our nation into chaos and retreat. But they have failed. Our country is strong. A great people has been moved to defend a great nation. Terrorist attacks can shake the foundations of our biggest buildings, but they cannot touch the foundation of America. These acts shattered steel, but they cannot dent the steel of American resolve. America was targeted for attack because we're the brightest beacon for freedom and opportunity in the world. No one will keep that light from shining... The search is underway for those who are behind these evil acts. I've directed the full resources of our intelligence and law enforcement communities to find those responsible and to bring them to justice. We will make no distinction between the terrorists who committed these acts and those who harbor them... America and our friends and allies join with all those who want peace and security in the world, and we stand together to win the war against terrorism. Tonight, I ask for your prayers for all those who grieve, for the children whose worlds have been shattered, for all whose sense of safety and security has been threatened. And I pray they will be comforted by a power greater than any of us, spoken through the ages in Psalm 23: "Even though I walk through the valley of the shadow of death, I fear no evil, for You are with me."

President Bush finished the speech by saying,

> This is a day when all Americans from every walk of life unite in our resolve for justice and peace. America has stood down enemies before, and we will do so this time. None of us will ever forget this day, yet, we go forward to defend freedom and all that is good and just in our world.

Within hours of the attacks, patriotism soared and American flags seemed to spontaneously appear at businesses and homes, on lapel pins, and as a mandatory accessory on automobiles [Note to self: Lapel pins did not appear on many in the mainstream media or on certain presidential candidates.] Thousands rushed to give blood for the survivors they prayed would be found at the WTC and the Pentagon, and thousands more took leaves from their jobs to go to New York City to look for or treat victims, clear the debris, and rebuild. Those working at "Ground Zero" amidst the toxic dust, debris, and body parts were hailed as heroes—a title they richly deserved.

On September 14, 2001, President Bush went to Ground Zero to see the damage and to thank those who were still looking for survivors. As the president started his impromptu speech, a voice yelled out, "President Bush, we can't hear you!" President Bush replied, "I can hear you. The rest of the world hears you. And the people who knocked these buildings down will hear from all of us soon." There was thunderous applause to the chanting "USA, USA..."

This was a momentous event in American history. For a brief moment after the horrific and unexpected attacks, Americans felt confident and united. This speech had the potential of becoming a speech that would rally and unite the country much as FDR's speeches had after the attack on Pearl Harbor. As will be seen, the potential was not realized.

On September 14, 2001, Congress passed a joint resolution authorizing the use of force against terrorists.

President Bush addressed Congress on September 20, 2001. He started by noting the Union was strong, as demonstrated by the passengers who had fought back against the Muslim *jihadists* on

Flight 93 over Pennsylvania. He also recognized the rescue workers who had worked beyond exhaustion, the prayers of a grieving nation, and those who had made the "grief of strangers their own." He then stated that grief had turned to anger, and anger to resolution, and that "justice will be done." Al-Qaeda was listed as the attacker and Osama bin Laden (OBL) as its leader. He then demanded the Taliban in Afghanistan turn over the leaders of al-Qaeda and close the terrorist training camps. He stated these "demands" were not open to discussion or negotiation, and if the Taliban did not act immediately, they would share the fate of the terrorists.

President Bush then made it clear al-Qaeda was not the only terrorist organization threatening the United States and that there were others which needed to be "found, stopped, and defeated." He then stated they had attacked us because they hated our freedoms. He continued:

> We have seen their kind before. They're the heirs of all the murderous ideologies of the twentieth century. By sacrificing human life to serve their radical visions—by abandoning every value except the will to power—they will follow in the path of fascism, Nazism, and totalitarianism. And they will follow that path all the way to where it ends: in history's unmarked grave of discarded lies.

President Bush stated this would not be like the earlier war in Iraq, which had ended quickly, or like the air war above Kosovo, which involved no American casualties. Rather, it was going to be "a lengthy campaign, unlike any other we have ever seen." The president also again informed other nations they were either with the United States or against it and that those harboring or supporting terrorists would be regarded as hostile regimes.

Continuing the speech, he noted the only way to defeat terrorism was to "stop it, eliminate it, and destroy it where it grows." He then said, "The hour is coming when America will act, and you will make us proud." Seeking allies, he stated this was not just America's fight, but the fight of all who believed in freedom. He also stated that terrorist acts could not go unpunished. Shortly after this, he repeated that it would be "a long struggle." Continuing the speech, the president stated,

> The advance of human freedom—the great achievement of our time, and the great hope of every time—now depends on us. Our nation—this generation—will lift the dark threat of violence from our people and our future. We will rally the world to this cause by our efforts, by our courage. We will not tire, we will not falter, and we will not fail.

He then shifted the speech to the first person and said,

> I will not forget the wound to our country and those who inflicted it. I will not yield; I will not rest; I will not relent in waging this struggle for freedom and security for the American people. The course of this conflict is not known, yet its outcome is certain. Freedom and fear, justice and cruelty, have always been at war, and we know that God is not neutral between them.

Yawn, Three Thousand Dead and Nothing Changed

Although those in the mainstream media and politicians initially expressed their outrage over the 9/11 attacks in magazines, newspapers, and on television programs, they seemed to speak from the same script which condemned those who attacked "innocent" children, men, and women. There were demands for retaliation, all followed with a large asterisk calling for restraint and stressing the dangers of overreacting. And then there was the mandatory sentence noting that most Muslims were moderate and peaceful. [Question to self: What percent of Muslims are not "moderate and peaceful," and what is the critical percentage of non-moderate and non-peaceful Muslims that places us in danger? Some believe there are one billion Muslims. If "only" ten percent are "radical," that is one hundred million terrorists, which is a lot! And recent surveys of Muslim attitudes and beliefs are not encouraging. For example, twenty-five percent of Muslims living in England approved of the 7/7 bombings, and thirty percent would rather live under Islamic law than English law. Also, how does a "moderate" Muslim differ from a "radical" Muslim? Do both still believe in "death to infidels" and that the world would be "better off" under Islamic law? Is a moderate Muslim someone who supports and has the motivation for *jihad* but is simply out of ammo or is waiting for the call to *jihad*? Second question to self: Why do we need be reminded after every attack by Muslims that Islam is a religion of peace and that most Muslims are moderate and peaceful? If the attack had been committed by an atheist, Baptist, or Catholic, would the same disclaimer be used?]

And even with the nation having been attacked and living under the threat of further attacks, it soon became apparent that in some ways nothing had changed. That is, one-sided political correctness had to be rigorously followed. This was clearly demonstrated the Sunday after the attack when President Bush stepped out of the presidential helicopter and told Americans, "This crusade, this war on terrorism, is going to take awhile." There was outrage that President Bush had used the word *crusade*, a word some believed Muslims found offensive, a word that perhaps created fear in the Muslim community of another crusade. The director of the Council on American-Islamic Relations[16] (CAIR), which many credibly believe is a front for Muslim terrorist organizations, stated, "A lot of people think that America is out to get Islam anyway" and "we've got to be careful of the words we use." To most Americans, the word probably meant nothing more than a "vigorous or worthwhile campaign." However, there was a warning that if Muslims might find a word offensive, then the word was not to be used. Those who were so fast to respond to the word *crusade* should have realized that (1) the United States did not exist during the time of the Christian Crusades (c.1095-1221), (2) the Christian crusaders lost, which would seem to imply Muslims might have a positive image of a conflict Islam won, and (3) Islam has been engaged in a crusade or *jihad* for fourteen hundred years. No one seemed to ask if Americans were offended by the words *jihad* or "*Allahu Akbar*" and if Muslims needed to be careful about the words they used. By Tuesday, a spokesperson at the White House had apologized for the president's remark. [Note to self: Remember to see when President Roosevelt stopped using the term "Nazi" because Hitler found it offensive.]

For some inexplicable reason there was also a warning about comparing the sneak attack by the Japanese on Pearl Harbor on December 7, 1941, to the sneak attack by Muslims on September 11, 2001. Some were worried the comparison would make Americans believe the Japanese were involved with 9/11. Others claimed Japanese-Americans might be offended by bringing up Pearl Harbor.

Then as the shock of the attacks started to dissipate, those in the mainstream media reminded their listeners, readers, and viewers the United States is a colonialist, homophobic, imperialistic, intolerant, racist, repressive, and sexist country which lacks universal healthcare and, if not directly or indirectly responsible for the attacks, it was at least deserving of them. Those in the mainstream media did not seem to perceive the irony in castigating one of the most tolerant countries in the world, the United States, while seemingly defending Islamic countries, which are among the most colonialist, homophobic, imperialistic, intolerant, racist, repressive, and sexist countries in existence. And unlike the United States, where laws and public opinion tend to prevent the few who hold these views from acting on them, in Islamic countries these views and the actions they generate are not only legal, but also openly accepted. Thus, for example, in Islamic countries women hold second-class citizenship and homosexuals are imprisoned or executed.

In an attempt to prevent any military response to 9/11, thirty-six million individuals participated in three thousand "peace" rallies in the United States, Europe, and the Middle East. These were attended mostly by individuals who did not act or look very peaceful. The nightly news video clips shown by the mainstream media demonstrated that most of the protesters were not proponents of global warming since they burned items such as American flags and images of President Bush. Back in the United States there were reports of parents being revolted over displays of patriotism in schools attended by their children, and many in the mainstream media refused to wear lapel pins with the American flag, claiming it would bias their already blatantly biased reporting. Many apparently saw 9/11 as a series of four one-time attacks rather than the continuation of a fourteen hundred-year *jihad*. One Democratic senator called the attack nothing more than a "nuisance."

Root Cause?

Next came the search for the "root cause" of the attacks. For those in the mainstream media, the root cause needed to have three characteristics. First, the root cause needed to be something that most people would not understand and would, therefore, readily accept, especially if it was repeated and simplified. Eight examples of the first characteristic will be presented.

First, some claimed the cause of 9/11 went back to the post-World War I era and the collapse and dissolution of the Ottoman Empire after which the British and French created artificial boarders for artificial countries which did not take into account ethnic, religious, or tribal differences. Since few Americans have much of an understanding of the history of the Ottoman Empire or of World War I and its aftermath, this was an explanation many readily accepted. There was no need to mention the *jihad* had started long before World War I and its aftermath.

Second, others believed the root cause was the Western exploitation of Islamic countries. This exploitation was, of course, largely done by the wealthy oil companies, an easy target to hate given gasoline prices. Ignored was the fact many Islamic countries became wealthy as a result of requesting Western companies to find, extract, refine, transport, distribute, and sell products the Islamic countries did not know how to find, extract, refine, transport, distribute, or sell.

Third, the mandatory Christian Crusades as a root cause of 9/11 was popular, especially the sack of Jerusalem in 1096. In reality, the Christian Crusades were simply a delayed response by Christians to the Islamic "crusade" or the Islamic *jihad* which had started four hundred years earlier. By the time the Christian Crusades started, sixty percent of the Christian world had fallen under Islamic domination.

Third-world poverty in wealthy Islamic countries was provided as the fourth root cause of 9/11. This, of course, ignored the fact that many Muslims involved in *jihad* were anything but poverty-stricken and that the United States had provided billions of dollars in assistance to Islamic countries.

A fifth root cause was the presence of American (a.k.a. Christian) soldiers in Islamic countries such as Afghanistan, Iraq, and Saudi Arabia. It is probably a waste of effort examining the time sequence and realizing that most American troops were in Islamic countries because of the 9/11 attacks. Additionally, the *jihad* is global and occurs where there are Muslims, not necessarily where there are American soldiers.

The sixth alleged root cause was that there had not been enough dialogue. Our arrogance and sense of superiority contributed to a lack of dialogue which alienated the Muslim world. How many times was Yasser Arafat a guest in the White House under former President Bill Clinton? How many useless Middle Eastern conferences have been held? Given the number of "peace" conferences, the Middle East should be the most peaceful place on earth!

The seventh root cause was Islamic "cultural regression." The regression is generally attributed to being colonized by the West with Britain, France, and Italy mentioned as some of the colonizers. Omitted from the discussion is Islamic colonization such as that in Spain or that by the Ottoman Empire. Prior to "colonization" by the West, these Islamic areas were not exactly "progressive" in areas such as human rights, the treatment of women, or economic or scientific development. In fact, colonization provided the missing infrastructure which could have been used to modernize areas such as economic development, education, and scientific advancement. Left unexplained is how Jewish refugees arrived from war-torn Europe; settled in a barren, desolate, and oil-free area that was a "colony" of England; and in a matter of years turned Israel into a free, highly educated, and wealthy country.

If colonization was the root cause of 9/11, we should probably ask, "Why didn't colonized Native Americans fly planes into the WTC?" We could also ask why the United States left Kuwait after the First Gulf War without establishing it as a colony of the

United States. The United States left Kuwait after liberating it from a Muslim attempt to turn it into a colony. And establishing independent governments in Afghanistan and Iraq hardly seems like an act of colonization.

The eighth root cause is the United States' support of Israel. Certainly there is Muslim anger and jealousy toward Israel, which occupies a minuscule part of the total land mass of the Middle East and which has a small population in comparison to its "neighbors." After all, Israel has repeatedly and successfully defended itself from simultaneous attacks from multiple Muslim countries. In reality, Israel has been provided support by the United States because it supports our values such as freedom. And Israel has directed Islamic aggression away from the West by serving as a buffer zone between Islam and the West. Thus, instead of Muslims detonating themselves in shopping malls in mid-Western U.S. cities, they do so in Israel. So, yes, the United States does support Israel. When Islamic countries stop treating women like second-class citizens, stop chopping off hands, and stop posing a threat to our existence, then perhaps they will receive greater support.

Using the support of Israel by the United States as the cause of 9/11 has another major problem. The *jihad* did not start after the United States started supporting Israel in 1948, but fourteen hundred years earlier, circa 622. Additionally, one of the major Muslim "terrorist" or *jihad* organizations is the Muslim Brotherhood, which was created in 1928 and is the breeder of newer organizations such as al-Qaeda and Hamas. The Muslim Brotherhood has the following as its motto: "Allah is our objective. The prophet is our leader. The *Koran* is our law. *Jihad* is our way. Dying in the way of Allah is our highest hope."

Earlier, it was mentioned the root cause of 9/11 needed to have three characteristics for the mainstream media. The first characteristic, which was just examined, dealt with making the root cause simple to understand. The second characteristic of the root cause is it can be eliminated by a simple solution. For example, if the Christian Crusades were the source of 9/11, we can apologize—again. If poverty was the cause of 9/11, we can send more money to oil-rich Muslim countries or to oil-poor Muslim countries if oil-rich

Muslim countries will not help them. If American troops need to be withdrawn from Muslim countries, then they can be withdrawn. Or if the lack of dialogue is the problem, there can be more useless conferences.

Generally, the simplest solution has been to deny the existence of a problem and to revert back to a pre-9/11 mentality. After all, once it is admitted that a billion Muslims want non-Muslims converted, dead, or in subjugation, there is no longer a simple solution. In fact, the reality is too horrific to think about. Another simple solution has been to look at symptoms of the problem, such as terrorist attacks, rather than the cause of the problem, Islam.

The third characteristic of the root cause required by the mainstream media is that 9/11 should be seen as (1) a normal response by Muslims to past abuses by America and the West, (2) a normal response by Muslims to present abuses by America and the West, or (3) a normal response by Muslims to future abuses by America and the West. In other words, it is not the fault of Islam; it the fault of America and the West. Thus, for many the searches for the root cause only needed to look in one direction, offer one interpretation, and occur only at certain historical periods.

Thus, the mainstream media was on a foolish quest to find the cause for 9/11 rooted in some aspect of Western behavior and culture. The search would have been more productive if those in the mainstream media would have looked to Islam. For example, the *Koran* in verse 2:193 commands Muslims to "fight them until there is no more *Fitnah* (disbelief and worshiping of others along with Allah) and (all and every kind of) worship is for Allah (alone)." Or reading verse 9:5 might have helped in the search for the root cause of 9/11. It says, "Then kill the *Mushrikun* [idolaters, polytheists, disbelievers in the Oneness of Allah, pagans] wherever you find them, and capture them and besiege them, and lie in wait for them in every ambush." If these two quotes were not enough, then perhaps they should have looked at verse 9:29, which reads, "Fight against those who (1) believe not in Allah, (2) nor in the last Day, (3) nor forbid that which has been forbidden by Allah and His Messenger (Muhammad), (4) and those who acknowledge not the religion of truth (i.e., Islam) among the people of the Scripture (Jews and

Christians), until they pay the *Jizyah* [a high tax imposed on non-Muslims living under Islamic domination] with willing submission, and feel themselves subdued."

These commands and more than one hundred similar verses might have provided the mainstream media with some clue as to the real root cause of 9/11. If these quotes were not enough, they could have examined Muhammad's behavior and the instructions to his followers to fight against non-Muslims until they testify that none has the right to be worshiped but Allah and that Muhammad is his messenger. If this was still not sufficient, the mainstream media could have examined Islam's bloody fourteen hundred-year history.

Responding to 9/11

While less than a month after 9/11 those in the mainstream media were still looking for the root cause, Operation Infinite Justice was in the final stages of planning. Part of the planning involved changing the name of the operation since some believed it might be offensive to Muslims who believe that only the Islamic god can provide infinite justice. Thus, Operation Infinite Justice became Operation Enduring Freedom and started on October 7, 2001. [Note to self: When will we spend less time worrying about offending terrorists and more time killing them?]

President Bush was clear that the purpose of the Operation Enduring Freedom was to destroy al-Qaeda terrorist training camps and the Taliban leadership which supported them. This would prevent the future use of Afghanistan as a base for terrorist organizations. In a speech on October 7, 2001, President Bush stated, "The battle is now joined on many fronts. We will not waver, we will not tire, we will not falter, and we will not fail. Peace and freedom will prevail."

Literally as Operation Enduring Freedom started, the mainstream media was reminding its listeners, readers, and viewers that no invading army had ever conquered Afghanistan with the former Soviet Union mentioned as the most recent example. Thousands of U.S. soldiers and tens of thousands innocent Afghani civilian casualties were expected in a long, drawn-out war which would end in disaster for the United States.

On the same day as Operation Enduring Freedom started, former President Bill Clinton gave a "root cause of 9/11" speech at Georgetown University. In the speech he blamed the United States for the 9/11 attacks. First he noted "we" had mistreated Native Americans and had owned slaves. He then went on and blamed the Christian Crusades for the attacks when he said, "Indeed, in the first Crusade, when the Christian soldiers took Jerusalem, they first burned a synagogue with 300 Jews in it, and [then] proceeded to kill every woman and child who was Muslim on the Temple Mount. I can tell you that story is still being told today in the Middle East and we are still paying for it."

Many conservative writers responded to Clinton's speech, noting that many countries mistreated Native Americans, including Britain, France, and Spain. However, the worse treatment of Native Americans was by other Native Americans. Concerning slavery, well, many countries allowed slavery, including Islamic countries. The United States had one of the shortest legalized periods of slavery of any country in history and fought the Civil War, which ended with the elimination of slavery. Some Islamic countries still openly practice slavery: Mauritania and Sudan. In other Islamic countries, slavery is more covert: Niger, Oman, Saudi Arabia, and Yemen. Also, Muhammad, the prophet of Islam, was a slave-owner and slave-trader.

And if the Muslims are still angry about the slaughter on the Temple Mount after more than one thousand years, why aren't Jewish pilots crashing planes into buildings to protest the burning of the synagogue and the deaths of three hundred Jews? Concerning Clinton's speech, these writers also asked, "Why should the United States be held accountable for something that happened before Columbus discovered the New World, and the United States was founded?"

The mainstream media was not asking, "Why aren't those in the West angry about the Islamic conquest of the holiest cities of Christianity or the invasion and attempted colonization, conquest, and infestation of Europe?" The Christian Crusades were directed at regaining control over cities that had deep religious meaning to Christians. They were not designed to colonize or conquer Islam's holiest cities.

[Note to self: In ten weeks, about the time it took former President Clinton to finish his speech at Georgetown and hit on some women in the audience, the Taliban was in retreat and U.S. forces were in Kabul, which is Afghanistan's capital and largest city.]

What Next?

Unfortunately, as will be seen, there would soon be a series of second attacks on the United States.

CHAPTER 11: SECOND ATTACKS: MAINSTREAM MEDIA

Muslims have been waging *jihad* on Western Civilization and other non-Islamic cultures for fourteen hundred years. The earlier chapters examined Islam's holiest religious documents to illustrate the ideological basis for *jihad*. Later chapters examined the behavior of Muhammad, Islam's prophet, since all Muslims are obligated to follow in his path, which included numerous *jihads* against non-Muslims. Based on Islam's religious documents and the behavior of Muhammad, it was demonstrated that Muslims are obligated to wage *jihad* until the world has been placed under Islamic domination and Islamic law.

Thus, the attacks on 9/11 were nothing more than the continuation of the Islamic *jihad*, and they should have been a wake-up alarm to Americans that, because of better financing and organization, the *jihad* has expanded globally. Additionally, 9/11 should have awakened Americans to the reality that on a daily basis the *jihad* is also taking place culturally as Muslims attempt to place the world under Islamic domination.

With this reality staring Americans in the face, the question which emerges is, "Why have so many Americans returned to a pre-9/11 mentality?" After all, public support of the "war" in Afghanistan and Iraq has been minimal. The public views issues such as the economy, education, and healthcare as the most important political issues rather than an enemy that is obligated to convert, subjugate, or kill them.

Part of the answer to the question is that there was a series of second attacks shortly after 9/11. The second attacks were carried out to prevent the United States from responding to the Muslim terrorists attacks on 9/11 and to return Americans to a pre-9/11 mentality. This chapter and the following chapter will describe and provide examples of these second attacks.

Second Attacks: Mainstream Media

The mainstream media has aided, assisted, enabled, and supported the Islamic *jihad* against the United States. Although those in the mainstream media are primarily secular in terms of religion, they are generally opposed to any religion associated with the West and are, generally, in support of any ideology or religion which is opposed to the West. By filtering and manipulating the news, the mainstream media attempted to turn off the alarms triggered by 9/11 and to prevent the United States from defending itself.

There have been many techniques used by the mainstream media to turn off the "Muslims are coming" alarm. One technique has been the reluctance to associate Muslims with any aspect of terrorism. For example, while news reports provide detailed descriptions of the age, marital status, and occupation of suspected Muslim terrorists, the reports often fail to mention their religion. This is referred to as the missing "M" word. For example, the riots in France were not by "Muslim youth" but by youth who were "angry" "disenfranchised," "poor," or "un-assimilated." This "reporting" ignored the actual cause of the riots—Islam—and provided the Muslim rioters the role of victim.

The "covering for Muslims" by the mainstream media started shortly after 9/11. One example occurred in 2002, with the "Beltway Snipers." Although one of the snipers had converted to Islam twenty years earlier, some in the mainstream media used his pre-Muslim name, John Allen Williams, rather than his Islamic name, John Muhammad. Five years after the attacks, a TV special on the snipers ignored Islam as a possible motive for the attacks and focused on child abuse and marital problems as the source for the serial murders. Ignored were the notes by the snipers stating they were "servants of

Allah" and "we will kill all in *jihad...Allahu Akbar.*" Also ignored were the demands for Islamic meals and copies of the *Koran.*

A Muslim who wanted to blow up a shopping mall was initially characterized as someone with possible "ideological motivations." Note the substitution of the word *ideological* for *religious.* Other stories have stressed the troubled backgrounds of terrorists rather than their religious backgrounds. And sometimes clues that would establish the religious identity of the individual, such as the individual's name or country of origin, are simply missing. In the last case it is simply a mystery as to why suicide bombers in the Middle East target Jewish men, women, and children. Or why someone in the United States would go to a Jewish center or an Israeli airline counter and start killing people while shouting "*Allahu Akbar.*" Equally mysterious is why Muslim drivers run over non-Muslim pedestrians in San Francisco or non-Muslim students in North Carolina. The liberal media reassures Americans that all of these instances are "isolated" and not part of a larger pattern. Some have referred to acts such as these as resulting from the "sudden *jihad* syndrome," where "normal" Muslims suddenly become violent.

There has been one additional missing "M" word, namely "mosque," and no mention of the hate-filled, radical literature and videos, and of the venomous and vile rants of the *imans.*

In addition to the missing "M" words, there has also been the missing "I" word, or "Islam." In searching for the root cause of 9/11, every aspect of a terrorist's life is examined except religion. The official announcement after an attack with a car bomb in England was that the attack could have been carried out by anyone, even though the terrorist was filmed fleeing from a flaming car yelling *Allahu Akbar.* This denial of reality continued when there was an alert about possible "dry runs" by terrorists probing for weaknesses in airline security. In testing the security system, these potential terrorists placed blocks of cheese, similar to blocks of explosives, with cell phones taped to them in their carry-on luggage. When this information was released, many wanted to know about the characteristics of owners of the luggage, specifically their religious affiliation. In other words, "Are those pesky Amish at it again?" The information released was that the potential terrorists were "diverse" and included both males and females.

In August 2006, President Bush used the term "Islamic fascist," which was met with howls of outrage for suggesting Islam might have violent individuals. The mainstream media often omits words such as *Islamic* or *Muslim* and replaces them with words such as *freedom fighter*, *fundamentalist*, *insurgent*, or *terrorist*.

Other examples can be seen in the terminology frequently used to describe the war. It is generally portrayed as a "war on terrorism." Many have reported that terrorism is obviously nothing more that a technique of waging war. World War II was not a war against the Nazi *Blitzkrieg* or against Japanese airplanes for their attack on Pearl Harbor. Rather, it was a war against specific countries, which is in some ways easier to fight than a war against a geographically diverse and violent ideology. When countries go to war with other countries, and where soldiers have uniforms, the enemy is easier to identify and to engage. This is obviously a new type of war with a diffused and diverse enemy, many of whom have selectively "integrated" into Western societies. To win the war, it is necessary to recognize the "cause" of the war and to call the enemy by name. The sensitivity to this issue can be seen in that allegedly one Western world leader has prohibited the use of the words "Islam" and "terrorism" in the same sentence.

Obviously words matter and certainly there has been discussion on how to define the war. Part of the "sensitivity" may be nothing more than an attempt to make it a war against a dictator or a repressive group rather than against a religion. As has been seen in Afghanistan and Iraq, thousands of Muslims actively assist American soldiers because they want their families to be able to live in freedom and peace.

Some History

The bias of the mainstream media can be seen in many ways. In President Bush's State of the Union speech on January 30, 2002, he stated Iraq was part of the "axis of evil," and by seeking weapons of mass destruction (WMD), it posed a "grave and growing danger." He continued stating the "price of indifference would be catastrophic." He stressed that he would not wait for Iraq to become an imminent threat before acting. During the president's speech, he said British intelligence had informed him Saddam Hussein had attempted to get uranium (yellowcake) from Niger. Shortly after the speech, the mainstream media spent weeks disputing this claim. Later there were accusations the Bush Administration had revealed the identity of a CIA agent. Both of these insignificant issues received endless attention from the mainstream media. Ultimately, it was concluded that Saddam had tried to obtain uranium and the Bush administration had not revealed the identity of the CIA agent.

In October 2002, more than a year after 9/11, the U.S. Congress approved a resolution to go to war with Iraq. The war started on March 20, 2003, more than eighteen months after 9/11. By the time the invasion of Iraq started, the climate for war in the United States had dramatically changed, and for most Americans 9/11 had become a distant memory with the only lingering consequence the necessity of leaving a little earlier for air flights. In fact, many had returned to a pre-9/11 mentality. Part of the change in the climate for war was because the mainstream media had stopped presenting images of 9/11. Gone were the images of the collapsing World Trade Center (WTC) towers and of the smoldering ruins in Washington and a Pennsylvania field. Gone were the images of men and women pressed against windows in the WTC, confronted with the unimaginable horror of burning or of jumping to their deaths. Gone were the images of the workers at the smoldering ruins of ground zero collecting family, friends, neighbors, and strangers piece by piece in plastic sandwich bags. In fact, one could say Americans had developed a collective amnesia of 9/11, or they had developed the Scarlett O'Hara Syndrome: "I can't think about that right now. If I do, I'll go crazy. I'll think about that tomorrow."

Well, it is tomorrow, and the United States and other non-Islamic countries are at war with a seventh century ideology that wants to destroy much of what we believe in, such as freedom. Part of the amnesia may simply be this is "too horrible" to think about. At least during the Cold War between the West and the former Soviet Union, both sides recognized "war" would bring about total mutual destruction. For the atheistic Soviets who were attempting to create "heaven on earth," this meant "winning" the war left them dead and with no place to go. Those in the West also realized mutual destruction was not an acceptable option, although for more humanitarian reasons. Thus, the United States and the former Soviet Union fought World War III with surrogate wars in places such as Korea, Vietnam, and Afghanistan. Today we are confronted by an enemy that is not constrained by the "too horrible to think about scenario."

Unable to prevent the war in Iraq with biased reporting, the mainstream media abandoned any pretense of balanced news reporting after the war started. The war was deemed a failure before any combat operations had taken place, when the American public was informed it would be too costly in lives and money, no doubt similar to the news reports issued in December 1941. From the first day combat operations started, the mainstream media had little but negative reports. Initially, the troops advanced too rapidly and, thus, were outpacing their supplies. Then, after a sandstorm halted the advance, the war was deemed a "quagmire" and the advance had "run out of steam." After this came the concerns about the possible war-related damage to archaeological or religious sites. When Bagdad fell in the shortest and probably least costly war in U.S. history, there were complaints that in relegating a dictator and his murdering, raping, torturing thugs into hiding, disarming an army, restoring basic services, and maintaining order, the American troops had not taken time to prevent the alleged looting of the National Museum of Baghdad. [Note to self: Does it seem ironic that the greatest achievements of Iraq are in a museum with relics from the Persian Empire, which Islam destroyed?]

Having been wrong on the length of the war and the number of casualties, the mainstream media now proclaimed the aftermath of the war was not going as planned, as if the aftermath of most wars went according to some pre-war plan. The war did end earlier than expected, which meant many fanatical Muslims were not killed and, thus, reemerged as terrorists. It also meant the U.S. military had to develop new equipment and tactics to fight the enemy, which it did successfully.

Another example of the attack by the mainstream media deals with Jessica Lynch, the American soldier who was captured early in the war. When she was rescued from captivity, the mainstream media reported the well-planned and orchestrated military operation as little more than a publicity stunt.

Additional coverage of the post-war occupation in Iraq focused endlessly on fraternity-style pranks at a prison, with Senator Teddy Kennedy proclaiming, "Saddam's torture chambers had reopened under new management, U.S. management." [Note to self: Was leaving Mary Jo in the backseat of a submerged Oldsmobile to drown, suffocate, or be "water-boarded" a form of torture, while the lifeguard of Chappaquiddick—and the liberal moral compass of the Senate—ran, hid, and called his lawyer?] After the prison episode, U.S. soldiers found real torture chambers operated by al-Qaeda. These stories had everything the mainstream media loves for a headline, such as blood and guts. The torture chambers included instruction booklets with pictures of how to torture using everyday devices such as blow torches, electric drills, hammers, and meat cleavers. And one of the torture chambers had five victims, and others had mass graves of the victims. The mainstream media was basically mute on these discoveries and on the verses of the *Koran* inscribed on the walls to motivate the Muslim torturers. However, alleged massacres by U.S. soldiers received a great deal of attention until they were debunked, after which the stories were largely ignored. Conservative writers have continued to be amazed at the willingness of the mainstream media to believe the distortions and lies about U.S. soldiers while ignoring almost daily unbelievably horrific atrocities by our enemy.

When President Bush landed on the aircraft carrier U.S.S. Abraham Lincoln in May 2003 while it was on its way home from the war, a banner flew with the words "Mission Accomplished." There was seemingly more anger from the mainstream media about this banner than about all of Saddam Hussein's atrocities from the time he came to power. It should be mentioned that the mainstream media knew about Saddam Hussein's atrocities but elected not to cover them. The previous sentence could be rephrased to read, "But elected to cover them up." It is fascinating that to keep a news office in Iraq, the mainstream media could not report on the news in Iraq. Anyway, nitpicking continued over whether the mission was really accomplished since there was still violence taking place.

The mainstream media was outraged after Secretary of Defense Donald Rumsfeld responded to a soldier's question, planted by a reporter, concerning the alleged lack of armor on vehicles. He said an army goes to war with the equipment it has. Rumsfeld was correct in his statement. If a nation did not go to war until it had the equipment needed, it would be conquered before it had a chance to go to war. Because each war and enemy is different, it is difficult to know what is needed until fully engaged. As we have seen in other wars, Americans have the unique ability of rapid innovation in both equipment and tactics to win wars.

Next was the claim the Patriot Act would result in violations of civil liberties. The ability to examine the list of books checked out of a library seemed to be the major criticism of the act. Basically, the Patriot Act allows the use of tactics against terrorists that are currently being used against those involved in organized crime. This is obviously a complex area which can be summarized as: civil rights can be infringed on, or we can be dead, in which case we don't need civil rights.

When the facts did not meet the anti-war agenda of the mainstream media, they openly used photographers and reporters who supported Muslim terrorist activities. This resulted in distorted or fabricated news stories and fake photographs which were all negative to the United States. Since the fake stories and photographs supported the mainstream media's liberal, anti-Bush, anti-war agenda, there was little reason for the mainstream media to question these sources.

Even "positive" stories were given a negative slant. For example, the emphasis on U.S. soldiers rebuilding a school was that it would now attract terrorists. Another example of the good news turned into bad news dealt with the decline in Iraqi deaths from terrorist activities in late 2007. Rather than portraying this as good news, the headlines were that there was unemployment among grave diggers who buried the terrorists' victims and among the taxi drivers who took the bereaved to and from the morgues. Amazingly, in late 2007 when the surge in American troops was clearly working, one of the mainstream media news organizations announced there was "no news from Iraq today." The announcement should have been that there were no American casualties, no car bombings, and the wonderful news was that America is winning the war!

Another example of good news becoming bad news deals with Ayman al-Zawahiri, the Muslim terrorist who was second-in-command to Osama bin Laden (OBL) in the leadership of al-Qaeda in Iraq and who personally beheaded hostages. The failure to capture or kill him was seen by the mainstream media as allowing him to continue to plan death and destruction in Iraq. The failure to capture or kill him was seen as a blunder by our inept troops, and it was stated that killing or capturing him would be a "major victory." However, after he was killed, the storyline was that his death was going to "enrage the insurgency," his death was "not very important," and his death would "increase the danger for U.S. troops."

There was a similar response when terrorist mastermind Imad Mughniyeh was killed in 2008. His death went largely unnoticed in the mainstream media, and one Western reporter even said the reaction to his death was "mixed."

Although the mainstream media was against the war, it could also be for the war if it could develop a negative slant to a story. For example, when a leaked memo revealed a raid on an al-Qaeda camp had been aborted, the mainstream media, which should have been jubilant the raid was aborted and no Muslim terrorists were killed, reported the story as a "missed opportunity."

Even a decrease in the deaths of U.S. service personnel was seen negatively. This was illustrated when a twenty-five percent decrease in total U.S. deaths in Iraq was reported as a thirty-six percent increase in deaths in one area.

There is one additional technique used by the mainstream media to further its agenda. Basically, numbers are used when they are useful. Thus, when there are increases in the number of deaths or roadside bombings, these figures are reported. However, when numbers are no longer useful, such as when deaths or roadside bombing decrease, the mainstream media relies on criticism, which cannot be measured. For example, they claim the war is creating more terrorists.

There are numerous other examples of the biased reporting. One recent headline was "U.S. and Iraqi Forces Raid Lollipop Factory." While technically correct, the former candy factory had been converted into a bomb-making factory. Inside the "factory" were tons of bomb-making materials. The factory was also equipped with an anti-aircraft gun on the roof.

The discoveries and breakups in the United States of terrorist plots to attack building, military bases, and airports are not given much attention by the mainstream media. And when the mainstream media actually covers the breakup of terrorist plots, the threats are often minimized. For example, the reports stress the plot was not very far along without mentioning that at one time the 9/11 plot had not been very far along. The plot to blow up the U.S.S. The Sullivans failed because it was not very far along, and the small boat filled with explosives sank. However, nine months later, the same plot was further along, with a bigger boat, and it succeeded in killing and wounding scores of service men and women and in almost sinking the U.S.S. Cole.

The Muslim terrorist threat has also been minimized by mentioning the physical structures that would be attacked, such as buildings and pipelines, and by not mentioning the number of people who would be in these buildings or near the pipelines during an attack.

Further attempts to minimize the threats portray the terrorists in one of three ways. First, the Muslim terrorists are portrayed as individuals who are not very smart, with the minimum I.Q. for using a box cutter not being specified. One of the Muslim terrorists involved in the first attack on the WTC in 1993 is often used as an example of an individual in the "not very smart" category. This individual was arrested when he returned to obtain his deposit on the rental truck which had carried the bomb that exploded inside the WTC. Thus, this "not very bright" individual had helped to successfully carry out the first attack on the WTC.

Recent attacks by Muslim terrorists have demonstrated the "not very smart" category does not apply to many Muslim terrorists since an analysis of their backgrounds has revealed advanced levels of education. Then they are characterized in the second way, namely as "crackpots" or "bungling fools." Unfortunately, the mainstream media also often reveals how these crackpots bungled their attempts at terrorism so that future bungling Muslim crackpot terrorists would have a higher probability of being non-bungling Muslim crackpot terrorists.

The third characterization of terrorists is as victims. Reports mention, for example, they are divorced, or they have not recently seen their children. Or perhaps at one time they were homeless. Sympathy must have been the intent of the article dealing with a Muslim terrorist who was removed from an airplane while on his way to a religious conference. The article seemed to be hinting he should have been allowed to attend the conference and then hauled off to jail. Another recent article showed Muslim terrorists as "family men." The article was complete with photographs of the terrorists relaxing at home with their children after a hard day of maiming and murdering. One photograph showed a terrorist walking hand in hand with his daughter, and another showed a terrorist in front of a television with his daughter on his lap. [Note to self: In a few years remember to look for articles about these Muslim terrorists performing honor murders of these daughters.]

Two Muslim college students were portrayed in sympathetic terms after being arrested with pipe bombs. The pipe bombs were referred to as "fire crackers," and readers were told the students were afraid of what might happen to them. One student said he was worried he would not be released from prison until after his father, who lived in the Middle East, had died.

The 2007 arrest of a Muslim medical student in Michigan around the anniversary of 9/11 generated little national coverage. This was even though the student was arrested wearing dark clothing, with camouflage paint on his face, carrying a loaded semi-automatic weapon, and he had just entered on his web page that he was going to start his personal *jihad.* Officials downplayed the incident because they were concerned the public might overreact or that it might turn into something about terrorism. [Note to self: How much publicity would this have received had the individual been an abortion clinic protestor or the member of a local militia?]

The mainstream media has also anxiously waited for any negative milestone, especially those involving military fatalities, as if each arbitrary milestone marks the failure of the war. For example, it anxiously waited for and responded quickly when the number of military war deaths exceeded the number killed on 9/11. The connection between almost three thousand civilians being killed by Muslim terrorists in the United States and three thousand soldiers being killed in Afghanistan and Iraq is uncertain, although almost certainly it was intended to convey the idea this was a negative milestone. Some in the mainstream media were so enamored with this "milestone" that rather than reporting the total number killed, some initially started reporting the number killed in excess of those killed on 9/11. [Note to self: Remember to look for similar news reports in late 1941 or early 1942 stating when the number of military deaths exceeded the number killed at Pearl Harbor.]

The mainstream media's fascination with milestones only relates to certain milestones. For example, toward the end of 2007, the mainstream media missed coverage of another milestone, namely the ten thousandth attack by Muslim terrorists since 9/11. These attacks have left approximately sixty thousand dead and ninety thousand injured.[17]

The mainstream media has also tried to divert attention from Islam as a cause of 9/11 by focusing on distorted, fabricated, or real instances of violence by Jews and Christians. The typical line has been that many religions have committed acts of violence. For Jews, the section in Deuteronomy (20:16-18) is cited where God ordered the Hebrews (c. 1,200 B.C.) to destroy several cities and to let "nothing that breathes remain alive." The Hebrews did as God ordained about three thousand years ago (Joshua 10:40). What the critics failed to mention was this God-given order related to a specific group at a specific time. In contrast, the Islamic *jihad* is open-ended in terms of group, place, and time. Essentially, any non-Muslim group can be subjected to the *jihad* at any time and in any place. As has been seen, there are numerous commands for Muslims to convert, subjugate, or kill non-Muslims.

For Christianity, the Crusades are frequently mentioned as one of its violent episodes. The Christian Crusades were simply a four hundred-year delayed response to the Islamic crusade, or *jihad.* The Crusades were an attempt to regain control over some of the holiest cities in Christianity, not to conquer the holy cities or land of Islam. Nor were they attempting to convert, kill, or subjugate non-Christians. The crusaders knew some of the violence they committed was not sanctioned by Christianity and they would ultimately have to answer for these acts. In fact, popes excommunicated many crusaders, sentencing them to an eternity in hell for some of their actions. The contrast between Christianity and Islam is simple: Christian Crusaders were sentenced to hell for committing atrocities, but the same actions guarantee Islamic *jihadists* immediate entry into paradise.

Next came the mainstream media's obsession with the failure to find weapons of mass destruction (WMDs). The list of politicians proclaiming their existence both pre- and post-war was extensive, and it includes former President Clinton and Vice President Gore as well as Senators Clinton, Edwards, Kennedy, Kerry, and Levin. Also conveniently forgotten is the fact that WMDs were only one of the reasons for going to war, and that each of the twenty-three resolutions for going to war was sufficient in and of itself. Thus, many criticized the war by distorting the basis for the war. Ignored was the fact Saddam Hussein had used chemical weapons at least ten times against his own people. Also, when sarin- and mustard gas-filled projectiles were found, they were dismissed as pre-Gulf War weapons and of no importance, even though Iraq was obligated to notify U.N. inspectors of their presence and destroy them.

Next the mainstream media focused on the failure to find OBL. The claim was that the search for him had been diverted by the war in Iraq, and if we had concentrated our efforts on finding OBL, then terrorism would end and harmony and peace would be restored. Few bothered pointing out that the allies won World War II even though they did not focus their efforts on finding Hitler and, in fact, never did find him. Also, OBL seems to have been relegated to a cave where he makes grainy and increasing incoherent videotapes and knows that making any electronic transmission will almost certainly be followed by a series of smart bombs.

Then there was the claim that U.S. soldiers were fighting in the wrong country and they should be in Afghanistan, Osama bin Laden's (OBL) former base, not Iraq. This claim left out two important items. First, shortly after 9/11 President Bush stated he wanted to protect the homeland, take the war to the enemy overseas, and spread freedom in the Middle East, which he hoped would take root and help to eradicate terrorism. Second, the U.S. Congress voted to support this plan. [Note to self: Wasn't FDR's first land attack in North Africa? Was FDR criticized because he did not immediately attack Japan?]

The biased and selective presentation by the mainstream media has created a negative attitude about the war among many Americans. After all, the mainstream media focuses on causalities, mistakes, scandals, and setbacks rather than on successes. The mainstream media seems to want an immediate retreat from what President Bush has stated is going to be a "long-term conflict." In some ways, this is similar to the American Civil War. By late summer 1864, the war had become very unpopular in the north. The death toll of Union soldiers was close to three hundred thousand which, if adjusted for the increase in population, would correspond to three million deaths today. In addition to the dead, there were thousands more Union soldiers who were horribly maimed or dying in Confederate prisoner of war camps. The platform of the Democratic Party in 1864 is very similar to its platform in 2008. They believe the war is lost, but that we should support the troops. In 1864, there were calls for peace, and the Democratic candidate for president was former General McClellan, who had been one of Lincoln's first commanders in the war. McClellan wanted some type of settlement with the Confederacy. President Lincoln could not bring himself to a settlement and the break-up of the United States. Fortunately, Union victories in early fall 1864 brought the realization that a successful conclusion to the war was close and talk of a settlement ceased.

The bias of the mainstream media can be seen in other ways. For example, there was a series of leaks about antiterrorism activities, much of which was published by the liberal, treacherous, and treasonous *New York Times* (*NYT*). Some of the leaks concerned ways the government tracked the financial transactions of terrorists. Others dealt with CIA interrogation methods, secret CIA prisons, and NSA wiretapping. Also, highly sensitive information on the vulnerability of certain areas, such as the Hudson River tunnels, to terrorist attacks was published. [Note to self: How many American soldiers needlessly died as a result of the release of this material? And why is it those in the mainstream media did not have a problem leaking sensitive information, but they were outraged when they incorrectly believed the name of a CIA agent was leaked by the Bush Administration?]

Toward the end of 2007, the mainstream media was outraged about the destruction of videotapes showing the water-boarding of two Muslim terrorists. It is somewhat uncertain if the outrage was over the destruction of the tapes or the destruction of the tapes before they had been leaked to and shown by the mainstream media. These tapes would have illustrated an ugly part of war and turned Muslim terrorists into victims. Although the blatant left-wing bias of the mainstream media has refused to show images of 9/11, it almost certainly would have shown images of the water-boarding. [Note to self: Can Muslim terrorists be water-boarded if they are fasting? Or would swallowing water nullify the fast?]

Not only has the mainstream media willingly assisted the enemy by providing information that would aid them in attacking the United States, but there are other instances where it has refused to provide assistance that might prevent future attacks. One example occurred in Seattle when the FBI requested information on two men who had been seen on the Washington State Ferries exhibiting "unusual behavior." One FBI official reported that rather than taking the typical types of photographs, they were seen photographing locked doors to sensitive areas on the ferries. In an attempt to resolve the issue, the FBI requested that newspapers publish photographs of the two men whose behavior it noted might be innocent. However, many refused to publish the photographs. Of course, there were cries of anti-Muslim and anti-Arab profiling even though the religion and ethnicity of the men were unknown. Al-Qaeda has previously selected ferries as targets, and two ferry attacks have recently taken place in the Philippines.

The mainstream media then demanded an exit strategy with a specific timetable. This defeat or retreat would be called "redeployment." It is difficult to imagine a timetable being developed during World War II for the return of the Pacific Fleet. And it is difficult to imagine General Patton being told his time was up and to turn around and return home. [Note to self: In 1945, shortly before the atomic bombs were dropped on Japan, American soldiers had the slogan "Golden Gate in '48." With the anticipated invasion of Japan, they expected winning the war would take time, not a timetable.]

Next came the suggestion that Iraq would have been better off under Saddam's leadership than under American occupation. The rationale was Saddam had kept the violence among the various factions in Iraq under control. The logic here seemed strange since Saddam engaged in mass murder, including the use of weapons of mass destruction to keep the various factions in Iraq under control. Thus, "secretly" massacring individuals was acceptable, while terrorists' publically massacring individuals was not acceptable.

Several individuals have had articles asking, "What if the mainstream media had reported on World War II in the same way it reports on the war on terrorism?" The basic question is, "Would we have won the war?" Too often the mainstream media has provided stories without context. The stories have dealt with the deaths and maiming of American soldiers, but they have failed to ask how these losses moved us closer to winning the war. President Bush has delivered numerous speeches where he has laid out our long-term strategy and how each operation moved us closer to our goal. The mainstream media has largely refused to cover the speeches.

Another attempt at ending the war by the mainstream media has been the unsubstantiated claim that fighting and killing terrorists is simply creating more terrorists, and if U.S. troops left Iraq, the terrorists would also leave. There was no comment on where the terrorists would go or if the terrorists would become emboldened by the retreat. There seems to be no recognition by the mainstream media that part of the rationale in attacking Iraq was to draw terrorists from around the world to one place—not the United States—where they could be killed.

Recently, several writers have noticed the heroes of the war have been largely ignored. Now, thanks to the mainstream media, we are more likely to know the names of those involved in a minor prison scandal or the names of anti-war protesters than of American military heroes. During World War II, the military heroes went on publicity tours and raised millions of dollars to support the war effort. Today few know the names of the heroes of Afghanistan and Iraq. Five who have received the Medal of Honor are Army Sergeant Paul R. Smith, Marine Corporal Jason L. Dunham, Navy Seals Michael Monsoor, Lt. Michael Murphy, and Army Pfc. Ross McGinnis. Corporal Dunham was killed on the same day as Pat Tillman, the former pro football player who believed defending his country was more important than playing professional football. Corporal Tillman died as the result of "friendly fire," a tragic but unavoidable occurrence in war. Corporal Dunham died by jumping on an explosive device which shielded his fellow soldiers from certain death. Both were heroic young men, but who do Americans know most about, Corporal Dunham or Corporal Tillman? Obviously Corporal Tillman since there were two aspects of his death the mainstream media could exploit: First, the friendly fire aspect, and second, the "cover-up" of his death. The friendly fire aspect made it seem as though his heroism and sacrifice were in vain. They were not! Then the mainstream media was outraged it took a little over a month for the military to complete its investigation and announce Corporal Tillman had been killed by friendly fire. One month to complete an investigation and announce the results is not an unreasonable amount of time—except to the mainstream media.

There was a similar lack of interest by the mainstream media when Lt. Michael Murphy was posthumously awarded the Medal of Honor. Although Lt. Murphy was from New York's Long Island, initially the *NYT* did not carry the story but did find room for a story on a military inquiry into civilian deaths in Afghanistan. Lt. Murphy and three members of his team had been sent to assassinate an al-Qaeda leader but were discovered by goat herders before they could accomplish their mission. They discussed killing the goat herders since they were probably members of al-Qaeda or, as a minimum, al-Qaeda informants and supporters. Thus, the goat herders threatened the completion of the mission as well as the lives of Lt. Murphy and his colleagues. Ultimately, they decided against killing the unarmed "civilians" and let them go. The goat herders immediately informed al-Qaeda operatives of the presence of the American soldiers, and within hours the four men were being attacked by hundreds of al-Qaeda fighters. Three of the four men, including Lt. Murphy, were killed. This story, detailed in the book *Lone Survivor* (2007) by Luttrell and Robinson, was largely ignored by the mainstream media because it did not fit the image they have of American soldiers.

When it was announced by the White House that Navy Seal Michael Monsoor would be awarded the Medal of Honor posthumously, the announcement was largely greeted with silence.

Feminists who seem to look for any imaginary, mediocre, or mundane accomplishments of women to publicize have not mentioned Leigh Ann Hester and Monica Brown, the first women to be awarded the Silver Star since World War II.

There were other attempts by the mainstream media to undermine the war. One was to label it a "civil war" in which the United States had no right to participate. When the civil war label proved false, it became an "unwinnable quagmire." After the "surge" made it a winnable war, the mainstream media defined the dying gasp of the enemy as resurgence by the enemy.

As both the military and political news from Iraq improved and could not be ignored, coverage of the war disappeared from the front pages of most newspapers. It was replaced by the consequences of the war in the United States. First, there were claims the trauma of the war was producing an astronomical suicide rate among returning veterans. This was easily and rapidly debunked. Next was the claim the war-crazed returning veterans were engaging in massive criminal activity after returning from the war. Again, within hours this was demonstrated to be false, and it was shown that the crime rate of returning veterans was a fraction of non-veterans. Still hoping to end the war, the mainstream media finally focused on its cost. There were claims the war was diverting money from education and healthcare. There was no attempt to compare the cost of the war with the cost of 9/11 or a series of 9/11s.

Another "whitewash" by the mainstream media deals with Islamic behaviors such as "honor murders." One recent murder in Canada was that of a sixteen-year-old girl who was strangled by her father for dressing "too Western." One of her offenses was refusing to wear the head scarf, the *hijab*. Her refusal to obey her father meant she was an out of control female who had to be killed to protect the family "honor." She had told her friends she was afraid of her father, and she had sought refuge in women's shelters. After being lured back home by someone she thought she could trust, her father strangled her with her *hijab*. The headline of her story was "Canadian teen dies: Father charged." A Muslim spokesperson stated, "I don't want the public to think that this is really an Islamic issue or an immigrant issue; it is a teenager issue." Another report stated it was an example of domestic violence which cuts across Canadian society and is blind to color, creed, ethnicity, race, or religion. And, of course, some blamed a racist Canada for the tension it creates in Muslim families.

Another honor murder in Canada was that of a fourteen-year-old girl whose uncle had raped her. Since she was not married and no longer a virgin, she had dishonored the family and had to be strangled by her father and brother to preserve "family honor."

There have been numerous other reports of honor murders in Western societies. At least twenty-five have recently been discovered in England. And in the United States the first reported honor murders of two teenage sisters have taken place. Most honor murders go unreported because of the closed nature of many Muslim communities and because the mainstream media is so politically correct it cannot attack a "protected group" no matter how vile the behavior.

In addition to the distortions of what is covered in the mainstream media, we also need to examine what is not covered. One example deals with the trial of the Holy Land Foundation. This trial dealt with the funding of Islamic terrorism both in and out of the United States through the Holy Land Foundation. Essentially, the mainstream media largely ignored reporting on this story. Also, Islam receives a "pass" from the mainstream media on its history of slavery. In the West there is collective white guilt and discussions of reparations. Ignored is the fact that almost twice as many blacks were taken from Africa to Islamic countries as were taken to the West in the trans-Atlantic slave trade. Yet blacks are a major source of converts to Islam. The issue of slavery has recently come into focus because Muslims living in the United States have been found to keep servants in their homes in "slave-like conditions." After being sentenced to a long prison term, one "slave owner" stated in his defense he had not committed a crime and that the United States was criminalizing "basic Muslim behaviors."

Another example of the bias of the mainstream media occurred in 2007 when two networks refused to run advertisements supporting the war. Later in the year they refused to run advertisements thanking U.S. servicemen and women for their service in the war. The advertisements also encouraged the American public to show their appreciation for the sacrifices servicemen and women have made on behalf of the U.S. One commentator noted, "Sometimes you cannot buy freedom of speech."

Recently, there has been another attempt to keep everyone on the same "What—me? Worry?" page. This occurred after the failed attempt by Muslim terrorists to destroy several large commercial airplanes over the Atlantic Ocean. In response to the planned attack, President Bush commented on the ongoing "war with Islamic fascists." He was immediately condemned for being insensitive, and his remarks were deemed "counterproductive." And when President Bush compared the current war to the war in Vietnam, an editorial in the *NYT* called the comparison "bizarre." Since the war started, the *NYT* has published more than three thousand such "bizarre comparisons."

An article in *City Journal* reported that shortly after the invasion of Iraq, fifty percent of the news stories were negative. Six months after the start of the war in Iraq, the percentage of negative stories increased to seventy-seven. By 2004, the percentage was eighty-nine. And by the spring of 2006, an amazing ninety-four percent of the stories were negative. Is it any wonder public opinion on the war has been negative?

Decisions need to be made on the basis of accurate information, not the blatant, biased, one-dimensional, one-sidedness of the mainstream media. Certainly, the Internet and more balanced news sources such as Fox News provide alternative views. However, there is a new trend emerging to censor these "alternative views." A number of individuals have reported that websites such as *Dhimmi* Watch, Hot Air, *Jihad* Watch, and the Middle East Media Research Institute are blocked at the organizations where they work. However, pro *jihad* sites such as that of the Council of American Islamic Relations (CAIR) were readily available. Individual organizations were not singling out websites to allow or block. Thus, it was being done by the Internet providers for these organizations.

Television and movies have also assisted in the second attacks on the United States. Recently, PBS refused to air one episode of the series *America at a Crossroad* titled "Islam vs. Islamists" largely because of complaints from Muslim organizations. Later, PBS made the program available to its stations as a "stand-alone program," meaning stations had the option to show or not show the program. Fox News eventually aired the program.

However, earlier PBS had aired the program *Muhammad: Legacy of a Prophet*, which was a "sanitized" biography. It even offered justification for the genocide of a Jewish tribe where Muhammad had six hundred to nine hundred men beheaded and the women and children sold into slavery. Meanwhile, CBC has hired a Muslim consultant to make certain its programs do not in any way insult Islam.

As the sixth anniversary of 9/11 approached, many asked when ABC would release its five-hour mini-series *The Path to 9/11* on DVD. Some believe Muslim organizations blocked the release while others claim it was Bill and Hillary Clinton since the documentary-drama portrays the Clinton administration's inept handling of terrorism.

In 2007, CNN aired a three-part series titled *God's Warriors*, with a part on Christian, Islamic, and Jewish warriors. One review said the parts on Christian and Jewish warriors could have been written by OBL. The part on Islamic warriors had a series of apologists who claimed they were fighting against oppression.

Movies such as *Kingdom of Heaven* have predictable leftist Hollywood formulas. One leading historian on the Crusades summarized *Kingdom of Heaven* as "rubbish." Another said it was OBL's view of history. It was also called *Kingdom of B.S.* The makers of the film *Crossing Over* removed the scene of an "honor murder" presumably because of objections from Muslims. Scenes offensive to Christians and Jews remained in the film.

The BBC dropped a fictional terrorist attack by Muslims in an episode of *Casualty* to "avoid offending Muslims." Animal rights terrorists were substituted. The same trend occurred with Tom Clancy's novel, *The Sum of all Fears*, where the Iranian-Palestinian terrorists in the novel were transformed into Neo-Nazi Austrians in the film.

Muslim groups in Western countries have been very effective with their propaganda. After 9/11 there were stories about hate crimes against Muslims or about Muslim men being singled out for extra scrutiny when boarding airplanes. Additionally, some of the more vocal critics of Islam have been sued by Islamic groups such as CAIR, which many believe is a front for Muslim terrorist organizations. The same has happened in Europe. For example, prior to her death in 2006, well-known author Oriana Fallaci could not return to her native Italy because of a lawsuit claiming her books, *The Rage and the Pride* (2001) and *The Force of Reason* (2004), constituted hate speech against and a vilification of Islam. Rather than a religion of tolerance, this religion is quick to be offended, to riot, and to sue.

An additional example of censorship deals with former French sex symbol and movie star Brigitte Bardot, who is on trial for the fifth time for "inciting racial hatred against Muslims." As an animal rights activist, Bardot has been critical of the Islamic practice of slaughtering animals on *Eid al-Adha.* As a French patriot, she has been critical of the Islamisation of France, stating that Muslims are destroying France.

The attempt to censor any material critical of Islam can be seen in other ways. For example, a book club stopped selling the book *The Life and Religion of Mohammed* by J. L. Menezes because an Islamic organization found it to be "a virulently Islamophobic book." The West has not called for the removal of the distorted, hateful material toward the West, which is distributed by mosques throughout the world, including those in the United States.

The corrupt and inept United Nations Human Rights Council has issued a resolution directed at preventing any criticism of Islam. Although the resolution claims to represent all religions, it only mentions Islam by name. This is because, according to the resolution, the United Nations is "alarmed at the continuing negative impact of the events of 11 September 2001 on Muslim minorities and communities in some non-Muslim countries, the negative projection of Islam in the media, and the introduction and enforcement of laws that specifically discriminate against and target Muslims." The resolution continues stating there is a "need to effectively combat defamation of all religions, Islam and Muslims in particular." The resolution continues stating that "Islamophobia today is the most serious form of religious defamation" and constitutes a threat to "world peace." The resolution states there is freedom of expression but that it needs to be "exercised with responsibility." However, if freedom of expression is not exercised responsibly, then it will be "subject to limitations as provided by law..."

Another attempt at the suppression of free speech can be seen in Canada, where human rights complaints have been filed against *Maclean's Magazine* by an Islamic organization. The complaint is based on an article by Mark Steyn titled "The Future Belongs to Islam," which is from his book, *America Alone: The End of the World as We Know It* (2006). The Muslim organization claimed the article subjected Canadian Muslims to hatred and contempt and that the book was "flagrantly Islamophobic." The complaints stated it was being filed to protect Canadian multiculturalism and tolerance. It is actually an attempt to prevent further criticism of Islam through fear, intimidation, and high legal expenses. Those writing in Steyn's defense have stated that confronting reality is not illegal. Within Canada there have been other unelected "human rights commissions" that have attempted to curtail speech critical of Islam.

Even the authors of children's books are not immune from criticism. One English author who gave his animal characters multicultural names recently had to change the name of a character from

Mohammad to Morgan. We can only hope Morgan will not be killed for apostasy.

In addition to charges of Islamophobia, another attempt by Islamic organizations at preventing the truth about Islam from being disseminated is censorship by lawsuits. One example deals with a Saudi billionaire suing Rachel Ehrenfeld for accusing him of funding Islamic terrorism in her book, *Funding Evil: How Terrorism is Financed and How to Stop It* (2005). She was sued in the English court system, where the burden of proof is on the defendant. Dr. Ehrenfeld lost the suit. She counter-sued in the U.S. system and won. Another example deals with the book, *Alms for Jihad* (2006), by Robert Collins and Millard Burr. The same Saudi billionaire sued the publisher of the book. In response, the publisher destroyed all unsold copies of the book and allegedly requested that libraries remove copies from their collections.

There are reports that some publishers are afraid to publish books critical of Islam. Once again, we see the attempt to intimidate critics of Islam and Muslims into silence. An article in the Counter Terrorism Blog reported that lawsuits are being used more frequently than most realize to suppress any negative portrayal of Islam. The most frequent charge is libel.

Not only can the authors of books and their publishers be sued, but so can the authors of emails, even if they are by voluntary subscription. One author sent out information about terrorism to about ten thousand individuals who had subscribed to receive them. One Muslim claimed the emails created a hostile work environment and sued for emotional distress. Bloggers are not immune. In England, a British blogger has been arrested based on comments he made about Islam, which Muslims claim stirred up racial hatred. He could face seven years in prison.

In 2007, there was an *Opus* cartoon strip which resulted in Muslim staff members becoming emotional after viewing it prior to publication. The strip was either cancelled or run selectively. A week earlier, the strip had included the Reverend Jerry Falwell. [Note to self: Were Christian staff members allowed to preview and vote on whether that strip should be released?]

In addition to attacking authors, Islamic organizations have also attacked radio show hosts they do not like. One is Michael Savage, who they allege made anti-Islamic comments. The Islamic organizations have attempted to call for a boycott of his sponsors until they cease advertising on his radio program.

Another attempt at suppressing any negative portrayal of Islam can be seen with the example of the Young Americans Foundation (YAF). Robert Spencer, who is a prolific author of books about Islam, and who created the Internet sites *Jihad* Watch and *Dhimmi* Watch, was invited to speak at one of its conferences. The YAF received a letter stating it would be sued if Mr. Spencer was allowed to speak. The attempt at legal intimidation did not work, and Mr. Spencer delivered his speech.

The YAF story was not yet concluded. When conservative columnist Mike Adams heard about the threat made to the YAF, he wrote a column asking his readers to call or write the attorney who had sent the letter to the YAF and ask the attorney to stop assisting "Muslim extremists." Dr. Adams also suggested faxing the attorney a copy of the First Amendment. The attorney sent Dr. Adams a letter suggesting a federal statute had been violated because the column had the intent of abusing, annoying, harassing, and threatening the attorney. In his response, Dr. Adams noted the attorney had voluntarily entered into an important debate and that many Americans were now engaging him.

Part of the reason for the biased coverage could be that the mainstream media is slowly being acquired by wealthy Muslims. One example deals with a wealthy Muslim who owns five percent of a news organization. When the news organization initially referred to the riots in France as "Muslim riots," one phone call to the company by the wealthy Muslim and the title was changed to "civil riots."

Fortunately, more Americans have been relying on the Internet rather than on the mainstream media for information about the war, and soon they were exposing the distortions and lies of the mainstream media. Not only were numerous fake photographs exposed, but also exposed were the "news accounts" by nonexistent Iraqi government and military authorities. Even "fake" anti-war blogs by U.S. soldiers have been exposed.

Unfortunately, currently not enough Americans are aware of the lies and distortions discovered by the bloggers, and the mainstream media is not about to inform its listeners, readers, and viewers that they are consciously, consistently, deliberately, and systematically being lied to.

One More Area

One additional area needs to be examined which deals with U.S. politicians and the government. In the 2006 elections, Republicans took political losses, which is common for this cycle in elections. However, many blamed the political losses on the "war on terrorism" or "Bush's war."

Thus, the Democrats decided to use the war, which is seldom popular, as an opportunity to make further political gains. In other words, Democrats consciously made the decision to place politics ahead of national security. Although voting for the war, many Democrats suddenly found reasons to withdraw from supporting the war. As American soldiers were in war zones and being killed and maimed, leaders from the Democratic Party, such as Senate Majority Leader Harry Reid, declared the war "the worst foreign policy mistake in U.S. history" and "lost." The Democratic leader in the House, Nancy Pelosi, stated the war has not made us any safer and that it was a "catastrophic mistake" and a "grotesque mistake." By establishing artificial benchmarks for the new Iraqi government and then providing limited time to reach them, the Iraqi government was also declared a failure.

Because of their gains politically, Democrats now had greater power to accomplish their goal of losing the war. The strategy appears to be to lose the war, gain politically in the next election, and then deal with the war. As noted earlier, this "war" has been going on for fourteen hundred years, and it is not an "optional" war. Too many politicians seem to want to say "no" to the war as though they were declining a dinner invitation.

The reticence of Democrats to approach the war can also be seen in the debates among Democratic presidential candidates where the words "Islam" and "terrorism" have been avoided. Also, the moderators of the debates have avoided "the war" and issues associated with it such as illegal immigration and a nuclear Iran. Presumably, the mainstream media does not want to expose the weaknesses of the Democratic candidates or the strengths of the Republican candidate on these issues. It is curious that while the issues of Islam and Muslims have been avoided in the debates, those debates which have allowed voters to ask questions have all had questions from Muslims, all of whom appear to have connections to CAIR, which many believe is a front for terrorist organizations. The Muslims asking questions at these debates have portrayed themselves as victims by talking about issues such as being singled out for airport profiling.

The Democratic candidates for president cannot even mention terms such as "Islamic extremism," "Islamic fanaticism," or "Islamic radicalism." They use terms such as "stateless terrorists." The Republican candidate has refused to back down from using the term "Islamic" to describe Muslim terrorists.

After forbidding the use of the term "Islamic terrorists" in 2008, the U.S. Department of State also forbade the use of the term "*jihadist*" to describe Islamic terrorists.

In addition to politicians in denial of the true nature of the war, the same is true for branches of the government. The U.S. Department of Justice was recently a sponsor of at a convention of the Islamic Society of North America (ISNA), which was an unindicted co-conspirator in an Islamic terrorism funding trial. The ISNA was founded by the Muslim Brotherhood in 1981. On its website it had slogans such as "Oh Muslims, There is a Jew hiding behind me, so kill him." At the convention, the U.S. Department of Justice had a booth staffed with attorneys to "educate Muslims about their civil rights." Thus, one set of U.S. Department of Justice attorneys is educating ISNA members while another set is prosecuting them. And, in 2007, President Bush had a board member of the ISNA deliver the "blessing" at the White House Ramadan dinner.

In 2007, the Democratic National Committee had a Muslim *imam* deliver the invocation at its winter meeting. The *imam* was known to have delivered anti-American and anti-Semitic speeches and attended pro-Hamas and pro-Arafat rallies featuring posters of the Ayatollah Khomeini. As Democrats listened to the *imam* with their heads bowed, he invoked "god" to guide people on the "right path," the path of the people god blesses, not the path of the people god dooms. He concluded by asking god for an end to war, violence, oppression, and occupation. Although there could be several interpretations of various parts of the *imam's* speech, from an Islamic perspective the "right path" is the path of Islam, and the people god blesses are those who follow the path. Christians and Jews are the people god dooms. The oppression and occupation refer to Israel and possibly to U.S. troops in Afghanistan and Iraq. The end to the war and violence refers to bringing the House of War into the House of Islam.

Just to demonstrate that Republicans can also act in stupid ways, President Bush plans to appoint an emissary to the Organization of the Islamic Conference (OIC) to "improve mutual understanding and cooperation between America and people in predominately Muslim countries." The OIC is a radical, pro-terrorist, anti-West, anti-Israel organization which is not likely to be moved by an emissary. The Islamic organization CAIR, which some believe is a front for terrorist groups, is helping in the appointment.

In 2006, a deputy defense secretary delivered a speech at the ISNA.

In Iowa in 2008, an Islamic cleric delivered the following opening prayer to the legislature. He said, "Give us victory over those who disbelieve" and "protection from the great Satan." He was asking the Iowa legislature, with bowed heads, to grant the Islamic god victory over non-Muslims and to grant Muslims protection from the great Satan, which includes Israel and the United States.

At the end of 2007, several congressional Democrats refused to vote for a resolution, stating that Christmas was a holiday celebrated by Christians throughout the world. Earlier these Democrats had voted in favor of a resolution stating that Islam was one of the great religions of the world.

The Pentagon recently fired its most knowledgeable specialist on Islamic law and Islamic terrorism because he would not "soften" his views on "Islamic extremism" for the Muslim aide to a deputy defense secretary.

How Far Have We Come?

In the last chapter it was mentioned that the original name for the invasion of Afghanistan was Operation Infinite Justice. However, the name was changed when some said the name might be offensive to Muslims. That was in 2001. In late 2007, a U.S. combat group was preparing to go to Iraq when it was discovered its call sign, "conqueror," needed to be changed because it might be offensive to Muslims. It was changed to Iron Knight. [Note to self: Keep the whiteout available because at some point a politically correct bureaucrat will discover there were knights who were Christian crusaders, and this might be offensive to Muslims. Again, when will we spend less time worrying about offending terrorists and more time killing them?]

The examples above make it look like the U.S. has not come very far since the start of the war. However, in 2001, American forces went into Afghanistan, and in 2003, they went into the heart of ancient Islam, Iraq. In both countries the enemy was defeated and constitutional republics were established. Almost sixty million individuals in these countries were given the opportunity to live in freedom for the first time. In addition, in two countries there is the potential for the growth and then the spread of capitalism and democracy, which will hopefully eventually spread throughout the Middle East. Capitalism and democracy are Islam's greatest fears.

Also, after 9/11 most anticipated further attacks within the United States. However, other than what might be called "lone wolf" style attacks, since 2004 there have been no successful Islamic *jihad* attacks in the United States or against U.S. interests outside the war zones. This is because Islamic terrorists groups such as al Qaeda and the Taliban were denied their traditional training areas. And, since al Qaeda stated that Iraq was the front for its war against the West, thousands of *jihadists,* including their top leaders, have been drawn into Iraq—not the United States—and killed.

More Second Attacks

In addition to the second attacks by the mainstream media, there have also been second attacks by Muslims. These will be examined in Chapter 12.

CHAPTER 12: SECOND ATTACKS: MUSLIMS

The last chapter examined the attacks against the United States since 9/11 by the mainstream media. This chapter examines the second attacks by Muslims.

Second Attacks: History 101

The attacks on 9/11 were not America's first wake-up call that it was under attack by Islam; it was only the most costly in terms of American lives and the closest geographically. There have been numerous "attacks" on the United States by "Muslim *jihadists*" both pre- and post-9/11.

What most Americans have not realized is that "the war," Islamic crusade, or *jihad* has been going on for fourteen hundred years, almost since the founding of Islam. Initially, the *jihad* expanded throughout what is now Saudi Arabia. Then it spread into what are now Egypt, Israel, Jordan, Lebanon, Syria, and Turkey. The Persian Empire, the cradle of civilization, fell, as did North Africa, followed by most of Spain. The expansion continued into parts of Europe and to the east into India.

Sometimes Western civilization successfully confronted and defeated Islam. One example was in France when Charles Martel, "the Hammer," stopped the Islamic invasion of Europe in 732. Islam had already conquered Spain and mandated much of the Spanish population to *dhimmitude* status, which meant they were a conquered people of low status, few rights, high taxes, and humiliating living conditions. In other words, they were slaves in their country. Without Charles Martel and his army, there was nothing in the way of the invading Muslim army to prevent it from taking over most of Western Europe. Then, just as it had spread across North Africa and into Spain, it could have gone into England. Writers have speculated what the world would be like today had the Muslim invasion succeeded. In literature, the works of writers such as Shakespeare and Milton would not have existed. Had a Muslim army then conquered Italy, artists such as Michelangelo would not have been allowed to produce their artwork. And the sciences would still be in the seventh century or earlier.

Two additional Islamic challenges were confronted and stopped. One was the defeat of the Islamic navy off the coast of Western Greece at Lepanto on 1571. Another was the repulsion of the Islamic attack on Vienna in 1683. After being repulsed at Vienna, the angry, defeated, and frustrated Muslim army, which had been assured of victory, marched back to the Middle East through southeastern Europe, leaving a path of death and destruction unparalleled in history.

Although Western civilization had many victories against the Islamic *jihad,* it also had many defeats. Christianity largely disappeared from the Middle East and North Africa, and many of the holiest cities in Christianity and Judaism became controlled and dominated by Muslims. The conquest and colonization of Spain for almost eight hundred years was another defeat. And, of course, another defeat was the conquest and sack of Constantinople in 1453, which brought about the end of the Christian Byzantine Empire.

Previously, those living in the West believed in the superiority of Western civilization and recognized the dangers it confronted. Charles Martel, for example, united Christians who often feuded and fought with one another to come together and fight a larger and more dangerous enemy. The same was true for Vienna in 1683, where feuding Christian European armies came together and assisted the city. They recognized Islam was the greater danger which needed to be confronted and defeated. Currently, the West does not have an ideology or a religion to unite it. In fact, too many have come to shun our ideological and religious past.

Previously, the West was also saved by superior technology. Freedom led to innovation in many areas, including the military. Thus, the West defeated some *jihads* because of its use of superior military technology. Whereas in the past information on military innovations often diffused slowly to Islamic societies, currently these innovations are passed on much more rapidly.

Many books mention the rapid expansion of Islam, which makes the expansion sound like Islam was an ideology that simply could not be resisted. In reality, the expansion and conquest was mostly by the bloody scimitar. Islam started its expansion and conquest at the same time the Byzantine Empire and the Persian Empire had been engaged in a series of wars that had left each financially and militarily exhausted. As a result, parts of both empires were left without military protection, which allowed the unopposed Muslim bandits, murderers, raiders, rapists, robbers, thieves, and thugs to systematically conquer towns and villages on the outer fringes of both empires. The only opposition was from craftsmen, farmers, shopkeepers, and their families. Many in the path of the Islamic *jihad* were killed, raped, or taken into slavery. Some were given the option of living under *dhimmitude*, which allowed non-Muslims to live under Islamic protection but be subjected to an inferior legal status, high taxes, and humiliating living conditions. If the *dhimmi* was unable to pay the high taxes, the choice became conversion or death. It was generally the *dhimmis* who produced the accomplishments within Islam.

Typically, however, the *jihadists* were less interested in mandating *dhimmitude* and more interested in rape, slaughter, and slave-taking, which resulted in an immediate benefit. That is, if the *jihadists* were victorious, they immediately received loot, slaves, and women. If killed, the Muslim *jihadists* immediately went to "paradise," where they got loot, slaves, and women—only in greater quantities in the Islamic god's paradise. Also, the heavenly life did not include some of the bothersome issues found in an earthly existence. For example, men did not have any sexual limitations, and there were always promiscuous virgins as partners. In paradise, they would not discharge any bodily material such as mucus or urine, and drinking from a river of wine did not produce drunkenness or hangovers.

The Islamic "expansion" meant large areas of the Middle East which had at one time been rich in agriculture and commerce became desolate wastelands due to the indiscriminate and wholesale slaughter and slave-taking. The few who managed to hide and survive the slaughter often died of starvation or from the plagues that frequently accompany mass death. Thus, much of the "cradle of civilization" became a wasteland under Islamic subjugation.

Shortly after the Christian Crusades, which the Christians lost, Islam went into dormancy as far as expansion through force. Basically, Western civilization advanced because of ideas such as freedom and progress which allowed for many advances, including military innovation. Some claim Islam regressed to medieval times, but in fact, it never advanced to the medieval stage of development. This was, in part, because it relegated fifty percent of its population—women—primarily to the kitchen and bedroom and, in part, because most Muslims believed all knowledge was in the *Koran.*

Even though it went into dormancy, the *jihad* had inflicted an unparalleled horror. The record of deaths is estimated at one hundred and twenty million Africans, sixty million Christians, eighty million Hindus, and ten million Buddhists.

The recent resurrection of the Islamic *jihad* came about for several reasons, two of which will be briefly discussed. The first reason for the resurrection of the Islamic *jihad* has been the Western demand for oil, which has allowed tremendous wealth to flow to Muslim countries. This wealth has often been used to fund *jihad* and radical Muslim schools and mosques.

The second was the realization by Muslims that Islam could successfully confront and defeat the major superpowers. For some this was demonstrated in 1973 when Black September, under the guidance of terrorist Yasser Arafat, took over the Saudi Arabian embassy in Khartoum and executed two American diplomats and a Belgian diplomat. Not only were there no reprisals, but within a year Arafat gave a speech at the United Nations flanked by four of the executioners. The terrorist received a thunderous applause from the U.N. audience.

Others believe it was the 1979 takeover of the American embassy in Iran followed by the belated and weak response by the United States when Muslims realized Islam could successfully confront and fight a superpower. Islam again demonstrated its ability to attack with impunity in 1983 with the retreat of U.S. forces from Beirut after an explosion killed two hundred and forty-one Marines. Several other attacks followed with no response. For example, in 1983, the CIA head in Beirut was kidnapped, tortured, and murdered. Also, in 1983, the U.S. embassy in Kuwait was bombed. In 1985, Flight 847 was hijacked by Muslim terrorists, and a U.S. soldier was murdered. In the same year, the cruise ship Achille Lauro was hijacked, and an American citizen was murdered. In 1988, Pan Am Flight 103 exploded over Scotland with two hundred and seventy dead.

In 1989, the Soviet Union withdrew its forces from Afghanistan, which demonstrated that not only could Islam confront and defeat a Western superpower, but also a non-Western superpower. The breakup of the Soviet Union also increased Islamic power since it had exercised a certain amount of control and influence over Muslim areas formerly under its control.

There was a bombing near Marine housing in Yemen in 1992. In 1993, the rapid withdrawal of U.S. troops from Somalia demonstrated again America was a "paper tiger." In the same year, there was an assassination attempt on former President George Bush while he was in Kuwait. In 1993, there was the first attack on the World Trade Centers (WTC), which the Clinton administration treated as a criminal rather than a terrorist act. In 1995 and 1996, there were bombings directed at Americans in Saudi Arabia; in 1998, there were bombings of the embassies in Kenya and Tanzania; and in 2000, there was the attack on the U.S.S. Cole.

Admittedly, there were a few responses to these attacks. For example, in response to the downing of Flight 103, President Reagan bombed Libya. And President Clinton had some missiles fired at suspected terrorists' targets, although in this case it is uncertain if the attack was an attempt to deal with terrorists or an attempt to distract people from his impeachment hearing.

Many debate the start of the Islamic *jihad*. For some it was Yasser Arafat in 1973. Others claim it was the takeover of the American embassy in Iran in 1979. For others, it was either the first attack on the World Trade Centers in 1993 or the second attack in 2001. These answers are all wrong. It was Muhammad in 622!

The Three Types of *Jihad* Attacks on the United States

Currently, Western civilization is under three ongoing attacks by the Islamic *jihad*. The first is violent in nature, such as the attacks against the U.S. military in Afghanistan and Iraq. The first type of *jihad* is also illustrated by the terrorists' attacks in countries such as France, Great Britain, Spain, Russia, and the United States. Previously, most Americans rested comfortably in the belief that Israel would be subject to the attacks, not the United States. Also, Israel would deal aggressively, forcefully, and successfully with the attacks and would provide a buffer zone for the United States, thus shielding it from attacks. We know this is no longer true.

Others falsely believe increased security measures have made us safer since there has not been a major attack on American soil since 9/11. This is a foolish belief which has created a pre-9/11 mentality. The lack of direct attacks on the United States is the result of four factors. First, the Muslim terrorists have realized another attack would temporarily increase American resolve and support for the "global war on terrorism" in Afghanistan, Iraq, and elsewhere, such as Iran. Therefore, the Muslim terrorists have directed their attacks at what they believed are weaker targets, such as England and Spain. The Muslim terrorists have also watched many U.S. politicians run away from support of the war. The Muslim terrorists have realized that if the Democratic Party makes political gains, it will remove U.S. troops from Afghanistan and Iraq. This would be similar to the hasty retreat from Somalia in 1993. It would demonstrate once again that America is a "paper tiger" whose citizens have no ideology or belief system for which they are willing to fight.

A second reason for the lack of physical attacks is that there is no need for them. The Muslim terrorists believe the second and third type of *jihads*, discussed below, will be successful. This does not mean there will not be other violent *jihads* against the United States. There will always be *jihadists* seeking an early entry into paradise. However, these attacks will be implemented to demoralize Americans and to gain further concessions. For example, if an attack takes place, those suggesting Muslims are behind the attack will be quickly criticized for Islamophobia. There will be calls for greater acceptance, tolerance, and understanding of Islam with mandated diversity, multiculturalism, and sensitivity training sessions. If Muslims are arrested, there will be lawsuits based on profiling. And liberal members of Congress will call for laws prohibiting any profiling by religion (Islam), country of origin (if it is in the Middle East), and appearance (only if it is Arab).

The third reason, and the most important, for the lack of violent *jihads* on the United States is the Muslim *jihadists* do not want to reawaken the United States, especially under the watch of President Bush. Many *jihadists* probably assumed the response to 9/11 by the United States would be similar to those of the past. There would be appeasements, concessions, conferences, criminal investigations, financial incentives, self-blame, and unfulfilled threats.

The fourth reason is the wars in Afghanistan and Iraq have lured thousands of *jihadists* away from the United States, where they have been killed. Thousands of others have been wounded, are in hiding, or are considering a career change. Two formerly radical Islamic countries are experiencing freedom, and almost sixty million people have economic and educational opportunities for themselves and their children. During the Clinton administration, terrorism was treated as a criminal matter and resulted in a handful of convictions in eight years. Under the Bush administration, terrorism has been treated as a war, and a slow day in Afghanistan and Iraq results in more Muslim terrorists being removed as threats to the United States than in eight years under the Clinton administration.

The second *jihad* is on the cultural front. For more than thirty years it has been assisted by educators, liberals, and the mainstream media, all of whom have been obsessed with condemning American society and getting rid of any vestige of Judeo-Christian beliefs and practices. These same individuals portray the United States as the only country to have experienced issues such as slavery, with other countries presumably living in utopian bliss with universal but substandard healthcare. We even learn some of the country's founders and signers of the Declaration of Independence owned slaves! The "cultural *jihad*" is also referred to as the "soft *jihad*" and "*sharia* by the inch." The goal is to gradually replace Judeo-Christian values with Islamic values and laws. This is what has been proposed by the Muslim Brotherhood, a terrorist organization that was formed in 1928. One of its documents has the following statement: "The *Ikhwan* [Muslim Brotherhood] must understand that their work in America is a kind of grand *jihad* in eliminating and destroying the Western Civilization from within and sabotaging its miserable house by their hands and the hands of the believers so that it is eliminated and Allah's religion is made victorious over all other religions."

The cultural *jihad* has been facilitated by three concepts: cultural relativity, diversity, and political correctness. The basic message of cultural relativity is simple and can be summarized by the question, "Who are we to judge the behaviors and practices of others according to some arbitrary, artificial, and culturally-imposed standard?" The exception to the rule is the United States and other Western countries. Here others can impose their arbitrary, artificial, culturally-imposed standards, and then be indignant when they are not met. Thus, with cultural relativity there is no difference between a culture whose accomplishments include freedom and liberty and one whose accomplishments include strapping bombs to their children.

The message of diversity is that we are to accept, appreciate, celebrate, tolerate, and understand the behaviors and practices of other cultures. Again, the exception is Western countries, where there can only be criticism, disgust, and hatred—especially of dead white males, the perceived source of all evil. In teaching American history, the positive stories or characteristics of those who founded this country are often ignored. However, any flaws—created, imagined, or real—are endlessly emphasized and probed. Often the achievements of these individuals are credited to others. While true heroes are ignored or slandered, they are replaced by insignificant individuals who have either fictitious accomplishments created or minor accomplishments embellished, but who meet some diversity quota in terms of disability (except able-bodied), ethnicity (except European), race (except white), religion (except Christian or Jewish), sex (except male), or sexual orientation (except straight). Others are elevated by half-truths or outright lies.

The West is at a crucial point in its history. Do those in the West consider their values, such as the freedom of religion or speech, to be worth defending? Or are Muslims gradually going to impose a seventh century ideology? President Bush may have been wrong in his speech on 9/11 when he stated the attacks failed in their attempt to frighten America into "chaos and retreat." Based on what has happened since 9/11, it seems like the attacks have been working as Muslim terrorists anticipated.

In addition to cultural relativity and diversity, there is a third concept that has facilitated the Islamic cultural *jihad*, which is political correctness. It has become socially unacceptable as well as often illegal to offend others on the basis of characteristics such as ethnicity, race, or religion. Essentially a "protected class" has been created that is immune from criticism. Technically, political correctness requires mutual sensitivity and tolerance. However, in practice, insensitivity and intolerance of anything Western is not only allowed but also often mandatory. Those who say anything critical about Islam are characterized by the term "Islamophobic" which, according to Islamic apologists, devalues the character and statements of those who have made "disparaging" comments about Islam. It is Islamophobic even if the comments are true. Being classified as Islamophobic can be as damaging to individuals and their message as being characterized as sexist or racist. This linguistic manipulation also transforms Islam into the victim. It is also used to intimidate those who are critical of Islam and to negate their comments. It also creates self-censorship since few want to be labeled Islamophobic.

At an Islamic conference in 2007, Islamophobia was described as "deliberate defamation of Islam and discrimination and intolerance of Muslims." Islamophobia was described as the worst form of terrorism that was creating further alienation. The conference concluded Islamophobia was the characteristic of a mental disorder. [Note to self: Look for a study of those who died on 9/11 to find out what they believe is the worst form of terrorism. Also, the mental disorder could be called "I want to live in freedom!"] A phobia is an irrational fear. There is nothing irrational about fearing Islam and its fourteen hundred-year *jihad* against all that is not Islamic, especially since Muslim terrorists use Islam to justify their actions. Muslim clerics have issued *fatawas*, or religious edicts, on a variety of issues, but not against Muslims who have committed acts of terrorism.

Those who want to report the news as only Muhammad would want it reported can purchase a media guide from the Council on Islamic American Relations (CAIR), which many believe is a front for Muslim terrorist organizations. The media guide is filled with instructions for the proper reporting of Islamic issues.

One writer recently asked, "Why do the mainstream media only focus on Islamophobia and not Infidelophobia, or the Muslim hatred of non-Muslims?" Looking at terrorism around the world, Infidelophobia is certainly the larger problem. Others have asked, "When was the last time you heard of a Christian filing charges of 'Christianophobia?'" This type of phobia only appears to be a crime which is applicable to one religion.

In addition to the military *jihad* and the cultural *jihad*, the third *jihad* is from the crib. Basically, Western families have a low birth rate. It appears that years of brainwashing with concepts of cultural relativity, diversity, political correctness, and the attack on anything Western has suppressed the birthrate in the West. No surprise there! Why bring children into a decadent, disgusting, materialistic, miserable, oppressive, and soulless society? We live in a society that has been largely stripped of its heroes and its ideology. Some writers have mentioned it is no wonder "they hate us" given the fact we seem to have a cultural hated of ourselves which has made us "morally enfeebled," thus incapable of responding to the attacks by Muslims.

Meanwhile, Muslim families have a high birth rate; more than two times that of Western families. This has been part of a plan since the 1970s, when an Algerian *jihadist* at the UN stated Muslims would move to Europe, not as friends but as conquers, and that their sons and the wombs of their wives assured them victory. Also, Muslim children have low rates of assimilation into certain areas of Western societies. It has also been noted that many young second generation Muslims seem to become "unassimilated" from Western values. It would probably be better to speak of "selective assimilation" and "selective unassimilation." Obviously, some assimilation is taking place since most Muslims in Western countries speak the native language, attend public schools, learn occupational skills, and participate in the economic sector of society. Additionally, they often wear Western clothing, use cell phones, drive automobiles, and know how to manipulate the welfare system to their benefit. However, assimilation is low in other areas such as interreligious marriage, which is creating parallel societies. Intermarriage rates are low because of arranged marriages, because of family pressure to marry within Islam, and because of religious pressures to marry within Islam. Even friendships outside of Islam are discouraged since they are seen as distracting Muslims from following Islam and as drawing weak Muslims from Islam.

Because of this it is expected that some European cities will become predominately Muslim in this century. This is not just a result of the high Muslim birthrate and the anemic Western birthrate, but also of migration. Muslims are migrating into Western societies often as part of family reunification programs. And Westerners, especially the young, are migrating out. Thus, we will soon see European cities with an aging Western population and a young, seething Muslim population probably unwilling to provide for the pension benefits of non-Muslims.

In fact, in some European cities Muslims are wearing shirts with dates such as 2030 or 2050, the year it is projected Muslims will make up a majority of the population. One indicator of the crib *jihad* can be seen in England, where the name "Muhammad," in one of its many spellings, is one of the most popular names for newborn boys. Given the cultural and crib *jihads*, there is little need for violent *jihads* on the United States and other Western countries. Change will be gradual but certain. Europe is increasing, becoming *Eurabia*;[18] can the United States be far behind?

The Muslims are Coming, The Muslims are... Oops, They're Here!

Islam has been at war with the non-Islamic world for fourteen hundred years. After a period of dormancy, the war has been renewed with seemingly unlimited financial resources. The outcome of the war is uncertain, but it does raise the question, "Why aren't Americans as worried about Islamic aggression as, say, they were about Nazi aggression or communist aggression?" We have seen that part of the answer is the mainstream media has refused to identify the danger or to even call the enemy by its name—Islam. This, coupled with Muslim organizations lying about Islam and attempting to distort the *jihad*, lulled many into a state comparable to the pre-World War II warnings of German and Japanese aggression during the 1930s. This was when Neville Chamberlain uttered, "Peace for our time," which is similar today to "Islam is a religion of peace" and "Most Muslims are not terrorists." We also hear about the elusive "moderate" Muslims.

After the attacks on 9/11, both Islam and Muslims needed damage control. Most expected that in public appearances they would be apologetic, contrite, embarrassed, and humbled by the Muslim attacks on 9/11. This was especially true since Americans saw images of Muslims dancing with joy not only in Islamic countries but also in Western countries on 9/11. However, almost immediately after the attacks on 9/11, spokespersons from Islamic organizations appeared on news programs, and rather then being apologetic, contrite, embarrassed, or humbled by the Muslim attacks on 9/11, they repeated with a straight face that Islam was a religion of peace and then listed a seemingly endless series of grievances which only seemed to appear after 9/11.

Thus, Muslims seem to have been awakened by their attacks on 9/11 and have gone on the offensive. Part of the offense is to prevent any criticism of Islam by creating fear among critics so they will self-censor their opinions. This silence of criticism is necessary because an honest and open discussion would reveal the true nature of Islam, which most non-Muslims would find abhorrent.

It has become comical to listen to the formulaic response by Muslim spokespersons who automatically appear whenever a Muslim terrorist plot is discovered or whenever Muslim terrorists commit acts of terrorism. First, we will learn Muslims everywhere are "shocked" that anyone could plan or commit such a horrible act because Islam deplores "senseless violence." The spokesperson will fail to reveal if Muslims believe this particular act was "senseless" or "sensible." Second, the spokesperson will claim Islam is in no way responsible for the planning or commission of the act. It will not matter if the Muslim terrorists cited Islamic religious documents as the justification for planning or committing the act. It will not matter if the Muslim terrorists posted a webpage stating they were starting *jihad* for the Islamic god. Nor will it matter if the Muslim terrorists were videotaped fleeing from a flaming car yelling, "*Allahu Akbar*," or "death to infidels." Third, the spokesperson will state the Muslims who planned or committed the act do not represent all Muslims. Left unstated is the percentage of Muslims they do represent. Fourth, in an attempt to devalue critics, it will be stated that those who see Islam as being responsible in anyway for the planning or commission of the act are "guilty" of Islamophobia. Fifth, the spokesperson will state, with a straight face, that Islam is a religion of peace. [Note to self: This is the shortest part of the response since there are so few examples to cite.] In the sixth stage, the spokesperson will turn Muslims into victims by claiming Muslims now live in fear of hate crimes and reprisals because of the actions of a misguided few. The seventh stage, and fortunately the last, is the call for non-Muslims to accept, appreciate, tolerate, and understand Islam and Muslims. There is no corresponding call for Muslims to accept, appreciate, tolerate, or understand non-Muslims.

Writers have summed up the "Muslim formulaic response" as one which pretends to oppose Muslim terrorism while using every means available to oppose those trying to prevent Muslim terrorists from carrying out more Muslim terrorist attacks.

The call for tolerance of Islam and Muslims seems unnecessary since in a nation of three hundred million people, the number of hate crimes against Muslims after 9/11 were zero or almost zero. This is even with Islamic organizations encouraging Muslims to create sympathy and a victim status by reporting imagined, manufactured, or real examples of hate crimes. In 2006, there were one hundred and ninety-one alleged hate-crimes against Muslims. In comparison, there were one thousand and twenty-seven against Jews. Some of the hate crimes against Muslims involved a *Koran* in a toilet and a trampled flower bed in front of a mosque. Many of the hate crimes reported were probably manufactured by Islamic organizations in an attempt to create sympathy for Muslims. A recent study on employment discrimination against Muslim-Americans called any claims of discrimination "pure fiction."

Large Scale Attacks

The Muslim terrorist attacks of 9/11 have taken the restraints off Muslims from expressing their grievances with the non-Islamic world. In contrast to the calm delivery of the Muslim spokespersons mentioned above, on a daily basis we see Muslims slowly arising from quiet prayer sessions and immediately transforming into outraged, red-faced, sword-shaking, death-chanting maniacs over trivial issues. Three examples will be provided.

The first example deals with the Muhammad cartoon-controversy. Basically, it started when multi-cultural and politically correct politicians in Denmark finally openly stated the assimilation of Muslim emigrants was a failure. There was rampant abuse of welfare benefits, horrific honor murders, and an astronomically high crime rate for young Muslims. Also, the "moderate" *imams* were openly issuing radical statements such as unveiled women—Muslim or non-Muslim—deserved to be raped.

In the midst of this discussion over the failure of Muslims to assimilate, the editorial staff of a Danish newspaper asked forty cartoonists to submit cartoons featuring Muhammad. Out of fear, most of the cartoonists declined, but ultimately twelve cartoons were published in September 2005. There was a five-month delay in Muslims' outrage over the cartoons, presumably to provide mosques around the world time to order Danish flags to burn during the obligatory protests. It also allowed time for Muslim groups to publish images of the twelve cartoons, with a few extra provocative cartoons added just to enrage the seemingly perpetually enraged Muslims. Thus, months after the cartoons were first published, there were a number of well-planned and orchestrated riots with the mandatory flag burnings. More than fifty individuals were killed. There were calls for boycotts of Danish products, which probably led to an increase in the sale of items from Denmark by counter-protesters. And, of course, there were the mandatory death threats toward the cartoonists, most of whom went into hiding out of a justifiable fear that members of the "religion of peace" would kill them. In defense of the basic Western value of "freedom of the press," a few newspapers published the cartoons. However, most newspapers, out of a justifiable fear of Muslims, which they spun as respecting other religions, refused to publish the cartoons. These same "religiously sensitive" newspapers have not had a problem publishing anti-Christian or anti-Jewish material.

A documentary film released in 2007 demonstrated that those responsible for instigating the riots had not seen the cartoons. And in late 2007, two Muslim terrorists were tried for attempting to blow up two trains in Germany because a German newspaper had reprinted the cartoon demonstrating the right of freedom of speech. One of the terrorists noted that the intent of the bombs was more to create fear than to kill.

While Muslims were still in need of anger management courses because of the twelve cartoons, the Middle East Media Research Institute issued a report in July 2007 on anti-Semitic cartoons in the Arab and Iranian press. The report included images of the cartoons with no reports of flag burnings, rioting, or deaths by outraged Jews. A summary of the cartoons noted there were recurrent themes which included "Jews as long-nosed characters of ultra-orthodox appearance, as killers of Christ, as serpents, or as Nazi soldiers. In addition, Jews were portrayed as having pervasive control and power, and as conspirators and instigators of wars, who are out to rule the world."

The cartoon controversy of 2006 was back in 2007, only it had moved to Sweden. This time a cartoonist drew a dog's body with Muhammad's head. There was swift outrage by Muslims, which resulted in the ambassadors from twenty Muslim countries demanding the Swedish prime minister change Swedish laws to prevent "Islamophobia." An al-Qaeda leader in Afghanistan offered one hundred thousand dollars for the murder of the cartoonist with a fifty thousand-dollar bonus if he was slaughtered like a lamb, which would mean his throat would be slit.

In 2008 Holland may have put an end to the cartoon controversy by accepting *dhimmitude* status. The Dutch police arrested a cartoonist and charged him with publishing cartoon that discriminated against "Muslims and people with dark skin." The allegation was that the cartoons insulted people based on their race and religion which might incite hate. Ten police officers went to arrest the cartoonists, proving that the pen is mightier than the sword.

A second example of Muslim intolerance occurred in September 2006, when Pope Benedict XVI gave an academic-theological presentation at the University of Regensburg in which he quoted a Byzantine emperor who died in 1425. The emperor wrote, "Show me just what Mohammad brought that was new and there you will find things only evil and inhuman, such as his command to spread by the sword the faith he preached." The pope continued quoting the emperor:

> Violence is incompatible with the nature of god and the nature of the Soul. God is not pleased by blood, and not acting reasonable is contrary to God's nature. Faith is born of the soul, not the body. Whoever would lead someone to faith needs the ability to speak well and to reason properly, without violence and threats... To convince a reasonable soul, one does not need a strong arm or weapons of any kind, or any other means of threatening a person with death...

There was the predictable Muslim outrage over the pope's speech. At least this time, unlike with the cartoon controversy, it was in a timelier manner. By mischaracterizing the pope's speech, Muslims claimed the pope had mischaracterized Islam. Initially, the pope issued a statement in which he attempted to explain the purpose of his presentation and the context in which the quote was used. When this was not sufficient, which few expected it would be, the pope issued another statement saying he was "deeply sorry for the reactions in some countries" to his speech.

The pope's speech resulted in Muslims around the world being outraged over the suggestion Islam might have violent tendencies. To demonstrate that Islam is a religion of peace, Muslims rioted, attacked, and burned Christian churches. This time, rather than asking the pope to apologize for the speech, there were demands by Muslims that the pope be killed for "blasphemous statements about

Muhammad." Apparently the pope was not available for execution, so the religion of peace killed a Catholic nun in Somalia.

A third example can be seen with internment. As noted earlier, part of the second attack is to obscure the real cause, nature, and purpose of the war, and to make certain the West loses the war. One of the techniques used is distraction, and an example of distraction was when the mainstream media raised the possibility the internment camps of the 1940s might reappear, only this time they would house Muslims. Since many have been indoctrinated to believe the internment camps were a national disgrace, this was an attempt to prevent any type of profiling, in this case religious profiling. Critics of internment camps noted that many of those relocated in the 1940s were sent to desolate places which often caused them financial hardships. [Note to self: Weren't many Americans relocated during World War II, often to desolate areas such as North Africa or the sunny Pacific islands of Iwo Jima and Okinawa? By leaving behind businesses and jobs, many of these Americans suffered financial hardships, not to mention being killed and maimed. Although isolated and rural, the relocation camps were probably safer than the beaches at Normandy, Iwo Jima, and Okinawa.]

There was probably no need to worry about internment camps or profiling since former Transportation Secretary Norman Mineta, who had been relocated from California to Wyoming in 1942 with his non-U.S. citizen Japanese parents, was not about to let internment or profiling happen again. Only ten days after 9/11, while the World Trade Center (WTC) ruins were still smoking, Mineta issued an order to airlines stating it was illegal to discriminate against passengers based on ethnicity, race, religion, and national or ethnic origin. The order also stated it was illegal to discriminate against passengers based on Middle Eastern characteristics, such as being Arab or Muslim. As a result of this mind-numbing stupidity, middle-aged Episcopalian women outfitted in the latest Brooks Brothers clothing and carrying matching Burberry purses and totes were more likely to be searched at airports than those fitting a terrorist profile. And who has not been outraged over the photograph of the intensive body search of an older Catholic nun by a young, *hijab*-wearing Muslim female TSA agent?

Critics of the Japanese internment often cite that it was not necessary since there were no instances of domestic sabotage by Japanese Americans during World War II. They neglect to mention that perhaps the lack of sabotage demonstrated internment worked!

The Consequence

These attacks, and others like them, are an attempt to prevent any criticism of Islam. The long-term strategy is create fear, and hence self-censorship, among critics by attacking a wide range of issues. The attacks might be over cartoons, a speech by the pope, or the name of a teddy bear. The attacks can also be over a false story about a *Koran* being flushed down a toilet, which resulted in riots killing about twenty individuals. [Note to self: Remember to find out the name and model number of a toilet capable of taking out a three-pound book since most federally mandated low-flush toilets have difficulty taking out far less waste.] The point is to make critics of Islam afraid to say or do anything, no matter how trivial, because it might trigger an attack. The consequence will be the slow replacement of Western culture and values with Islamic "culture" and "values." As noted earlier, some have called this "*sharia* by the inch" or the "soft *jihad*."

Even with Muslim attacks taking place in Western countries and with numerous other attacks being prevented, many in the West still don't get it. They seem more concerned with an imaginary backlash against Muslims as a result of Muslim terrorism than with actual attacks or planned attacks by Muslims.

The Future?

We need to remember that history is little more than a graveyard of civilizations. Some of these civilizations existed for centuries, while others existed for shorter periods of time. All of these civilizations had a time when they were at the pinnacle of their power. Their armies were strong and powerful; their borders were secure; their citizens were united; and their enemies were dead, in retreat, or in subjugation. At this time, it must have been difficult for either friend or foe to conceptualize a future in which this civilization would cease to exist. In fact, it would have been incomprehensible to believe that over time this civilization would be added to the list of dead civilizations.

Some of these civilizations were destroyed by outside forces. The majority, however, were destroyed by internal forces. For most, if not all, of these dead civilizations there must have been a turning point, an event that would doom them to a slow or rapid death. The event did not have to be something that seemed important at the time and, in fact, it may have gone largely unnoticed. The event may have initially been seen or portrayed as something positive, something that would benefit these civilizations. But this event would set in place a series of other events which, one by one, like a snowball gaining in size by rolling down a hill, would doom these civilizations to being little more than footnotes in history books, Trivial Pursuit questions, and the sites for future archaeological digs.

Western civilization is facing an immediate and severe threat to its existence. This threat will determine for Western civilization if or how soon it becomes another dead civilization. The threat is not "extreme," "fascist," or "radical" Islam. The threat is not an Islam that has been "hijacked." Rather, it is the Islam that has existed for fourteen hundred years.

Apologists for Islam, liberals, the mainstream media, and a fifth column of Islamists incorrectly separate Islam into radical and moderate categories. This is like separating those belonging to the Nazi Party or the Klu Klux Klan into radical and moderate categories. One either believes in the basic doctrine or one does not believe in it. A Christian does not have the option of selecting any five of the Ten Commandments any more than a Muslim has a choice to select only certain verses from the *Koran*. Were there Nazis who were too lazy to get off the couch to throw Jews into the gas chambers? Of course! Were there members of the Klu Klux Klan who decided to get drunk and go to bed early most nights rather than to go out and lynch, rape, and terrorize blacks? Yes! Did this make them moderate, and thus, acceptable? Of course not!

This book is a warning to those who believe in the superiority of Western civilization. It is a warning that we are in jeopardy, both culturally and physically. Many things we take for granted would vanish in a society controlled by Islam. As noted earlier, there were numerous warnings before 9/11 which were ignored. In addition to some of the specific terrorist attacks mentioned earlier, another warning was Steve Emerson's classic 1995 documentary on PBS titled *American Jihad: The Terrorists Living Among Us*. Emerson's early investigation and warnings have resulted in him being called the "Paul Revere of Terrorism." Another warning was in the July 1998 issue of *Reader's Digest*, which had an article on Osama Bin Laden (OBL) subtitled "This Man Wants You Dead." This should have attracted the attention of the American public. There were other warnings that should have been alarms to Americans that the United States and Western civilization were engaged in a life and death struggle. Unfortunately, as have dead civilizations before us, we soon returned to assuming we were too great, or too powerful, or too dominant to be defeated and destroyed, even after numerous alarms. Additionally, there was the belief that the enemy was not a threat. Many Muslims had funny-sounding names, they lived in countries our military could easily defeat, and we believed they would be lured over to the Western lifestyle before they became dangerous. And, to be honest, most of us after 9/11 had our own lives and problems to deal with and it was easier to simply put it out of our minds. Let others deal with it and maybe it would just go away. After all, once we recognize it as a "problem," we have to do something.

And Last?

The next chapter will provide examples of the Islamic infestation of the schools and the community.

CHAPTER 13: THE ISLAMIC INFESTATION OF THE WEST

In the last chapter it was mentioned that Islam is attempting to slowly replace Western culture and values with Islamic "culture" and "values." Some have referred to this as "*sharia* by the inch" or the "soft *jihad*." Examples of Islamic inroads in education and the community will be examined in this chapter.

Education

There are numerous areas where Islam has been making demands in education at all levels, some of which will be examined in this section.

Prayer in public schools has long been a controversial issue. There are numerous examples of Christian children being prohibited from saying prayers. While Christian children are forbidden from praying in public schools, special prayer rooms have been set aside for Muslim students. However, apparently one room is not enough for Muslim students attending schools with multiple buildings since they have demanded multiple prayer rooms, claiming the number of mandatory daily prayers creates a burden with only one prayer area. Muslim student organizations have also requested courses be scheduled in ways that do not conflict with prayer times.

On college campuses there have been reports of generic religious facilities being "taken over" by Muslim students and transformed to meet their needs, such as separate prayer areas for males and females. Additionally, when non-Muslims have attempted to use these *de facto* mosques, they have been turned away, threatened, forced to comply with Islamic rules such as removing their shoes, and prevented from bringing items into the room such as rosary beads or *Bibles*. While many colleges have "generic" religious centers with generic "ministers," Muslim students have demanded mosques with *imams*.

While Christian students have been prohibited from saying prayers or mentioning God at athletic events and commencement ceremonies, a predominantly Muslim high school in Michigan allowed its football players to pray in the huddle.

Separate prayer rooms are only the beginning. Muslim students have also demanded separate housing facilities since integration with non-Muslims was disturbing the pious from becoming more pious and drawing the weak from Islam.

Even the names of school athletic teams need to be changed. In California, a Christian football team was pressured to change its name from the Crusaders while Muslim football teams were allowed to have names such as Sword of Allah.

Although the celebration of Christian and Jewish holidays is prohibited in public schools, students are instructed in the meaning of Muslim holidays since this is seen as a "cultural exercise," not religious indoctrination. And while Christian and Jewish holidays can no longer be acknowledged, there have been demands that colleges and schools observe Islamic holidays.

Muslim students have demanded colleges and schools install foot-baths so they can wash before prayers. If religious accommodations were made for Christian or Jewish students, there would be lawsuits, but the liberal ACLU has called foot-baths a "reasonable accommodation" because of the safety issue. The ACLU is concerned Muslims might slip and fall if one foot is on a wet floor and the other is in a normal height sink being washed. [Note to self: Remember to look at the fine print in the Establishment Clause for the "health and safety" exception.] School administrators have defended the installation of foot-baths—probably out of fear—claiming they could be used for other purposes, such as bathing babies. First, how many babies are there at high schools and colleges? Second, hopefully most parents would not bathe their babies in public foot-baths. Third, it is questionable if Muslims would "purify" themselves in an area that had recently washed a baby's butt. In fact, Muslims would not be able to use a foot-bath which had been used by non-Muslims until it had been purified. And the foot-baths would have to be cleaned by Muslims since a non-Muslim would leave them unclean. [Note to self: This will make for interesting "Muslim-only jobs" in union contracts.] Fortunately, schools will not have to supply towels since Muslims "drip dry" after washing (e5.25).

Muslim student organizations have demanded college and school cafeterias provide separate foods for Muslims. This will require separate food storage and preparation areas so Muslim food does not become contaminated by that of non-Muslims. Food preparation utensils also need to be kept separate. Obviously pork is not allowed in Muslim diets. This includes products that contain gelatin since it might be made with pork byproducts. Separate eating rooms have also been requested. The need for separate rooms for dining can be seen in two examples. First, after a Canadian college provided acceptable Muslim food, the Muslim students complained the environment was "unsuitable" since non-Muslims drank alcohol and listened to music. And at a public school a ham sandwich recently committed a hate crime against Muslim students.

Other demands by Muslim students have included developing educational practices and rules around Islamic religious practices. For example, exams should not be scheduled during periods of fasting because this might place Muslim students at a disadvantage. Additional practices and rules are needed for the times Muslims are to refrain from sexual thoughts and behaviors. During these times any scheduled academic material which could provoke sexual behavior or thoughts, such as material in biology or sex education classes, will have to be postponed. And mandatory swimming classes should not be scheduled during times of fasting since swallowing water would nullify the fast. [Note to self: Can the water-boarding of terrorists take place during a time of fasting?]

Many of these demands for the Islamisation of schools come from the Muslim Student Association (MSA), which has chapters on six hundred college campuses. It is widely believed by many that the MSA is a front for the terrorist organization the Muslim Brotherhood, which created Islamic terrorist groups such as al-Qaeda and Hamas. As mentioned earlier, the strategy of the Muslim Brotherhood is to destroy the United States from within. A starting place for the destruction of the United States is in education.

The MSA has an online publication titled "Your Chapter's Guide to Campus Activism." The guide states, "We are a nation elected by God to lead humanity" and "We are obligated by God to enjoin the right and forbid the wrong within any society we establish ourselves." The guide instructs the chapters on how to "educate" the campus community. One suggestion is to "speak in language that resonates with your audience. Most Americans identify with concepts such as 'justice,' 'self-determination,' 'human rights,' and 'democracy.' These terms will be constructive when delivering your message, regardless of the issue." The guide continues by saying, "Don't alienate with words like 'us' and 'them.' Make use of terminology like 'our country,' 'our security,' and 'we the American people.'" The chapters are instructed to make the topics relate to non-Muslims. For example, when talking about the dress of Muslim women, "broaden the topic to women's rights or women's status in Islam."

Muslim student organizations have been effective in preventing those with whom they disagree from giving presentations or speaking at colleges and schools. Sometimes they have disrupted presentations and speeches. Other times they have protested outside of the buildings where the events were going to take place in an attempt to keep those who wanted to attend from attending. After some Internet videos were released showing members of the religion of peace not looking or acting very peaceful, Muslim student organizations attempted to curtail the freedom of speech in other ways. One technique was to prevent the presentation or speech from taking place by accusing the speaker of hate speech against Islam and Muslims. Just in case the hate speech accusation was insufficient, it would be mentioned that if the hate speech was allowed, it would create a potentially violent situation, thus placing those in attendance in danger. To alleviate this danger, the recommendation was to increase the level of security, the cost of which would prevent the presentation or speech from taking place. And to make certain there is no freedom of speech or diversity of ideas, one last claim is that if the presentation or speech takes place, it will initiate future hate crimes against Muslim students. This has been called the "sneaky censorship tactic." It worked at one university campus when a speech linking Islamic anti-Semitism and Nazism was cancelled for security reasons.

Classes and assemblies must be separated by religion according to some Muslim student organizations. It is not separation that is sought here but censorship. As noted above, Muslim student organizations have shown considerable intolerance of speakers they find unacceptable. Since attendance at these presentations and speeches is optional, it is obvious separation by religion is not what the Muslim students want, but censorship of anyone and any ideas they find objectionable.

There also needs to be sex segregation with athletic events. When a Chicago Muslim high school's *burka*-clad girls basketball team played against non-Muslim teams, males were prohibited from attending the games, even as referees.

There have been demands from Muslim students that all female teachers wear head scarves.

Muslim students have demanded that sexually integrated sports and gym classes be prohibited, especially if "touching" is involved. If showering is necessary after a gym class or sports event, then private showers and changing rooms must be provided for each Muslim student since it is indecent to be seen naked or to see others naked. The "touching" issue has resulted in Muslim female-only proms! Try holding a Christian-only prom and see what happens. Dancing classes are prohibited, especially if they are sexually integrated or if touching is involved. Music classes must be limited to only the human voice and selected instruments. And those in art classes are not allowed to create anything that could be deemed an "idolatress" figure.

A school in England banned a Christian female student from wearing a "purity ring" because it was a "religious symbol" but allowed Muslim students to wear clothing reflecting their religion.

One school recently had non-Muslim female students wear *burkas* to see what it was like to be stared at and be the object of discrimination. It was also to demonstrate this was a "liberating" style of dress. Shouldn't the experience have been to demonstrate how this style of dress oppresses women? Or the experience could have been to demonstrate how only a misogynistic ideology would impose this on women. It could also have been used to demonstrate that in Western societies women have options in terms of how they dress, whereas in Islamic societies it is one size and one style fits all. Another school in New Hampshire created an Arabian Bedouin tent community where students took on Arab names, ate Arab foods—separated by sex, of course—and wore Arab clothing. This was done as a "cultural exercise" rather than a sexual apartheid exercise.

Non-Muslim students have also been forced to learn verses from the *Koran*, fast during lunch hour, and memorize the five pillars of Islam. Some schools have also started special programs to help non-Muslim students understand Muslim students. These programs often deal with "misconceptions" and "stereotypes," and they include material on women in Islam, such as why they are veiled, as well as material on why Muslim students need to disrupt classes by leaving to pray. The shortest section of these programs deals with famous nonviolent Muslims. [Question to self: Shouldn't the program be to help Muslim students assimilate by understanding non-Muslim students?]

Muslims are also forcing changes in the way certain topics are presented in colleges and schools. One example deals with coverage of the Holocaust. Some colleges and schools have eliminated coverage of the Holocaust because the topic is offensive to Muslim students. Others have omitted coverage of the Holocaust because the material contradicts what is taught in the local mosques. [Note to self: The teaching in the mosques is probably that the Holocaust was "too little too late" or "you haven't seen anything yet."] For others, coverage has been omitted out of fear Muslim students will make anti-Semitic remarks. However, the "real" reason coverage is omitted is the fear it will provoke threats and violence.

Textbooks are conscious of the way material on Islam is presented. One junior high textbook defined *jihad* as either Muslims fighting to protect themselves from harm or attempting to convince others to take up a worthy cause. The same book was noted to exhibit "contempt for Christians and Jews."

Muslim medical students in England have requested they be exempt from reading, attending lectures, or taking exams that conflict with their faith. Two areas where they want exemptions are with sexually transmitted diseases and alcoholism. Other Muslim medical students have refused to treat patients of the opposite sex. And female Muslim medical students are refusing to follow basic hygiene rules by rolling up their sleeves when washing their hands. They claim it violates basic rules of modesty within Islam although when washing before prayers five times a day, they are obligated to wash their hands up to their elbows.

Some English schools have eliminated material on Winston Churchill to make way for "modern issues," which is presumably a code for cultural relativity, diversity, and political correctness. Some English colleges and schools have rewritten English history to reflect other cultures. For example, the English defeat of the Spanish Armada in 1588 is now credited, in part, to the Muslim Turks delaying the departure of the Spanish fleet.

While Islamic student organizations have demanded "toleration" of their behavior and beliefs, they have been incredibly intolerant of any behavior or beliefs they find objectionable. The disruption of speeches by those they opposed was mentioned earlier. Another example occurred when a university student group supplemented the "educational experience" during Islamic Awareness Week. The supplement consisted of posting factual statements about Islam and then requesting "peaceful Muslims explain or justify these astonishingly intolerant and inhuman facts." One example in the supplement quoted part of the *Koran*, which says, "I will cast terror into the hearts of those who have disbelieved, so strike them over the necks, and smite over all their fingers and toes." Another example asked Muslim students to justify Muhammad having sex with a nine-year-old girl. And it requested Muslim students explain why all of the nations, which punish homosexuality with death, have fundamentalist Muslim governments. There was the inevitable complaint from an intolerant, perpetually outraged, and whining Muslim student organization. The complaint was referred to a committee on student life which, by unanimous consent, found the student group guilty of harassing Muslim students, guilty of creating a hostile environment for Muslim students, and guilty of intimidating Muslim students. Perhaps to discourage the types of freedom of speech the committee found unacceptable, it recommended that future funding and recognition of student groups be based on their behavior. Finally, after finding the student group guilty of freedom of speech, the committee stated students should feel free to engage in freedom of speech, even if others might find the speech hurtful or offensive.

In October 2007, the David Horowitz Freedom Center held Islamo-Fascism Awareness Week. The event was held on more than one hundred college and university campuses and had a number of goals, such as opposing the oppression of women in Islam and opposing *jihad.* The MSA was outraged and called the event a hateful assault against Muslims everywhere. Others called Islamo-Fascism Awareness Week a form of Islamophobia. Although the MSA objected to Islamo-Fascism Awareness Week, several authors, including Christopher Hitchens, pointed out that Islam and fascism have nine unmistakable similarities. First, they both have cultures which stress death and violence and reject the development of the mind. Second, with the exception of weapons, they reject modernity. Third, they are nostalgic over a mythological past. Fourth, they are anti-Jewish. Fifth, both worship one great leader, who can be dead or alive. Sixth, they are sexually repressed. Seventh, they hate art and literature and see it as degenerate. Eighth, both believe they are part of a "master" race. Ninth, they repress women.

Muslim students have also demanded the presentation of any material on Islam be done from an Islamic perspective since others "misrepresent Islam." In fact, there have been demands that the Islamic perspective be incorporated into literally all courses since Islam has perspectives that differ from those in the West. Presumably, this means Muslims would have to instruct these courses. Some colleges are taking money from wealthy Muslims to create centers with titles such as "Center from Muslim and Christian Understanding." It is doubtful these "centers" will present material in a balanced or diverse manner.

Additionally, Muslim students needed to be "protected" from ideas that might make them question their beliefs or cause them stress. To assist colleges and schools with this goal, Saudi Arabia has provided a "teaching resource" which has been described as "practically proselytizing" and a "piece of propaganda." The teaching resource offers an uncritical view of Islam while criticizing Christianity and Judaism. In addition, a Saudi Arabia oil company has sponsored free tours to Saudi Arabia for K-12 teachers. No doubt the guided tours were similar to those the Nazis provided the Red Cross when it toured the "model" concentration camps.

The Muslim Council of Britain called for a ban on "un-Islamic activities," which included playground games, swimming, and school plays. There are demands that Muslim students receive educational grants or interest-free educational loans since Islam is opposed to usury and interest-bearing loans.

In the United States, the publically-funded Khalil Gibran International Academy in New York was designed to be an "Arab language" school, but allegations of ties to Islamic extremists created concern about the real purpose of the school. In California, an "experimental school" was created where there are Muslim prayers and foods. We can assume with a high degree of confidence that the ACLU would be more responsive if the publically funded schools were catering to Christian or Jewish students.

Community

In the section on education, it was mentioned that the MSA is believed by many to be a front group for the Muslim Brotherhood, which has as its goal the destruction of the United States from within. The MSA is attempting to achieve the goal through education. There are numerous Islamic community organizations—such as the Council on American Islamic Relations (CAIR), the Islamic Society of North America, and the North American Islamic Trust—attempting to achieve the goal through the community.

For example, noise laws have been changed to allow the "call to prayer" in cities that ban church bells.

The "cross" has caused all types of problems. Muslims in England do not like the British flag because of its red cross. The international organization, the Red Cross, considered changing its trademark and name since the "cross" was offensive to Muslims. Even the addition sign in mathematics was offensive as a "Christian" symbol. Anecdotal reports have emerged of Muslims being offended by Mont Blank pens because they incorrectly believe the image of a snow-capped mountain on the end of the pen is a Jewish symbol.

Also, if Muslim teams cannot win on the sports field, there is a chance they might win through the court system via the Islamophobia or victim card. A Muslim soccer team recently lost a match to an Italian team. The Muslim team has requested the courts cancel the win because the Italian team had red crosses on their shirts.

Muslims in England have suggested eliminating the Holocaust Memorial and replacing it with "Genocide Day," which would include material on Muslims, especially the Palestinians.

In Western countries polygamy is illegal. However, polygamous Muslim men migrating into many of these countries are allowed to bring all of their wives. In many Western countries the polygamous men receive welfare benefits for these "dependents," which means Western taxpayers subsidize harems. To increase the number of polygamous marriages *imams* started performing telephone marriages where one partner was in a Western country and the other in a country where polygamy was legal. After the marriage the new partner would move to the Western country. Now *imans* are performing polygamous marriages in Western countries stating that Western laws cannot make them go against Islamic law.

Muslims have demanded that freedom of speech be limited if the speech is critical of Islam. One example was in Australia, where two ministers were convicted under the "vilification law" for holding conferences and posting material critical of Islam. And in the United States a man accused of placing a *Koran*, which was owned by a library, in a toilet was charged with two felonies: aggravated harassment and criminal mischief. This may be the first time in U.S. history where a felony has been committed against an inexpensive book.

In England, public libraries have acquired large inventories of books by Islamic terrorists. These books, purchased with taxpayer monies, glorify Islamic terrorism and the *jihad* ideology.

There have been reports about Muslims wanting to learn how to drive public school buses, and videotapes have been found in Afghanistan with al-Qaeda terrorists training to capture school buses. An al-Qaeda spokesperson stated, "We will kill two million American children." And Osama bin Laden (OBL) promised Beslan style attacks in U.S. cities. [Note to self: Will the FBI become interested when the Muslims only want to learn to drive forward and going very fast?]

A fast food chain was forced to recall packaged ice cream when Muslims claimed the "spinning swirl" on the lid was "sacrilegious." An opera in Germany became a "security risk" and was cancelled because Muslims objected to the way it portrayed Muhammad. When it was announced that the acronym of two merging companies was SIRA, Muslims became outraged and demanded the name be changed. This is because *sira* in English means "a biography of Muhammad, the prophet of Islam." The name was quickly changed. There was also objection over the construction of a cube-shaped building in New York because it "resembled" a cube-shaped Islamic religious shrine in Mecca. There was also concern that once the building was completed, it might sell alcohol or pork.

The Muslim crusade against fake pigs has had quite a run recently. In England, Muslims found Winnie the Pooh's friend, Piglet, to be offensive, which led to a ban on Piglet in several areas. Also in England, the traditional piggy bank, which has been given to children to encourage them to start saving money, was found to be offensive to Muslims. Tolerance would suggest having a piggy bank for Christian children and something else for Muslim children. Nope, even the thought of an unseen plastic pig lurking under the counter in a bank was too much for Muslims who demanded that all piggy banks be banned. A bank in Belgium eliminated its pig mascot because it "did not meet the requirements that the multicultural society imposes on us." Muslim cashiers in some grocery stores have refused to touch items with pork. Nursery schools have purged their libraries of children's books with images of pigs with the same vigor of the book-burnings that took place in Nazi Germany. And one school changed a play about the "three little pigs" to the "three little dogs." A news update: Muslims don't like dogs either, and those books and plays will have to go next. Perhaps the play could be titled *The Three Little Camels*?

Not only have there been problems with piggy banks but also with teddy bears. An English teacher in the Sudan was threatened with forty lashes and two weeks in prison for allowing her students to name a teddy bear Muhammad. Thousands rioted in the streets, calling for her death. The president of the Sudan finally pardoned the teacher. The Muhammad teddy bear incident also demonstrated once again the bias of the mainstream press. Rather than portraying this as another example of the insanity of Islam, the mainstream media blamed the teacher for not being more knowledgeable about Islam so she would not give offence.

The examples go to the point of absurdity. Muslim women have demanded their driver's license photographs be taken while wearing head scarves that come down to their eyebrows and face scarves that end at the tops of their noses. Obviously, these photographs cannot be used for identification since only two hate-filled eyes can be seen. In California a Muslim woman sued the police after she was arrested and had her head scarf removed when she was booked for a crime. She claimed her religious liberty had been violated.

In England, a man who murdered a police officer escaped the country using his sister's passport while clad in a *burka*. In both England and the United States, there have been robberies by *burka*-clad individuals who have discovered the tent-like garment is not only a great disguise but also a great place to hide weapons. In Michigan, a ban against riding on public transportation with a face mask was quickly lifted when a veiled Muslim woman screamed discrimination. The ban was to make those who committed criminal acts on buses easier to identify. In Canada, a controversy has erupted over whether Muslims should be allowed to "vote while veiled." [Notes to self: What would happen if a KKK member wanted a driver's license photograph taken while wearing the clan's hood? Does anyone remember that one of the Muslim terrorists on 7/7 was wearing a *burka* when he blew up an English bus? Perhaps it is only a question of time before we find out *burka*-wearing Muslim men are transvestites, and this is the only way they can fulfill their "sexual orientation" without being killed.]

Clothing is one of the ways Muslims separate themselves from non-Muslims. This is especially true for women, who seem to have very different interpretations of what is acceptable under Islamic law. There have been some interesting developments in the area of Islamic clothing for women. One is the *burkini*, a combination of a bathing suit and a *burka*. It was designed initially for Muslim women who wanted to be lifeguards in Australia. There has also been the development of what could be called "Muslim chic." Here there are images of attractive, sexy young women wearing "fashionable Islamic clothing" which, if worn in public in an Islamic country, would result in their being beaten by the religious police.

Some of the "traditional" clothing worn by Muslim women has generated security concerns which have resulted in discussions over whether certain types of clothing should be banned from public areas. This is obviously a sensitive area, one in which groups have equal clothing rights, but not special rights.

The ignorance, or perhaps indifference, to terrorism was recently demonstrated when a clothing company marketed a *kaffiyeh*, which is the scarf worn by Palestinian terrorists. When there was public outrage, it was marketed as a "peace scarf," and when the outrage did not go away, it was finally termed a "Euro scarf." What should have never been produced and marketed was finally withdrawn, but then it returned first as the "Riviera scarf" and finally as the "PLO Palestinian scarf."

Muslim taxi drivers have refused to transport passengers with alcohol or dogs. They have also refused to transport women who were not with a brother, father, or husband or who were dressed "inappropriately." They have also demanded that foot-baths be installed for their use in airports and for the right to park without being ticketed during prayers. There are also claims that Muslim taxi drivers are taking over the break rooms used by drivers and turning them into mosques. Also, airports are under pressure to create mosques for passengers. Apparently, Muslims believe generic religious centers are not sufficient.

The demands being made by Muslim medical students were noted in the previous section. Muslims visiting hospitals have refused to use anti-bacterial hand gel because it contains alcohol. Thus, they risk taking infections into and out of hospitals. Related issues deal with Muslim males, who have refused to be seen by female physicians, and Muslim females, who have refused to be seen by male physicians. Hospital gowns had to be created which met the "Muslim dress code." Also, Muslim clerics have told their followers not to have their children vaccinated against diseases such as measles, mumps, rubella, and tetanus since the vaccines were unlawful because they were made from animal or human tissue. In England, nurses were ordered to turn the beds of Muslim patients toward Mecca five times a day. They were also ordered to bring them water for washing. Some female Muslim dentists in England will only see women who wear head coverings.

The staff at a hospital in England was recently informed they were not to eat at their desks when Muslim co-workers were fasting. This was because their Muslim co-workers would be offended by their lack of "cultural awareness." Worried that non-Muslims might give in to temptation, the hospital had the food vending machines removed during the time of the fast. It should, of course, be automatically assumed these same culturally-sensitive bureaucrats have sent out memos informing the staff not to eat pork in front of Jews, beef in front of Hindus, or any type of meat in front of vegetarians.

In addition to Muslim cashiers refusing to touch items with pork, the same is true of alcohol. In fact, Muslims working in stores have refused to stock items such as alcohol. When Muslim workers walked off their jobs to take prayer breaks at times that did not coincide with authorized breaks, their supervisor told them they were being paid to work, not pray. This resulted in a civil rights lawsuit. In Canada, Muslim parlor owners were given an exemption from non-smoking laws because the judge ruled that smoking helped Muslims deal with depression.

There are demands, and rapid concessions, when Muslims want "Muslim only" hours at beaches, gyms, and swimming pools. Or, if special hours cannot be scheduled, there must be as a minimum separation by sex, and non-Muslims must dress according to

Muslim regulations. And at swimming pools only female lifeguards will be allowed during female hours and only males during male hours. There are also demands that during "Muslim Only" hours the viewing areas of swimming pools will be closed. There have been demands that public beaches have some type of barrier between the Muslim and infidel sections. Almost certainly the same standard would be applied if a conservative Baptist requested that thongs be banned from public beaches and pools. [Note to self: Remember to order the *DVD Muslim Girls Gone Wild: Spring Break* and the follow-up video *Muslim Girls Gone Wild: Wet Burka Contest.* Also remember to order the last DVD in the series, *Muslim Girls Gone Wild: Honor Killings.*]

Incarcerated Muslims in England have demanded toilets be repositioned so they do not face Mecca while relieving themselves. The prisoners have also demanded separate food preparation and eating areas, as well as separate utensils involved in food preparation, consumption, and serving since they do not want to consume food that may have contacted forbidden foods. A Muslim convict in England recently won a lawsuit because the prison refused to offer him an acceptable substitute when bacon was served. Another Muslim incarcerated criminal sued because his "substitute" meal was a peanut butter and jelly sandwich, and the jelly may have contained gelatin, which may have had pork byproducts.

In England, some police departments do not allow officers to go into Muslim homes during prayer hours. Also, they will not allow dogs into Muslim homes to sniff for drugs or explosives since Muslims consider dogs to be filthy and unclean. And, of course, the police officers must remove their shoes before entering the homes of Muslims. Also, in Europe, a judge recently ruled in favor of a wife-beating Muslim husband by citing a provision in the *Koran* which allows Muslim husbands to beat their wives. This is now referred to as the "*Koran* made me do it" defense. A police handbook in Australia instructs the police to deal with domestic abuse in the Islamic community in a manner consistent with Islamic culture and traditions. And in Italy a young woman was beaten and imprisoned by her father and brothers because they felt she was becoming "too Western." The father and brother were acquitted because they did not harbor ill-will toward the young woman. Rather, she was living a lifestyle "unsuited to their culture," and in response to the young woman's behavior, her brother and father followed their cultural values.

The Los Angeles Police Department announced in 2007 that its counter-terrorism bureau was planning to identify Muslim areas susceptible to "violent, ideologically-based extremism." Muslim groups quickly stopped the implementation of the plan. In 2008 a program for law enforcement officers titled "The Threat of Islamic *Jihadists* to the World" was met with outrage by Islamic groups who stated the program linked a religion to terrorism. The program was designed to teach law enforcement officers about the development of Islam, the various branches of Islam, and how to respond to terrorism.

Recently there were demands that the schedule for the summer Olympics be changed if its schedule conflicted with Islamic holy days because it placed Muslim athletes at a disadvantage due to fasting. [Note to self: Muslim athletes? Find out when the Olympics added cutting off heads, pillaging, raping, cutting throats, and oppressing women to the list of Olympic events.]

After 9/11, airplane and airport security became a major concern for many Americans. Recently, there were audacious and bold attacks on this security by Muslims, perhaps indicating the level of confidence they have in attacking our culture and then, if necessary, using the legal system to defend themselves. Muslim airline passengers pushed the security limits by buying one-way tickets, having no luggage, praying loudly prior to boarding, sitting in the wrong seats, castigating the United States prior to boarding, and asking for unnecessary seatbelt extensions which could be used as weapons. When non-Muslim passengers became concerned for their security and the Muslims were escorted from the plane, there were cries of religious profiling with pre-prepared law suits and demands for sensitivity training of all non-Muslims involved. Lawsuits were even filed against the airline and the passengers who dared to voice concern. And, to intimidate other airplane passengers into silence, there were demands that the names of the passengers who voiced concern be made public so they could be made examples of by threatening them into hiding or suing them into bankruptcy. To some extent, the attempt to turn the terrorists into victims backfired. This was too much for most Americans, who must have had images of 9/11 replaying in their minds as well as remembering personal experiences where they had concerns about some of those they were traveling with. The backlash and lack of sympathy caused the lawyer of the Muslims to go from demanding maximum public exposure to requesting limited media access to the case because it was "stressful" to his clients.

Connected to the above is the proposed "John Doe Law." This would protect the identity of those who reported suspicious terrorist activity, which is demanded by law. Democrats oppose the law, probably out of fear of offending trial lawyers.

Another issue with air travel emerged. This time it dealt with Muslim females who were seated next to males they did not know. One flight had left the gate and was getting ready to take off when the Muslim males accompanying the Muslim women left their seats to protest where the women were seated. Three hours later, most of the Muslims were "escorted" off the plane to the cheers and jeers of the other passengers.

Western countries that have large unassimilated Muslim populations are now finding an epidemic of gang rapes on Western women by males with "non-Western backgrounds" (a.k.a. Muslims). An *imam* in Australia said the women deserved to be raped based on the way they acted and dressed. This has brought about the suggestion by some Westerners that countries need to assimilate to the values of the Muslims rather than the Muslims assimilating into the society which they have infested—oops—migrated to. To some extent, this is happening. For example, some non-Muslim women are afraid to be in public areas without head scarves since they know they will be subjected to harassment by Muslim males.

This hatred of Western women can be seen in the recent attempt to blow up a nightclub in England. Several writers have noted the Muslim men attempted the attack on "women's night."

There is one other area that has recently received greater attention: the "honor" killings or murders of young Muslim women. In the past, the murders of these young women often went unexplained and unsolved. Interestingly, most Western liberal women's groups do not seem concerned with the epidemic of these murders. Now, however, many of the unexplained deaths of previously healthy young Muslim women are being explained as honor murders. The details of these murders, when they emerge, are shocking. Family members, generally the brothers, father, and mother, actively participate in the murders. The reasons for the murders are often based on who the young Muslim women were dating or who they wanted to date. The murders might have been because of the reluctance to agree to an arranged marriage. Some young Muslim women have been murdered for acting or dressing too Western. Often the murders are very bloody, and younger sisters are forced to watch to learn what happens to women who "dishonor" their families. Just when one thought this "religion" could not produce more degenerate, depraved, disgusting, reprehensible, and vile behavior, we find the "honor" murders are sometimes preceded by an "honor" gang rape of the victim. Again, this is with the approval and participation of family members.

Because of increased recognition of honor murders and greater investigations, some families are sending their daughters back to their country of origin to be murdered.

Female genital mutilation (FGM) is also emerging as an issue in Western countries. Because FGM is illegal in Western countries, young girls are often sent back to their country of origin to be mutilated. There have been reports of parents mutilating their children using scissors. FGM is seen as a way of making the female pure for her husband. It is estimated that in England more than sixty thousand Muslim girls have been sexually mutilated. There are also accounts of "cutters" being flown into and out of the country.

Forced marriages within Islam are also coming under greater scrutiny in Western societies. In the traditional patriarchal Muslim family, females do not make decisions about marriage. Note the word *female* was used instead of *women*. This is because arranged marriages can involve an underage female being forced to marry a male many years her senior. Within Islam, marriage is more of a contract between clans, families, or tribes than a contract between consenting adults. For many Muslim females who have been raised in traditional surroundings, this type of marriage seems "normal." But for many Muslim females who were raised in Western societies, arranged marriages conflict with newly acquired values concerning dignity and freedom of choice.

Although it has received virtually no attention from the mainstream media, the proposed memorial to the victims on Flight 93 has raised both eyebrows and the blood pressure of many who have seen it. Flight 93 was fifteen minutes' flying time from Washington, D.C., when it crashed into a field near Shanksville, Pennsylvania. The proposed memorial is titled the "Crescent of Embrace" and features a large crescent, which is a symbol of Islam and is present on the flags of Islamic countries. Leading up to the "crescent" are forty-four markers, one for each person on the plane: forty crew and passengers and four terrorists. One of the designers said the design was more of a bowl than a crescent and was intended to promote bonding and healing. Outrage brought about a modification in the design, although it still includes the crescent. Rather than honoring the crew and passengers who fought back against the Muslim terrorists and who sacrificed their lives, this "memorial" seems to honor the Muslim terrorists. Almost certainly if the design was in the shape of the Star of David or a Christian cross, the ACLU would already be involved in protesting the design. One outraged critic asked, "What's next, a swastika at a holocaust memorial?" [Note to self: Todd Beamer's last words were not "let's negotiate," "let's appease," or "let's tolerate." Rather, they were "let's roll!" It is about time we start emulating the actions of this heroic young man.]

For twenty years, Muslims have held a parade in New York City on the last Sunday in September. However, in 2007 the date was changed to Sunday, September 9, two days before the sixth anniversary of 9/11. Also in 2007, the Empire State Building was aglow in green to mark the end of Ramadan.

Recently, Muslim scientists have stated Mecca time should replace Greenwich Mean Time (GMT). This is because GMT was imposed on the rest of the world when Britain was a strong power in the world but Islam was now becoming more powerful. Also, they claim Mecca is the center of the world.

There is one other area that has received a great deal of attention in Europe, namely the creation of *de facto* Islamic states within European countries. Essentially, there are Muslim communities which are "no-go" zones because they are too dangerous for non-Muslims to venture into.

What Next?

There is a basic question that Americans need to ask themselves in terms of the tolerance of Islamic demands. Namely, how many concessions are you willing to make? And are you aware that every concession will result in another demand?

A recent Pew poll found there are only two million three hundred and thousand Muslims in the United States. That is under one percent of the population. As a young population, Muslims represent less than half a percent of those of voting age. Yet this less than one percent of the population is demanding the other 99-plus percent of the population capitulates to its demands. The prayer rooms in schools, the repositioning of toilets, and the Muslim only swim and gym hours are only the beginning. If these are accepted, then next comes the concession that Islamic beliefs are superior to Western beliefs. And Muslims can then demand and expect America will make thousands of further concessions. [Question to self: Will Muslims be okay with a *burka* and hood covering the Statue of Liberty or will they simply blow it away like the two priceless 1,500- to 1,800-year-old statues of Buddha in Afghanistan? Also, remember to do an Internet search on how many were killed in the Buddhist riots following the destruction of the statues.]

Does anyone really believe the cashier who will not scan alcohol or pork will accept an openly gay colleague coming to assist? At what point will there be demands that restaurants which serve alcohol or are near mosques be forced to move, or that Muslim waiters or waitresses not be obligated to serve alcohol or pork to customers? Oh, that has already happened!

These demands are generally orchestrated efforts to "push the limits" and to see where we "flinch" and where further inroads can be made. When they go too far, they temporarily pull back. But when we do not flinch or even hesitate, they demand further concessions. The West keeps trying to appease, placate, and demonstrate tolerance of Muslim demands, which are seen as signs of weakness. Islam will only be satisfied when non-Muslims have been converted, killed, or subjugated. The sooner the West recognizes this fact, the sooner it can start to fight back.

If taxi drivers are allowed to only transport those who observe Islamic customs, then how about public bus drivers? Will bus and taxi drivers also be allowed to refuse women they believe are dressed inappropriately or women who are not accompanied by a brother, father, or husband? When a Muslim teacher demands all female students cover their heads, will that be tolerated? The next demand will be that "unclean" female students not attend classes. Then, of course, will be the demand that all females be removed from the classroom.

At what point will all criticism of Islam or of the behavior of Muslims be illegal because of "religious intolerance laws," the fear of lawsuits, or the fear of violence? Any criticism of Islam or of Muslim results in an immediate claim of victimhood and a charge of Islamophobia. It may also result in a lawsuit. All of this means there can be no debate, no disagreement, no discussion, and especially no criticism of Islam or Muslims. No such rules apply to criticism of Judeo-Christian beliefs.

Some claim that 9/11 changed everything. It did, but not in the way many would have predicted. If you compared the changes you thought would take place immediately after 9/11 with what has happened, you almost certainly would have been wrong. Prior to 9/11, most Americans could not distinguish between "Islam" and "Muslim." Nor did they care. On 9/11, nineteen Muslims attacked America. A few years later, airport security personnel fear civil rights lawsuits when singling out Muslims who fit a terrorist profile. Numerous accommodations are made to deal with Muslim demands in schools and other areas. Many of those who have dared to criticize any aspect of the religion find death threats sending them into hiding or expensive legal costs accumulating. And, having learned nothing about the enemy, many pathetically ask, "Where are the moderate Muslims?"

While spokespersons from Muslim organizations seem to be everywhere, decrying the profiling of Muslims and the fear of hate crimes, two Muslims now serve in the House of Representatives. This brings up interesting questions such as, "How can these congressmen take an oath to support and defend the Constitution when their religion commands them to bring the United States under Islamic control?"

The Dangers

To see the danger we face and to see the evil of Islam, those in the West need only examine Islam's religious doctrines, the behavior of its founder, and its history, which is a history of a continual series of offensive wars of expansion. It is a history of slavery. It is a history of the lack of freedom. It is a history of intolerance. It is a history of the oppression of women. These are not aberrations of a religion that has been hijacked by extremists, but actions mandated by the Islamic god and the prophet of Islam. Christianity grew because of the power of its beliefs and the blood of its martyrs and converts. Islam grew because of the strength of its *jihadists* and the blood of those who refused to convert. Christianity grew for more than three hundred years without an army. Islam grew only after creating an army to force non-believers to convert.

It is also the history of a lack of progress. Imagine all the money that has flowed to the Middle East in the last sixty years. How many life-saving drugs have come from Islamic countries? Other than innovative ways of engaging in terrorism, what other inventions have come from Muslim countries? Other than oriental carpets, what about art and music? Where is the Shakespeare, Tolstoy, or Poe of Islam? This is a vapid, void culture that thrives on a mythical "golden age" and an envy and hatred of Israeli and Western success.

The question many need to ask is "Do you want the future history of the world to be written in English or Arabic?"

NOTES

[1] Citations will be primarily from three sources. The first is the *Koran*, where citations are by *sura* or chapter and verse, such as 5:23 meaning chapter 5 verse 23. In different versions of the *Koran* the numbering may be slightly different. The second source is the *hadith* reports. Three *hadith* report collections will be used in this book: Bukhari, Dawud, and Muslim. Citations are preceded by the first letter of the last name of the collector followed by the *hadith* report number, such as B100, D100, or M100. In different versions of the *hadith* reports the numbering may be different. The third source is *sharia* or Islamic law. Citations are preceded by the chapter, which are A - Z, followed by the number of the law. Law 1.15 in chapter A is cited as A1.15.

[2] See Bat'Ye'or's books *The Dhimmi: Jews and Christians Under Islam* (1985), and *Islam and Dhimmitude: Where Civilizations Collide* (2002). See also Robert Spencer's book *The Myth of Islamic Tolerance: How Islamic Law Treats Non-Muslims* (2005).

[3] In Arabic *hadith* means report and is singular. *Ahadith* is plural. In this book *hadith* report and *hadith* reports will be used.

[4] *The Translation of the Meanings of Sahih Al-Bukh ri* (Arabic-English), Translated by Muhammad Mushsin Kha alam Publishers, 1997.

[5] *Sahih Muslim With Explanatory Notes and Brief Narrators* (Arabic-English), Translated by Ab Adam Publishers & Distributors, 2003.

[6] *Suan Abu Dawud: English Translation with Ahmad Hasan*, Kitab Bhavan, 1990.

[7] There are numerous versions of the *Koran*. The citations for this book are from The *Noble Koran.*

[8] See, for example, Ibn Warraq's (ed.) book *The Origins of the Koran: Classic Essays on Islam's Holy Book* (1998), Bat Ye'or's book *The Decline of Eastern Christianity under Islam: From Jihad to Dhimmitude* (1996), R.G. Hoyland's book *Seeing Islam as Others Saw It* (1998), and M. Cook and P. Crone's book *Hagarism: The Making of the Islamic World* (1980).

[9] See, for example, Ibn Warraq's (ed.) book *The Quest for the Historical Muhammad* (2000).

[10] See volume 2, pages 30-33.

[11] See Edward Gibbons *The Decline and Fall of the Roman Empire*, volume II, Chapter L, page 231, in The University of Chicago, The Great Books.

[12] See Ibn Warraq's book *Leaving Islam: Apostates Speak Out* (2003).

[13] See, for example A. G. Bostom (ed.), *The Legacy of Jihad: Islamic Holy War and the Fate of Non-Muslims* (2005), M. Gil, *A History of Palestine 634 - 1099* (1983), and Bat Ye'or's three books *The Dhimmi: Jews and Christians Under Islam* (1985), *The Decline of Eastern Christianity Under Islam: From Jihad to Dhimmitude* (1996), and *Islam and Dhimmitude: Where Civilizations Collide* (2002).

[14] See http://answering-islam.org.uk/Books/Muir/Life1/index.htm.

[15] See WWW.CSPIPUBLISHING.COM.

[16] Omar Ahmad, CAIR's founder, said in 1998 that, "Islam isn't in America to be equal to any other faith but to become dominant. The *Koran* should be the highest authority in America, and Islam the only accepted religion on earth."

[17] See www.thereligionofpeace.com.

[18] See Bat Ye'or's book *Eurabia: The Euro-Arab Axis.*

Printed in the United States
203629BV00002B/103-1176/P

9 781606 473078